MANAGEMENT INFORMATION SYSTEMS

**A Framework for
Planning and Development**

Prentice-Hall
Series in Automatic Computation
George Forsythe, editor

PRENTICE-HALL INTERNATIONAL, INC., *London*
PRENTICE-HALL OF AUSTRALIA, PTY. LTD., *Sydney*
PRENTICE-HALL OF CANADA, LTD., *Toronto*
PRENTICE-HALL OF INDIA PRIVATE LTD., *New Delhi*
PRENTICE-HALL OF JAPAN, INC., *Tokyo*

MANAGEMENT INFORMATION SYSTEMS

A Framework for
Planning and Development

SHERMAN C. BLUMENTHAL

President
Libra Data Systems, Incorporated

PRENTICE-HALL, INC.

ENGLEWOOD CLIFFS, N.J.

© 1969 by Prentice-Hall, Inc.
Englewood Cliffs, New Jersey

Current printing (last digit):
10   9   8   7   6   5   4   3   2

Library of Congress Catalog Card No. 69-19168

Printed in the United States of America

FOREWORD

I first met Sherman Blumenthal in 1962, when he was President of National Computer Analysts. At that time I was organizing a program for an American Management Association seminar covering on-line, real-time systems, and I needed a speaker to discuss OLRT software. Sherm was recommended to me because of his contract software work for Teleregister Corporation on OLRT banking systems. Real-time software was then in its infancy, yet in the seminar Sherm managed to touch in a quantitative fashion on all of the keys to real-time software problems and their solutions. Today's experts are still discovering many of these keys. As always, Sherm was several years ahead of the field.

A year or so later he joined our Advanced Business Systems staff at Touche, Ross, Bailey, & Smart, where he continued his pattern of a thoroughgoing, quantitative attack on all of his projects. Two of his advanced research efforts were in the fields of the checkless society, and on-line communication between top managers and management information systems. Again, he was ahead of the field. His major contributions to the concepts of a system for Automatic Value Exchange, and Management Control Center Systems will be appreciated by many for some years to come.

For Sherm, this book was a labor of love. It represented the culmination of a number of his thoughts and contributions assembled in an integrated fashion as he reached maturity in his overall approach to management information systems. In a sense, it is representative of what is happening and what will continue to happen to many of us as individuals, and to our organizations.

We have progressed through the stages of computer technology: computer systems and computation, electronic data processing, integrated data processing, on-line, real-time systems, management information systems, long-range systems planning encompassing total management information systems and management science; and we have finally come to understand the organizational and management problems in the management information systems function, and how they are related to corporate planning.

During his career in information systems Sherman Blumenthal as engineer, programmer, entrepreneur, consultant, researcher, and manager acquired the requisite knowledge and experience to produce this book. It will be an invaluable reference and guide for those in the information-systems field for many years. For those of us who knew him well it will be a continuing reminder of his brilliant contributions.

Richard E. Sprague
Hartsdale, New York

PREFACE

There is an extensive literature on the planning and design of specific kinds of computer-based business systems. However, one searches it in vain for useful documentation of an approach to the kind of systematic planning for an entire range of business systems which is required in enterprise—particularly in large and diversified organizations. There have been many attempts to formulate structures for so-called "total-management-information-systems," usually commencing with a sometimes naive, sometimes sophisticated theory of the firm, but these attempts usually fell short of translating what is merely perspective and overview into something concrete, in the form of a comprehensive and integrated corporate-wide plan.

This book, too, starts with an overview—a theoretical foundation, if you like—and then attempts to bridge the gap between theory and practice by detailing the specific technical and organizational steps which must be taken to synthesize a comprehensive, integrated systems plan for the corporate enterprise, in its parts and as a whole. The book is not a series of independently conceived chapters, thrown together as a compendium of suggested practices and approaches to different aspects of the planning problem, chapters which, by their juxtaposition, convey the illusion (but not the reality) of a consistent and systematic point of view. There is a definite structure to the book; a common thread runs from the first chapter to the last. To the extent the book succeeds or fails in its purposes, it is a success or failure not of the parts, but of the whole. It is my hope, therefore, that the reader will find himself in agreement with most of the premises, arguments and conclusions in these pages, and that he will understand the need for and the role played by the expression of those things with which he may not entirely agree. I am under no illusion that this work represents an ultimate formulation of an extremely complex set of ingredients, a set which encompasses human, technical, economic, and organizational elements. However, since I have relied heavily on the work of others, most notably on the work of J. W. Forrester, Harold Sackman, Robert Anthony, and Herbert Simon, I trust that whatever contribution may be considered to have been made here is, in its essentials, solidly based.

The author wrote under the assumption that his audience would seek, as did he, a theoretically well-founded but practical approach to planning for systems in enterprise, an approach that could be adapted to many situations and circumstances. This ruled out a "cook-book" approach or elaborate case studies, although one chapter is devoted to a case study. Instead it attempts to equip the reader with carefully justified principles and techniques necessary to construct and carry through a "systematic" plan for systems development. Although the focus is often on large industrial enterprise, most of the principles can be carried over into other kinds of richly structured business organizations, and to a lesser degree to government, to educational and medical institutions, and the like. The increasing tendency in business to diversity and decentralization as a concomitant of growth and change makes much of what is said here about divisionalized industry highly appropriate to large organizations in general. Had the author had the time and knowledge, additional chapters might have been appended on the specific application of principles to transportation, retailing, banking, government departments, and other kinds of organizations. As it is, the discussion of such extensions is confined to relatively few passages.

The book is addressed equally to the systems professional, the advanced student of business, and the manager with important responsibilities for the successful employment of computer technology in his organization. Although there is very little here that is narrowly technical in scope or treatment, parts of this book will require close study for complete understanding. A complex and widely misunderstood subject unavoidably requires precise, carefully reasoned, and often complex explication. The reader is expected to bring some prior understanding of computer systems, business functions, management sciences, systems analysis, organization theory, and management control to the study of this work.

The author wishes to acknowledge the support and encouragement of his wife, who sacrificed many evenings and weekends over the past year; to Miss Theresa Hasson for her typing assistance; to his colleagues, most of whom by their sheer number must remain nameless, but to whom much of what he has learned over the past seventeen computer-saturated years is due; and finally to his children, Thomas, Richard, and Susan, the costs of whose education was not a negligible factor in prompting him to undertake this work.

Sherman C. Blumenthal
New York City

ACKNOWLEDGMENTS

The publishers wish to express their gratitude for the work of the two men who, after the author's death, assumed the responsibilities of seeing his book through production: Dr. Leon Davidson, of Metroprocessing Consulting and Design Services, who reviewed the author's manuscript, and Professor Norman R. Nielsen, of the Stanford Computation Center, who read the proof.

The publishers also acknowledge the cooperation of the following:

The Division of Research, Harvard Business School, Boston, Massachusetts, for permission to cite material from *Planning and Control Systems, A Framework for Analysis,* by Robert Anthony,

Harper and Row, New York, for permission to cite material from *The New Science of Management Decision,* by Herbert A. Simon,

John Wiley and Sons, Inc., New York, for permission to cite material from *Computers, System Science and Evolving Society,* by Harold Sackman, and

The M. I. T. Press, for material reprinted from *Industrial Dynamics* by Jay W. Forrester by permission of the M. I. T. Press, Cambridge, Massachusetts. Copyright © 1961 by the Massachusetts Institute of Technology.

CONTENTS

IX THE MANAGEMENT OF CHANGE 196

MANAGEMENT INFORMATION SYSTEMS

**A Framework for
Planning and Development**

Any worthwhile human endeavor emerges first as an art. We succeed before we understand why.

Jay W. Forrester, *Industrial Dynamics*

▌ INTRODUCTION

COMPUTERS AND THE SYSTEMS-PLANNING FUNCTION

It has become a commonplace observation that the "present generation" of computers will always vastly eclipse its forebears in its sheer potential for information collection, storage, processing and display. What may not be equally apparent is the kind of managerial upheaval which has accompanied growing use of computers in the business enterprise. The first decade of the widespread application of stored-program electronic digital computer systems in non-scientific areas was characterized by their use as adjuncts to, or more efficient replacements for, the regular clerical processes within business organizations. Computers were swallowed up by existing organizational and procedural frameworks, performing such traditional functions as payroll, inventory reporting, accounts payable and receivable, etc. Later we saw increasing application of the unique capabilities of computer systems to communications switching, manufacturing control, production scheduling, order processing, passenger reservations, information retrieval, and the like. In areas like these, which tend to be operationally oriented rather than bookkeeping in nature, computers perform not merely as more efficient surrogates for clerks and calculators, but in a role never fulfilled by their more primitive predecessors. Today one enterprise after another has already integrated, is in the process of

1

integrating, or plans to integrate heretofore disparate uses of computers into larger data collection, processing, retrieval, display and control complexes that cross over the functional and departmental boundaries of traditional organizations. The problems encountered in this more advanced employment of the computer are not solely or primarily technical and procedural, as they were before; rather they are to a very significant degree managerial and organizational.

Information-systems planning as a significant business activity is a phenomenon coeval with this recently expanded employment of the computer. Even today it is difficult to find an organizational locus for it in many enterprises. Nevertheless, wherever there is computerized information handling, some form of conscious planning or choice making has preceded it. That such planning has often not been a formalized process, a process guided by a specific goal-centered policy, is attested to in part by what one observer has called the "small islands of mechanization" [1] that have been and are so typical of the business use of computers. This is not necessarily a critical observation. It can be argued that the manner in which information-handling systems have been applied in business until recently has been practical and even salutary. The pressure for planning on other than an *ad hoc,* one application at a time basis could not have occurred until available technology, and an accompanying body of experience in its successful use, permitted a more comprehensive approach. The efforts of the past two decades in the measured exploitation of information-processing technology have given rise to a healthy situation, in which ever more ambitious plans feed on, and are made possible by, the very appreciable successes that have been achieved to date through a prudent, experimental approach. We have every right to believe that this approach has been correct, seeing that the computing industry is well on its way to becoming one of the three or four largest industrial categories, following only automobiles, petroleum and, perhaps, aerospace in sales.

Is it possible to characterize broadly what the future has in store for heavy users of computing machines in business? There are four sources at hand for this purpose: extrapolation of existing trends; the prognostications of authorities; what the users say they are going to do; and what a thoughtful appraisal leads one to believe can be done. Each of these sources will be used in the ensuing discussion. We are told that the past is prologue,* that there are better things to come. We ought first to examine the justifications for this contention, subject to tests of reasonableness, before characterizing the future of computer use in the firm and the role that formal systems planning might take in furthering this use.

---

* Theme of the 1967 National Conference of the Association for Computing Machinery (Shakespeare, *Tempest,* II.i.248).

A study of 33 firms made in 1966 by a prominent management consulting firm[2] predicted that in a few years these companies would devote close to 70% of their computer resources to operating areas and applications other than finance and administration. The study included firms in the fields of consumer, industrial, and fabrication and assembly products. The more experienced firms placed relatively more emphasis on applications in marketing, distribution, engineering and research. Regardless of prior length of experience with computers, the companies placed relatively little emphasis on top-management planning and control applications as important areas for future concentration. Most of the firms defined their ultimate systems goal as some form of close integration of applications, if not in one totally integrated system, at least in a series of integrated systems. A later study of 108 manufacturing companies by the same management consulting firm indicated that decentralized organizations in this group of companies expected to achieve in three to five years the *same* level of integration of computer systems as the centralized organizations in the group. However, most of the companies studied, including those with the most computer experience, did not expect to achieve "total-management-information-systems" in this time frame.[3]

In another survey conducted at about the same time,[4] 100 top managers of firms, utilizing altogether more than 120 computers, reported that without exception they made no direct use of the computer for decision making at the corporate or division level. The survey uncovered hardly any top manager who received information of any form directly from the computer. The investigator who made this survey concluded that only the decision-making process at the middle-management level in these companies was being affected by the computer directly; that top management was affected, if at all, through the intermediation of lower echelons who filtered computer-generated information on the way up. He felt, however, that by 1975 the computer would have a substantial impact on top management in large research-and-development and manufacturing companies, where special analyses of a non-repetitive kind are involved in the decision-making process. Routine, repetitive types of computer reports would continue to be produced for the middle-management level, to which there would be increasing delegation of control by top management. In particular, the investigator felt that the use of simulation models in exploring alternative courses of action by top management would increase significantly.

A later reported survey, conducted by the Diebold Group, Inc., which dealt with over 100 U.S. and foreign firms, predicted that by 1973 these companies would spend more than twice what they spent in 1965 on data-processing equipment and activities. The study indicated also that 10% of new plant and equipment investment in 1970 would be in computer systems, as compared with 4% in 1960 and 8% in 1966. Performance per dollar was expected to increase eight-fold, and capability 17-fold, between 1964 and 1973.[5]

This sampling of users' opinions and plans argues strongly that the steady penetration of computers into the basic operating and administrative functions of the corporation, together with further growth in "scientific management" applications in unique and complex problem areas as an aid to top-management decision making, will continue. To judge by these studies, little more than passing acknowledgement has been paid to the widely promoted concept of a management information system as a single, total system, or as a highly integrated set of subsystems. Anthony, among others, has said that such a system is the goal, and that those interested in improving management control systems will work toward it. At the same time he cautions those who would interpret his statement as a plea to collect data routinely in elemental building blocks, blocks which can be combined in various ways to answer all conceivable questions, that they are being completely unrealistic.[6]

There is considerable evidence of a spreading tendency toward the integration of what have heretofore been "islands of mechanization," at least in the area of logistical operations, i.e., order processing, physical distribution, inventory control, production, purchasing, etc. The pioneers in the development of large-scale, integrated "logistics" systems in business were the airlines. The concept behind the SABRE Airline Reservation System of American Airlines dates back to the middle 1950's, and the system became operational in the early 1960's. Most major airlines have embarked on, or are operational with, systems of similar magnitude. There were especially severe pressures behind this development, primarily the perishability of the commodity inventoried, airline seats. Similarly ambitious programs were later undertaken by industrial firms, banks, and utilities. Examples of such developments include IBM's Advanced Administrative System, the Westinghouse Telecomputing System, the INTER-LOC System of Lockheed Aircraft, the Ohio Bell customer-service system, and many others. Indeed it is difficult now to find a major firm without corporation- or division-wide logistics systems in being or in advanced stages of implementation.

ORGANIZATION AND THE SYSTEMS-PLANNING FUNCTION

Excellent systems planning has been done in the past on a decentralized basis. While many systems will continue to be functional or divisional in scope, rather than company-wide, it can be argued that systems planning should *not* remain so—but many would plead otherwise on both practical and philosophical grounds.

It is unlikely that the various management centers in a traditionally decentralized organization would willingly relinquish any significant part of their planning prerogatives to a central group. Where centralized systems have emerged, they have been limited to certain functional areas; they were usually initiated by top management as special one-of-a-kind efforts. It would be naive to assume, regardless of its merits, that centralized systems planning of a broader kind would be readily accepted in the typical company. In the thinking of many managers, any centralization of planning may foreshadow general organizational centralization, which they consider bad business practice as well as a personal threat. Since this book advocates a hopefully enlightened form of corporate-wide systems planning, and since, presumably, some significant centralized systems would emerge from this, does the book then stack the deck in favor of organizational centralization? The answer is very emphatically not, although a predisposition to centralization (or recentralization) might certainly be abetted and accelerated by any substantial degree of systems centralization. A predisposition to the opposite, sustained or increasing decentralization, can be equally supported by centralization of systems planning and development. How this is possible will emerge in the succeeding chapters of this book.*

It is perhaps unfortunate that some segments of the systems community have acquired a reputation for advocating a reimposition of the more unenlightened and authoritarian forms of organization by calling for development of so-called "total" systems. This may be undeserved. Some especially eager systems designers are probably guilty of no more than a desire to work on the newest, largest and most advanced developments. They may, however, be misleading their managements in their zeal for the all-encompassing "total-management-information-system." It is one thing to centralize routine, rigorously prescribed, well understood, relatively easily developed, and "managerially unsensitive" types of information-processing operations like payroll or inventory reporting; but there is quite another set of implications to a concommitant centralization of management control of previously separate activities, especially where the development of "big" systems is involved. The quantum jump from many small systems to *the* one "big" system is technically and financially risky, even for the biggest firms. The apparent penchant in some quarters for advocating a single great leap, rather than slow escalation, to the large, integrated systems goal has contributed to the unprofessional aura in altogether too many

---

* See especially Chap. IX, section entitled "Speculation on Corporate Organization."

of the breezily written articles on "total-management-information-systems." A due regard for good engineering practice, which means exploiting available and proven technology to the fullest, has too often been lacking in both theory and practice when it comes to systems design. But even assuming past sins in this regard will be forgiven, and that increasing resources will continue to be devoted to the development of larger systems aggregations, as predicted in the studies cited, what of the organizational implications for the enterprise? The already copious literature of the computer's influence on organization and management attests to the concern that is felt about this problem in many quarters.

One of the more thoughtful inquiries into this matter was reported on in a collection of original papers presented at a conference convened in April 1966 at the Sloan School of Management at M.I.T.[7] In his paper T. L. Whisler observed that:

> The current impact of information technology is to centralize the control structure in organizations or in the parts of them to which it has been applied. The technology is too new for us to conclude with complete assurance that its long-term effect will be the same . . . the evidence we have to date, especially the observable developments in the military, make the case for immediate centralization a strong one. In the long run, professionalization of the labor force and (in the case of business) separateness of markets may set limits on the degree of centralization.[8]

At the same conference John Dearden stated his belief that centralization is related to the similarity of product lines among the separate product-oriented divisions of an enterprise. As he put it:

> Where a company is divisionalized by product line, logistics will tend to be centralized by division. Where several divisions are involved in the same product line (as in the automobile business), the logistics systems will tend to be centralized at the group or corporate level.[9]

Whisler, however, would qualify this:

> [The] independence [of product-line organizations] is rarely realized in practice. Residual problems of interdependence among divisions are usually substantial; coordination and control remain important concerns of corporate management. The computer stands by to move in on problems of this kind; but, when it moves in, former divisional boundaries may be penetrated and control partially recentralized.[10]

Whisler illustrated his point by citing two actual examples among large divisionalized corporations. The first is an unnamed company which he had studied, where a corporate distribution center was established and "a substantial chunk of the former responsibilities of division managers has shifted to this center." [11] The second case cited is that of Westinghouse, where, he stated, ". . . quite a bit of centralization is going on among completely independent divisions; e.g., Consumer Products and Defense." [12] Whisler characterized the organizational effect of the computer-stimulated centralization in terms of the elimination of "organizational slack." [13] He said that the individual has increasingly to meet computer-imposed deadlines.[14] As his area of discretion is narrowed, as his behavioral alternatives become more and more prescribed, his company increasingly suffers from lack of innovative initiative, for fewer professionally qualified people elect to work in such an environment, or to function creatively once in it. Whisler saw a limitation to this trend toward centralized authority, focused on highly integrated computer systems; he observed that "the increasing professionalization of the U.S. labor force will surely set limits on the degree to which it is possible to design highly centralized organizations and find people willing to participate in them." [15] But at some stage in this development the point of no return may be reached, for the corporation may find it no longer has the option to withdraw power that has been centralized and cede it back to the psychologically emasculated individual.

All this certainly does not make retention of either centralization or decentralization in their classic forms a positive virtue. The problem should perhaps not be expressed in terms of the dichotomy of centralization versus decentralization, in which maximum employment of the computer inevitably leads to the former. This is too much like so many "either/or" intellectual traps that subsequent experience has proven to be merely frightening chimeras. Is it possible to have quite a bit of centralization within an essentially decentralized organizational structure? Yes, if the decentralized structure loses much of its hierarchical character, if traditional staff-line distinctions are blurred, if participative decision-making and profit responsibility are organizational goals—if, in other words, the computer revolution is seen to be able to support a truer and more extensive management partnership. That the principle of human primacy in the corporate context should be enhanced rather than destroyed by the computer is a premise of this book. The final effects of the "computer revolution" are far from being tallied at this point. We ought, however, to avoid thinking in absolutes about these matters prematurely.

SYSTEMS PLANNING—PRACTICES AND NEEDS

Although a very considerable amount of planning has accompanied the development of large, integrated systems, one can discern no underlying body of *formal* planning principles in what has been written about the genesis of these systems, or in the literature of business systems development generally. One might have expected management science to have addressed itself to this problem, since it is possible in principle to postulate formal systems-planning objectives. Robert V. Head, for one, has stated that "systems planning can be viewed as a managerial tool for obtaining . . . assurance that [systems resources] will be allocated in an optimum fashion." [16] This immediately raises the question of what is optimum. In management science the measures of effectiveness have usually been borrowed from classical economics—profit maximization or its various proxies. In this view optimum allocation of systems resources is obtained when return on investment is maximized. But perhaps by "optimum" is meant something less tangible, since major systems involve so many imponderable elements—imputed value, organizational acceptance, consonance with corporate objectives, etc. This may be among the reasons that the problems of acquisition, communication and processing of information have been excluded from management science models, as Ansoff and Brandenburg have pointed out.[17] They think that, while ". . . historically [management science] has been heavily biased toward the physical resource conversion process in the firm . . . [a] recent important and encouraging trend is toward the removal of this bias and [toward] a balanced view of physical, social, and informational aspects of organizations." [18] Head recognizes the dilemma posed in his previous postulation, for in another article he states that

> . . . most of the benefits of a management information system are of [an] "intangible" nature. Clearly, what is needed are new methods of justifying information-systems costs by somehow quantifying these heretofore "intangible" benefits. Until this can be done, it is difficult to see how management can be persuaded to commit substantial company resources to truly effective information-systems development.[19]

Forrester remarked upon the possible futility of this quest for objectivity when he observed, ". . . the economist . . . looks upon the entrepreneur as a man who maximizes his profit without asking whether or not he has the available information sources and the mental computing capacity to find the maximum." [20]

We have seen that where management has willed it, large, functionally integrated information systems have been and will continue to be developed. The attitude among the managements of these firms is clearly that "computing technology is here to stay, is advancing rapidly, with the competition active; let us then ensure that we maintain a prudently progressive posture." It would be difficult to sustain the view that if this is a reasonably fair representation of management's attitude, then their organizations forthwith receive maximum benefit from the investment in computers and related information-handling technology. In fact there is no prescription even for what this level of investment ought to be, regardless of whether the return from it can be maximized.

Referring to one of the investigations cited earlier, the values of installed computers in the companies studied ranged from $47,000 to $16 million, and from 0.05% to 0.59% of sales. The median was 0.22%, and the average 0.54% of sales. Total computer costs—machines, personnel, and operating—varied from $128,000 to $50 million annually. These companies ranged in size from under $100 million to several over $1 billion in sales.[21] While there was no projection of what these costs were likely to be several years hence, Booz, Allen's study of 108 manufacturing companies indicated that only four expected computer costs to remain at the same level or to decrease.[22] Doubtless few would claim that because they are spending a certain percentage of sales on computers and related costs today, that these same ratios are the correct ones for the future. If the typical firm is now emerging from the period of limited exploitation of the computer, one may expect these ratios to increase, even though the measurable return from the increased investment will become ever more difficult to identify as the applications grow in scope and complexity. In a way this is perhaps no more paradoxical than the situation with respect to the increasingly sizeable telephone bills these same firms pay every year without formal economic justification. But this observation does not lay the matter to rest.

Most companies would rightly deny that growth in their use of computers has been haphazard. Most have a fairly well defined target for computer systems application over some future period. Generally this target is not conceived as an integrated whole, but evolves from an ever-changing collection of systems-development proposals which come from all over the organization. Occasionally these independently proposed systems become organically related in larger complexes, when imagination, opportunity and internal politics permit. Requirements generally continue to be expressed in terms of the observed needs of the internal customers for systems, although these customers are often prodded into appreciating their opportunities by members of the systems organization. The competition for systems resources that arises in this situation is not always resolved on the basis of relative return on investment or other objective measures. Systems staffs are often found to complain that they are working on the wrong problems—an accounting system, for example, when there are greater unmet needs in inventory or distribution control, with far greater dollar potential.

Pressures for more rational planning have increased as the opportunities for doing even a little better than before have become so manifest as to be incontrovertible. At the same time that dollar investments in information technology are increasing in both absolute and relative terms, the technological necessity for planning on a more ambitious scale than heretofore has become apparent to business managements and their systems staffs. The technological prerequisites for broader planning goals now exist. These include the roughly contemporaneous emergence of compatible families of computers, mass storages, remote terminals, data communications, comprehensive operating systems, real-time processing, new programming languages, and a new spirit and substance of professionalism in the computer community.

THE OBJECTIVES OF SYSTEMS PLANNING

Planning has been described ". . . as a process of setting formal guidelines and constraints for the behaviour of the firm." [23] In another context we are told, "Strategic planning [cf. page 28 below] is the process of deciding on objectives of the organization, on changes in these objectives, and on the policies that are to govern the acquisition, use, and disposition of these resources." [24] Cyert and March state that ". . . plans take the general form of an intended allocation of resources among the alternative activities available to the firm or its subunits." [25] A little later the same authors list the parts of a plan as: a goal (prediction), a schedule (the specification of intermediate steps to the predicted outcome), a theory (a relationship between factors), and a precedent (a decision that is fixed for the planning period).[26] These definitions apply to the more limited context of information-systems planning, as well as to general business planning, since:

1. A systems plan constrains the behavior of that portion of the organization charged with the design and implementation of those systems specified in the plan.
2. Systems planning is a form of strategic planning wherein objectives are formulated in terms of proposed systems authorized for development, resources assigned to authorized systems projects, and policies formulated to guide the manner in which these resources will be used—for example, documentation standards, choice of hardware vendors, and the like.
3. Selections have to be made among proposed systems competing for the use of limited resources. Such choices are nothing other than the allocation of these resources, whether such allocation is "optimum" or not.
4. A systems plan is not merely the enunciation of a set of operating goals in terms of systems, but contains a prescription of how the goals are to be achieved by means of a scheduled series of projects and subprojects.
5. There are relationships between factors in a systems plan, although

these are not always explicitly set forth. These are what should be called rules of thumb. One such rule might state the probability density of debugged instructions that can be expected per unit of programming time, given a system of certain characteristics (e.g., large or small, real-time or batch, etc.).

6. A systems plan is finally a precedent, although a flexible one, more often honored in the breach than not. Few systems plans remain unchanged for long.

In one view, far from being motivated by rational assessments of return on investment, the usual objective of a systems plan is the lowest common denominator of what the technicians know can be done, what the data processing managers believe can be done (and what they try to sell to corporate management), and what corporate management understands and will allow to be done.[27] The path of least resistance through this skein of conflicting levels of understanding, and often self-serving interests, usually results in a limited systems proposal, confined to a preferably small segment of the organization, and not having an impact too high up even within that segment. That, in spite of such organizational barriers, so many computer users have moved so far beyond this confined and unrisky level of application is a tribute to the inherent management appetite for innovation in many of our industries. The planner can hope for such an innovative predisposition on the part of his management, but he can only recommend—he has neither the responsibility nor the authority for making the final choice. That this final choice is often motivated as much by the politics of the situation as by the objective virtues of the planner's recommendation is part of the ignominy of his lot, a fate of which the rueful but realistic planner should be ever mindful. He should, however, never attempt to anticipate what is saleable politically; rather he should leave that to others and should always set forth an undiluted picture of what he considers objectively the best course of action for management to take, and why.

Although the planner should be objective, and therefore heavily reliant on scientific methodology, he differs from his colleagues in the management sciences in several important respects. These have been identified by Ansoff and Brandenburg.

1. His interest is directed to models which are of direct relevance and usefulness to the firm. In that compromise between "formalism" and "realism" which each management scientist has to make, the planner inclines toward the latter.
2. The planner's job is "on line." As a part of management he is a daily "real-time" participant of the continuing management process. By contrast, many other management scientists within firms operate "off line" (in operations research or management science groups) on special problems and assignments.

3. A consequence of his on-line responsibility is the planner's concern with programming, again in contrast to many other management scientists who consider the problem "solved" when the preferred alternative is chosen.

4. Similarly the planner is concerned with organizational acceptance of planning, with implementation, with measurement, and with feedback into the planning process.[28]

If one reflects on the kinds of changes which have an impact on a firm, and the increasing rate of those changes—changes in the emergence and disappearance of products, in kinds and numbers of markets, in world-wide dispersion of operations, in sales growth, in investment per employee, in opportunities for acquisition and diversification, in the number of different skills necessary to operate the company, and in virtually every other measure that can be conceived—it is clear that the central need of the firm, both today and for the future, is to innovate continuously, and through innovation to ride the crest of engulfing change. Maladaptation to change in the biological organism leads to homeostatic collapse. In the social organism it leads to anarchy and chaos. In management hierarchies it leads to the Peter Principle,[29] wherein every post tends to be occupied by a person incompetent to execute his duties, and in enterprise as a whole it leads to the well known buggy-whip syndrome.* Forrester likens the firm to an information-feedback system,[30] in which appropriate adaptive behavior is related to appropriate information systems. This notion, which will be pursued in detail in the next chapter, suggests the key role information technology must play in the era of change. It suggests further that information-systems planning is important enough to be formalized, and not left to emerge merely from the interplay of interests that are narrower than those of the business as a whole, although this interplay will remain an important regulating mechanism. Therefore, this book will discuss systems planning in that larger perspective, rather than in terms of this or that functional or organizational subunit.

Given the above I believe it is possible to formulate the specific objectives of the systems-planning function around the needs for conserving systems resources, prolonging systems life, achieving greater efficiency in systems performance, and permitting the company more easily to adapt to change. Systems planning should accordingly serve to insure a business against the uncoordinated development and proliferation of islands of information-systems mechanization. One source of the multiplication of systems

---

* Executives who think too narrowly of the market for their products fall prey to the "buggy-whip syndrome." In the classic example, manufacturers of buggy whips —or so we are told—failed to see that the survival of their companies was tied to the future of the overall transportation market, and so they went broke when the horseless carriage took away all their customers.

has been the inability to systematically assess points of contact between existing or potential applications separately conceived by different organizational units in the firm. A second source has been the lack of a consistent and uniformly applied approach to the integration of related systems into larger entities of appropriate scope. An aggravating concommitant to this "disintegrative" approach to systems development has been the tendency to allocate resources on a first-come first-served basis. The systems-planning function must therefore encompass the review of proposed systems in terms of planning criteria designed to minimize the number of systems, to broaden their scope, and to place them in the proper sequence for development. All these requirements can be expressed by the following list of systems-planning objectives:

1. To avoid overlapping development of major systems elements which are widely applicable across organizational lines, when there is no compelling technical or functional reason for difference.
2. To help ensure a uniform basis for determining sequence of development in terms of payoff potential, natural precedence and probability of success.
3. To minimize the cost of integrating related systems with each other.
4. To reduce the total number of small, isolated systems to be developed, maintained and operated.
5. To provide adaptability of systems to business change and growth without periodic major overhaul.
6. To provide a foundation for coordinated development of consistent, comprehensive, corporate-wide and interorganizational information systems.
7. To provide guidelines for and direction to continuing systems-development studies and projects.

"SYSTEMATIC" SYSTEMS PLANNING

What activities should come within the scope of systems planning? This question is still very much a matter of arbitrary definition. Perhaps the long-range, macroscopic human consequences of pervasive automation are too much a matter of speculation to be formulated and included in the planning process. Since this is not a book of prophecy, further discussion of organizational matters will tend to be rather specific, with a single exception at the very end of the book. We do intend, however, to take a broad view of *systems* planning, i.e., the whole of that universe of business information processing in the firm which is in principle subject to computerization to the potential profit of the firm. This probably excludes *most* forms of business information, because most forms of information in business are not in principle subject to profitable computerization. The problem of designing systems to handle telephone calls, notes scribbled on margins of memoranda, looks on a customer's face when he says "maybe," knowledge of which people work together well, advertisements in trade journals, the availability of money, the probable impact of a competitor's new product on your market share, *ad infinitum,* is not likely to be of wide interest to those who, at the moment, are still wrestling with questions about how many inventory control systems they need if their product lines include a thousand different kinds of items, and so forth. If the scope of systems planning is, then, limited to the more pedestrian and tangible forms of information, is a structured, formal approach to planning over even this less extensive universe possible? As Beckett asks, ". . . can the process of conceiving, designing, constructing, and installing operating systems itself be formalized and crystallized into a system?"[31] He goes on to say in reply:

> Systems sophisticates are at once fascinated and baffled by this question. They recognize the process as being creative in large part, and in this sense perhaps not reducible to formal routine. On the other hand, they know that much of their art relies on a scientific search for clear understandings of the issue, a piece-by-piece identification of its components, a step-by-step analysis of the possible solutions, and a building-block approach to solutions. All of which implies a systematic approach to the solution of systems problems.[32]

This entire book is an affirmation of the belief that defining and solving business systems problems can itself be a systematic process. And not only a systematic process, but also a scientific one, in the sense that a hypothesis-experiment-confirmation approach to systems definition and development is possible to a large degree.

REFERENCES

1. "Planning for Data Processing," *EDP Analyzer,* Vol. 4, No. 6 (June 1966).

2. Booz, Allen, and Hamilton, Inc., "The Computer's Role in Manufacturing Industry," *Computers and Automation,* Dec. 1966, pp. 14–19.

3. Booz, Allen, and Hamilton, Inc., "The Computer Comes of Age," *Harvard Business Review,* Jan.–Feb. 1968, pp. 83ff.

4. Rodney H. Brady, "Computers in Top-Level Decision Making," *Harvard Business Review,* July–Aug. 1967, pp. 67–69.

5. The Diebold Group, Inc., "Research Study Conclusions," *Computer Digest,* Aug. 1967, p. 8.

6. Robert N. Anthony, *Planning and Control Systems—A Framework for Analysis* (Boston: Division of Research, Harvard Business School, 1965), p. 64.

7. Charles A. Myers, ed., *The Impact of Computers on Management* (Cambridge, Mass.: The M.I.T. Press, 1967).

8. Thomas L. Whisler, "The Impact of Information Technology on Organizational Control," in Myers, ed., *The Impact of Computers on Management,* pp. 47–49.

9. John Dearden, "Computers and Profit Centers," in Myers, ed., *The Impact of Computers on Management,* p. 188.

10. Whisler, "The Impact of Information Technology . . . ," p. 35.

11. Whisler, p. 36.

12. Whisler, p. 50.

13. Cyert and March, *A Behavioral Theory of the Firm* (Englewood Cliffs, N.J.: Prentice-Hall, Inc., 1963), p. 36.

14. Whisler, pp. 48–49.

15. Whisler, p. 37.

16. Robert V. Head, "Planning for Real-Time Business Systems," *Systems and Procedures Journal,* July–Aug. 1967.

17. H. Igor Ansoff and Richard C. Brandenburg, "A Program of Research in Business Planning," *Management Science,* Vol. 13, No. 6 (Feb. 1967), pp. B-219ff.

18. *Ibid.*

19. Robert V. Head, "Management Information Systems: A Critical Appraisal," *Datamation,* May 1967, pp. 22ff.

20. Jay W. Forrester, *Industrial Dynamics* (Cambridge, Mass.: The M.I.T. Press, 1961), p. 99.

21. Booz, Allen, and Hamilton, Inc., "The Computer's Role in Manufacturing Industry."

22. Booz, Allen, and Hamilton, Inc., "The Computer Comes of Age."

23. Ansoff and Brandenburg, "A Program of Research in Business Planning."

24. Anthony, *Planning and Control Systems,* p. 24.

25. Richard M. Cyert and James G. March, *A Behavioral Theory of the Firm* (Englewood Cliffs, N.J.: Prentice-Hall, Inc., 1963), p. 104.

26. Cyert and March, *A Behavioral Theory of the Firm,* pp. 110f.

27. Justin A. Perlman, "Centralization vs. Decentralization," *Datamation,* Sept. 1965, pp. 24–28.

28. Ansoff and Brandenburg, "A Program of Research. . . ."

29. Raymond Hull, "The Peter Principle," *Esquire,* Jan. 1967, pp. 76f. (After Dr. Laurence J. Peter)

30. Forrester, *Industrial Dynamics, passim.*

31. John A. Beckett, "The Total Systems Concept," in Myers, ed., *The Impact of Computers on Management,* p. 217.

32. *Ibid.*

Render unto man the things which are man's and unto the computer the things which are the computer's. This would seem the intelligent policy to adopt when we employ men and computers together in common undertakings.

Norbert Wiener, *God and Golem, Inc.*

 # AN INFORMATION-SYSTEMS PERSPECTIVE ON THE CORPORATION

INTRODUCTORY DISCUSSION

WHAT IS AN INFORMATION SYSTEM?

We shall seek a rigorous definition of what an information system is later in this chapter. First, however, a working definition is needed to undergird a preliminary discussion. Splendid definitions abound for this purpose. Sackman, for example, does not refer to information systems *per se,* but to what he prefers to call "man-machine digital systems." [1] Beforehand, with a certain purpose in mind, he defines the concept of a "system" as something which has a very definite informational aspect accompanying it, viz.:

> . . . [a] *system* refers to any related set of events and objects, the collective organization of information these possess, and the means for acquiring, storing, transforming, transmitting, controlling, or otherwise processing such information—all in relation to, but distinct from, the external environment in which the behaviors and history of the object system are embedded.[2]

Later he defines a man-machine digital system as:

> . . . an evolving organization of people, computers, and other equipment, including associated communication and support systems, and

their integrated operation to regulate and control selected environmental events to achieve systems objectives.[3]

This will be used as our working definition of an information system. Later
in the book we shall refer to on-line, real-time (OLRT) systems. Here, too,
Sackman comes to our aid (my italics)

> . . . a *realtime* [sic] computing system is one capable of following and
> controlling selected events in its related environment at the time they
> occur. *Online* [sic] man-computer communication refers to direct man-
> computer coupling with message rates approximating the speed of
> ordinary human conversation.[4]

Unless something more specific is meant, we shall hereafter generally dis-
pense with the locution "information system" and its variants, in favor of
the word "system," with a meaning coextensive with the former.

Systems are the planning entities, and before planning begins they
must be identified. The process of identification must be consistent with
the planning objectives outlined in Chapter I (page 13), and equally they
must make sense in terms of the real world of the company. In considering
an approach we shall repeatedly harken back to these two touchstones.

The real world does not often conform to what we would wish it to
be. The set of systems under development and in operation, together with
the existing arrangement of development and operating resources allocated
to them, is, in the absence of a plan consistent with the objectives described
in Chapter I, a plan by default—or, perhaps, a plan partially by design,
and partially not. What exists in the way of systems in being or under
development is the point of departure—one of the key inputs to the planning process, the other key input being the planning target itself. The
planning output is a periodically updated version of a program of work,
expressed ultimately as a series of approved systems projects, for bridging
the gap. Each version or "model" of the plan amplifies or refines parts of
the previous model, preferably incorporating work already completed as
a result of prior models without requiring major change.

The planning target is that postulation of systems entities and their
overall relationships which can serve as a review vehicle aimed toward a
less random development process. Proposed systems, regardless of where
they originate in the company structure, would be reviewed for "fit to plan."
Since in large, complex enterprises a systems plan cannot issue forth as a
product of armchair logic, *the review of existing and proposed developments is a most important input to a systems plan; and, in turn, the systems
plan is a most important input to the review process.* Figure 2-1 is an
illustration of two key elements of the review process, viz.:

1. New proposals for systems are matched against an *evolving* and *orderly* classification of systems. The matching process serves to segment new proposals to fit the pigeonholes in the existing systems classification, or, failing that, to aid in the creation of new or revised pigeonholes.
2. Similarly pigeonholed proposals are compared with each other and with systems in being or under development, to obtain measures of commonality and difference.

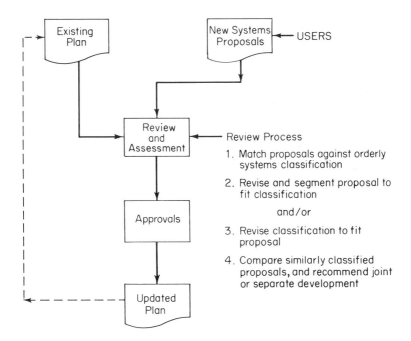

Figure 2–1. Relationship of systems plan and systems review.

The second step in this review process helps to determine the number of data-processing (as opposed to product-line) "businesses" the enterprise must actually conduct. It may be in fifty identifiable, profit-center-oriented, product-lines; but, for example, only in three fundamentally different saleable-product-inventory-management "businesses," etc.

AN ORDERLY CLASSIFICATION OF BUSINESS SYSTEMS IS FUNDAMENTAL
TO RATIONAL SYSTEMS PLANNING

A number of methods for achieving orderly classification have been suggested. These suggestions tend to fall within one or another of six basic types. Most procedures that have been followed in practice are actually a combination of two or more of these types of approach. I shall give them the following names, and then amplify upon them briefly:

1. The organization chart approach
2. The data-collection approach
3. The management survey (or "top-down") approach
4. The data bank approach
5. The integrate later approach
6. The integrate now (or "total systems") approach

The organization chart approach assumes that systems generally follow organizational boundaries. In a divisionalized enterprise organized along product lines, this would tend to displace the systems-planning problem from the corporate to the divisional level, especially if the divisions each have a rich internal functional structure: finance, production, personnel, procurement, marketing, etc., all within each division. Opportunities to develop common systems to serve similar functions in more than one division would depend on a higher-level coordinating responsibility with appropriate corporate-level backing. In a centralized enterprise, or within the context of a single, functionally rich division, the organization chart approach tends to equate functional and systems boundaries. Thus, there are conceived financial systems, marketing systems, etc. The points of information interchange among them, and between them and higher levels of operating management having cross-functional responsibilities, are then dealt with on an *ad hoc* basis. Certain fundamental transactions in the business, such as sales orders, which are vital to many functions, in this approach tend to be dealt with redundantly and separately by each functionally oriented system. Sales orders, for example, may be fed into several independent systems—a billing/accounts-receivable system, an inventory-reporting system, a production-planning system, a sales-analysis system, etc.

The data-collection approach assumes that a systems classification is best done after one has all the facts in hand. Before embarking on such a program the systems taxonomist (classifier) might pay heed to the historical development of other descriptive taxonomies. Only four thousand species were known to Linnaeus when he developed his scheme for biological classification in the eighteenth century, a scheme which enabled his successors to classify the over one million species known today. Rather than proceeding, like Linnaeus, inductively, the data-collection analyst, who asks for representative samples of every kind of information that flows within an organization, is faced with a number of imposing problems. He must postulate sensitivity criteria by which the unique aspects of similar pieces of information can be submerged in previously defined class characteristics.

Without these criteria the task becomes impossibly large. Zipf described the problem very well when he asked:

> . . . how can we accumulate [the sizeable quantities of current and historical source data needed]? The first and very expensive approach is to manually collect, compile and convert to usable form the massive amounts of data required for a given study. The second approach is to concentrate on converting the basic accounting functions to computer-based systems and thus have a larger portion of the data readily accessible in machine language as a by-product of normal processing . . . it is the only economically sound course of action.[5]

In order to make the data-collection task manageable, he must do some classification ahead of time—the very dilemma he wished to avoid in the first place. Secondly he must decide the minimal element of data to be collected and identified: a "transaction," a portion of a transaction, data fields, or what not. Third, he must decide whether he wants "raw" data, processed data, or both. Fourth, as Dearden and McFarlan might ask at this point, he must consider whether he wants action or non-action, recurring or non-recurring, documentary or non-documentary, internal or external, and historical or current data (this itself constitutes 2^5 or 32 categories).[6] Rather than assume he knows nothing, the sophisticated analyst should always capitalize on what he knows about his subject. If he does, he needs to collect only the data necessary to confirm (or disconfirm) his hypotheses. Besides, many arbitrary classifications of a given body of data are possible after the fact, as any statistician knows. There are no "right" ones, only more or less useful ones.

Forrester makes the following comments on the data-collection approach:[7]

> In formulating a model of a system, we should rely less exclusively on statistics and formal data and make better use of our vast store of descriptive information.
>
> . . . many persons discount the potential utility of models of industrial operations on the assumption that we lack adequate data on which to base a model. They believe a first step must be extensive collecting of statistical data. Exactly the reverse is true . . . a model should come first. And one of the first uses of such a model should be to determine what formal data needs to be collected. We see all around us the laborious collection of data whose value does not equal the cost. At the same time highly crucial and easily available information is neither sought nor used.
>
> . . . before we measure, we should name the quantity, select a scale of measurement, and in the interests of efficiency we should have a reason for wanting to know.

The management survey or "top-down" approach assumes that once the kinds of information that management needs have been determined, the systems necessary to supply the information can also be determined. Given that it is possible to determine these needs, and once determined, that they would tend to remain relatively stable in terms of content, levels of detail, and periodicity (a dubious proposition), it is quite likely that systems could then, and only then, be designed to fulfill the management information requirements. At the level of management control of operations there is probably no information needed that is not based ultimately on data routinely collected for purposes of running the business on a day to day, transaction by transaction basis. However, were this data to be captured, put in machine readable form and processed solely for the purposes of abstracting it into summaries or reports for management, the price might prove to be intolerably high. On the other hand, if the data were computer processed in order *first* to fulfill operational needs, and only secondarily for purposes of generating management control information, this would begin to make more economic sense. But we would no longer be dealing with a "top-down" approach.

The data bank approach is a rather theoretical one that presents great practical difficulties. The underlying theme is the establishment and maintenance of a vast pool of highly detailed data containing everything conceivably necessary for operational and management control of the business. Specific systems would utilize this pool by accessing data relevant to their purposes at will. The data bank would be shared among all systems, as any specific datum might potentially be relevant to several systems. Data would presumably be associated in many intertwining files or sets by being tagged with one or more attributes specifiable by and sensible to the systems using them. On an a priori basis the possible associations, into sets, of even 100 types of data elements is combinatorially tremendous—they exceed the number of grains of sand in the world. There is one set of all of them, 100 sets of 99 of them etc., 4950 sets of 98 of them, etc., altogether amounting to 2^{100} distinct sets of data elements. (This does not even take into account the variations in value of the data elements themselves.) The technical and theoretical problems are many, but they will doubtless some day be solved; perhaps we shall ultimately have the grand, generalized, cosmic data management system so much promised and never realized. Until then we would be well advised not to embark in this direction.

The integrate later approach makes its appeal on the basis of hardheaded practicality. This approach calls for continuing with design and implementation of individual systems as needed in the business, without waiting for a comprehensive plan or classification to be developed. The argument here is that if we were to wait to implement anything until we understood how everything ties together in one grand scheme, nothing would ever be done. Quite true. Unfortunately it is not often that independently developed systems coalesce into larger, nicely interlocking aggregations. It usually happens that later, after determining how some things (if not everything) should have been tied together, a major systems overhaul or complete redo must be undertaken to achieve meaningful integration. This is the historical pattern. We should be able to learn the lesson without repeating the experience ourselves. At one time it was plausible, practical, in fact healthy, to proceed thus. It guaranteed much of the success experienced in the earlier use of computers in business. This is no longer necessarily so.

The integrate now or "total-systems" approach is at the opposite extreme. It has had a particularly clamorous coterie of proponents, although they have become somewhat more muted than they once were. The devotees of the total-systems approach start with the premise that all things and processes within the firm, and between the firm and its environment, are interrelated, and that, therefore, the information networks can and should be similarly interrelated by conscious design, before implementation. Many have come to realize the shortcomings of this perspective. Myers has pointed out: ". . . the total systems concept, applicable to operations, hardly applies to non-operations." [8] Dearden and McFarlan support this view:

> The assignment of the responsibility for the logistics information system is not nearly so well developed and thought out in the typical company as the [financial and personnel] systems are. For one thing, being an operating control system, it has not required the degree of top-management involvement which is characteristic of the other two systems. The main concern of top management is that production schedules are being met and that costs are properly controlled. (If they are not, this condition is reflected in the financial information.) A second factor is that the responsibility for coordinating the entire logistics system is almost never assigned to a single executive. As a result, the system in many companies is relatively uncoordinated and far from optimum. In fact, much of the so-called "total systems" development has been designed to overcome problems in the logistics field. Careful examination of the description of a typical "total system" will reveal that it is concerned almost exclusively with the logistics system. [9]

We have the specific caveat of top management, too. Hershner Cross, Executive Vice-President of the General Electric Company, tells us:

> . . . no one really knows how to design, build, and install a single comprehensive system that will cover the vast complexes of today's industry. The result is that management with its existing systems will tend to resist any all-inclusive take-over, and for very good reasons.

And this means that the Integrated Management Information System will have to be developed step by step . . . .[10]

It is clear, and it has been demonstrated in practice many times, that at the lowest, most tangible, most definable level of operational control, "total-systems" are possible and even desirable and necessary. But such a "total-system" is in fact only one of many systems in the firm, i.e., it is basically the logistics system. The problem of classifying *all* of the systems remains, as well as the probable necessity for some sub-classification within the logistics area itself.

At this point we need to remind ourselves of the objective of our search for an approach. It is to define the entities in a systems plan. There is little profit in begging the question at one extreme by insisting that there is only one entity—a "total-system"—or at the other by claiming that the entities are whatever they accidentally turn out to be in the "integrate later" approach. It is also not sufficient to use the traditional pictures of a firm, such as the organization chart, in order to rationalize the information network into its component systems. We need a special perspective suitable to our special requirements—a *systems* perspective. And with this perspective our aim is to create an evolvable model of the information network in the business, a model which consists of systems and their relationships. In evolving the model, we want to analyze, synthesize, test, and reanalyze and resynthesize, until all potential information-systems needs have been addressed while at the same time the planning objectives set forth in Chapter I have been satisfied. In the next section a basis for analysis will be explored.

AN INFORMATION-SYSTEMS PERSPECTIVE FOR THE
BUSINESS ENTERPRISE—A FRAMEWORK FOR ANALYSIS

Three concepts undergird the development of the systems perspective proposed in this section. The first is Jay Forrester's information-decision-action model of the enterprise. The second is the distinction between programmed and non-programmed decisions, most notably expounded by Herbert Simon. The third is the precise characterization of the levels of management planning and control proposed by Robert Anthony. These concepts complement each other so naturally that this synthesis of them into a single, consistent view of enterprise is no great or original feat. In fact, this has already been done in part by several workers in the field whose comments will be cited in the following discussion.

INFORMATION-DECISION-ACTION

Forrester observed that social systems, including business enterprises, are "strongly characterized by their closed-loop (information-feedback) structure."[11] Later in the same work he amplifies this notion:

> The industrial system . . . is a very complex multi-loop and interconnected system . . . . Decisions are made at multiple points throughout the system. Each resulting action generates information that may be used at several but not all decision points. This structure of cascaded and interconnected information-feedback loops, when taken together, describes the industrial system. Within a company, the decision points extend from the shipping room and the stock clerk to the board of directors.[12]

And, further:

> The interlocking network of information channels emerges at various points to control physical processes such as the hiring of employees, the building of factories, and the production of goods. Every action point in the system is backed up by a local decision point whose information sources reach into other parts of the organization and the surrounding environment.[13]

Forrester defines management as the process of converting information into action—a process he also equates with decision making.[14] There are several information-feedback networks in the industrial company in which the management process takes place, viz., materials, orders, money, personnel, capital equipment, and information. The "information network" will be dealt with at some length later in this chapter. Each of these networks is composed of *levels, rates,* and *decision functions.* The definitions of these components as set forth by Forrester are freely excerpted from his book *Industrial Dynamics* and presented in the following paragraphs.

Levels are the present values of business variables (inventory, manpower, open orders, money, etc.) that have resulted from the accumulated difference between inflows and outflows in certain parts of the network.[15] *Rates* define the present, instantaneous flows of these variables between the levels in each network. The rates correspond to activity, while the levels measure the resulting state to which those parts of the network have been brought by the activity.[16] The *decision functions* (also called rate equations) are the statements of policy that determine how the available information about levels leads to decisions. All decisions pertain to impending action and are expressible as flow rates (generation of orders, construction of equipment, hiring of people, etc.). The decision functions determining the rates are dependent only on information about the levels.[17] In principle, rates are not determined by other rates.[18] This means that, for example, the information on which rate decisions are based is not usually the instantaneous measure of rates of flow, but depends rather on the short-run average of what the rates have been over some past period.

Levels exist to permit the inflow rates to differ, over limited intervals, from the outflow rates. By contrast, a delay is thought of as a special class of level in which the outflow is determined only by the internal level stored in the delay.[19]

The information network is itself a sequence of alternating rates, levels, and delays. It is raised to a position superior to the other networks because it is the interconnecting tissue between all of them. It transfers level information from other networks to the decision points in those networks, and rate information from the other networks to levels in the information network.[20]

A policy is a rule that states how the day by day operating decisions are made. Decisions are the result of applying the policy rules to the particular conditions that prevail at any moment.[21] The actual decisions involve three things: a desired state of affairs, the apparent state of actual conditions as reported by the information network, and the generation of the kinds of action that will be taken in accordance with any discrepancy which can be detected between the apparent and desired conditions, within applicable policy. This entire process is highly non-linear and noisy.[22]

PROGRAMMED AND NON-PROGRAMMED DECISIONS

"Programmed" and "non-programmed" are the terms used by Simon[23] to denote two kinds of decision making that others have called *implicit* and *overt,*[24] and *analytic* and *synthetic.*[25] First, Simon:

> Decisions are programmed to the extent that they are repetitive and routine, to the extent that a definite procedure has been worked out for handling them so that they won't have to be treated *de novo* each time they occur . . . .
> Decisions are non-programmed to the extent that they are novel, unstructured, and consequential. There is no cut and tried method for handling the problem because it hasn't arisen before, or because its precise nature and structure are elusive and complex, or because it is so important that it deserves a custom-tailored treatment.[26]

We can conclude that programmed decisions, no matter how complex they seem, can be automated, while non-programmed decisions, except perhaps at a very primitive level, cannot. Programmed decisions are, in a sense, all made at once. That is, a procedure is established (the catchword is "heuristic") which, if slavishly and undeviatingly followed by a computer or a human being, automatically makes all choices that arise in certain situations, i.e., those whose alternatives are previously specified. Non-programmed decisions are called for in those situations where a heuristic has never been developed because of the one-of-a-kind peculiarity of the problem, or because all of the relevant parameters are not fully known, or where their measures are uncertain, or because the variables in the problem are too numerous for adequate rationalization in the time available, or, as is usual, because of some combination of these factors.

Forrester does not believe there is a sharp break between the two kinds of decisions:

> The majority of managers will argue that the region of the intuitive-judgement decision is so subtle that no reasonable approximation can be made to it through formal decision rules. Yet . . . when faced with a decision . . . lying beyond the capabilities of their intuitive judgement, [they] will once more fall back on formal decision-making procedure.[27]
>
> The intuitive judgement of even a skilled investigator is quite unreliable in anticipating the dynamic behaviour of a simple information-feedback system of perhaps five or six variables . . . the human is not a subtle and powerful problem solver.[28]

If planning is to result in the development of a durable edifice of systems, one that need not undergo repeated overhaul to remain viable in a climate of frequent organizational rearrangement, then designers must fully understand how to make systems adaptable to the human variable in decision making. The first prerequisite is an understanding of which kinds of decisions should be built-in, and which should remain in the province of man-machine interaction. Decision making in the enterprise is hierarchical. The two kinds of decisions discussed above are clearly at the extremes of this hierarchy—it is in the in-between levels that we have a problem of making valid distinctions.

THE HIERARCHY OF PLANNING AND CONTROL IN THE FIRM

Simon visualizes three layers in the firm: at the bottom, a layer of physical production and distribution processes; next, a layer of programmed decision processes controlling the routine operation of the physical processes; and finally a layer of non-programmed decision processes for monitoring and redesigning the lower-level processes.[29] Another commentator on management reminds us in no uncertain terms that "one cannot, through centralization, computerization, or otherwise, create one big brain. The facts of human scale require that decision making be subdivided." [30]

One level in the decision-making hierarchy, *strategic planning,* has been defined in Chapter I (page 10). Anthony identifies two other levels as well, *management control* and *operational control.*[31] Table 2-1 distinguishes among these levels in the decision-making hierarchy based generally on Anthony's characterization. The extrapolation represented in the table is an attempt to extend this concept beyond the behavioral area to include an information-systems perspective: inputs, outputs, tempos, systems types, etc.

One cannot do systems planning, in the sense in which this term is used here, to support the strategic planning level unless one can describe how to encapsulate a universe of information in the kind of data bank we know how to construct today. Strategic planning decisions are based on more than the historical record traced out by transactions within the company, on more than old market surveys, etc. There are no predictable boundaries on the type of information top management will attempt to bring to bear in their considerations. The existing data base and previously developed operations research approaches may be called upon among other things to aid in "backgrounding" the decision-making process. This is far from being a process amenable to handling by a consciously designed system in readiness, able to supply all information, or any major part of it, on demand. The strategic planning level is included here for purposes of completeness and to set the other two levels in proper context. It will not form an important part of the subject matter in the balance of this book. However, management control and operational control will.

Management control systems derive their source data from operational control systems. The reverse is not true. What flows in the reverse direction is not data, but changes to operational control systems, stemming from management control decisions based on information supplied by the control system—plus, of course, decisions on the handling of exceptional situations which are beyond the existing capabilities of the program (but not necessarily incapable of being programmed!). This strongly suggests that operational control systems are a part of management control systems. In addition, management control systems include a process whereby concrete data are abstracted into "management information," by aggregation or other reductive methods, to produce summary reports, forecasts, etc.

The bottom level, that of operational control systems, is defined by Anthony to be:

> . . . a *rational* system; that is, in general, the action to be taken is decided by a set of logical rules. These rules may or may not cover all aspects of a given problem. Situations not covered by the rules are designated as exceptions and are handled by human judgement.[32]

Activities at this level are handled on a transaction by transaction basis; that is, prescribed actions are taken with respect to each event—in

Table 2-1. An Information Systems Perspective on the Corporate Hierarchy

Level	Organizational Identity	Activities	Characteristics	Tempo	Inputs	Information Systems	Outputs
Strategic Planning	Corporation & Division Top Management	Set objectives Determine resources to be applied	Unpredictable Variable Staff-oriented External perspective	Irregular	Staff studies External situation Reports of internal achievement	Special "one-time" reports Simulations Inquiries (unrestricted)	Goals Policies Constraints
Management Control	Corporation & Divisional Departments Profit Centers	Allocate assigned resources to tasks Make rules Measure performance Exert control	Personal style Organizational change Line-oriented Judgmental Internal perspective	Rhythmic quarterly monthly weekly	Summaries Exceptions	Many regular reports Format variety Inquiries (restricted) "Data-bank" oriented Abstract	Decisions "Personal" leadership Procedures
Operational Control	Supervisors Foremen Clerks	Use resources to carry out tasks in conformance with rules	Stable Logical Predictable Prescribed	Real-time	Internal events Transactions	Formal Fixed procedures Complex Concrete	Actions

29

part as it arises, in part at subsequent intervals, in batches or otherwise, as appropriate. This includes initially capturing and recording certain data about the event, thereby creating the processable transaction.

SYNTHESIS

A synthesis of the three concepts of (1) information-decision-action, (2) programmed and non-programmed decisions, and (3) the hierarchy of planning and control, will now be undertaken. Since each of the concepts overlaps the others, such a synthesis already exists in part. It remains only to formalize and amplify upon the preceding discussion. It is necessary to attach some rigor to the notions of operational and management control systems, and their component parts, since these are the planning entities —what a plan is about. To this end, primitive concepts such as *data* will be definitionally related, and progressively more complex concepts will be defined in terms of simpler, previously defined ones. This is not meant as an idle exercise in axiomatics, since we have no intention of proposing a formal language for business systems planning in which theorems are derived. But the same words have frequently been used before, often to stand for somewhat or even very different concepts. Strict clarification of the sense in which they are to be used here is, therefore, essential, if confusion is to be avoided.

In the definitions to follow certain formalities are observed: (1) the word in boldface to the left of the "is" is the term being defined; (2) the phrase to the right of the "is" is the definition; (3) the word "is" in the definition is to be interpreted as meaning "is made equal to by definition"; (4) explanatory comments may follow a definition, and, if so, will be set off from it; (5) where the definition contains previously defined terms, these will be in boldface too, followed by the number of the definition in which they were defined in square brackets.

1. A **datum** is an uninterpreted raw statement of fact.
2. **Information** is **data** [1] recorded, classified, organized, related or interpreted within context to convey meaning.
3. A **level** is a pool of resources (manpower, money, materials, capital equipment), a backlog of demands on resources (orders), or a file of **information** [2] about the status of resources and demands.
4. An **activity center** is one of the basic organizational entities in an enterprise under the common and direct supervision of a first line manager, supervisor or foreman, which regulates the flow between **levels** [3], and may transform the flows between **levels** [3]. (An activity center is not itself a level although it may consume resources stored in a level.)
5. An **action** is a prescribed regulative-transformative response of an

activity center [4] to **information** [2] about the **levels** [3] with which it is concerned.

6. A **decision center** is one or more management-level people, together with his or their supporting staff assistants, who (1) prescribe the decision rules that govern the **actions** [5] of one or more **activity centers** [4], (2) make decisions for **activity centers** [4] to execute (as actions) in situations where the scope of prescriptions (decision rules) is exceeded, non-existent, or where a prescribed **action** [5] was not properly responsive and further adjustment is deemed necessary.

The latter part of Definition 6 expresses the fact that decisions are characterized by their intention to thread a path between undesirable extremes, and to do so a sequence of "adjusting" decisions is often required in routine activities. A decision center may also consist of higher management echelons accountable for decision centers rather than activity centers; see Definition 8. Some or all of the people in a decision center at a certain "decision-time" may be part of another decision center at another "decision-time." For example, a production planning committee may meet quarterly to promulgate a production plan for the forthcoming period; its individual members may also have day to day production-scheduling responsibilities. Therefore, certain groups of people are not to be confused as being identical to certain decision centers, even though they may constitute a decision center at a certain time for a certain purpose.

A management control decision is a judgment made by a decision center for the purpose of instructing an activity center on the basis of information about the effect of previous actions on the status of a level. Management control decisions are distinguished from "programmed" decisions—in the latter case the choices are always made by applying prescribed rules or procedures to data without the intermediation of managerial judgment. They are also distinguished from decisions which, while they must be made, are indifferent in their consequences; e.g., the choice between sequences in which two or more operations are to be performed when the order does not matter. However, the original promulgation of "programmed" rules and procedures is the result of a management control decision.

7. A **functional unit** is an **activity center** [4] and its **decision center** [6]. (The general structure of a functional unit is depicted in Figure 2-2.)
8. A **management control center** is one or more management people together with his or their supporting staff, which acts as a **decision center** [6] for a group of **functional units** [7], or for a group of subordinate **management control centers** [8].
9. An **operational function** is a CLASS of any one or more TYPES of **actions** [5], carried on by the same or different **functional units** [7], which regulate the inflow and/or outflow to or from sequences of **levels** [3] as a group.

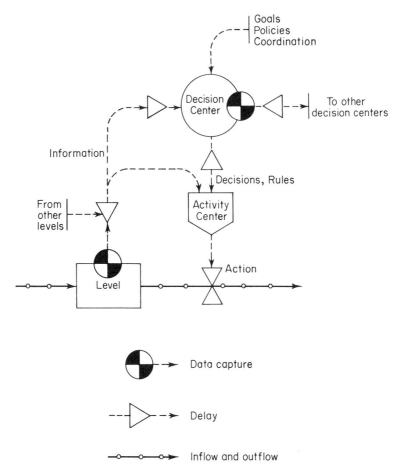

Figure 2–2. General schematic of a functional unit and its environment. (Freely adapted from Forrester, *Industrial Dynamics.*)

Alternatively an operational function can be defined in a more complex way as: a class of any one or more types of actions that are interrelated by the flow of information between the levels with which they are concerned and the decision centers which are part of the same functional units as those in which the actions take place, and between the levels and the management control centers accountable for the functional units in which the actions take place, and which regulate the inflow or outflow to or from sequences of levels as a group.

A functional unit may participate in more than one operational function, with the same or different groups of other functional units.

The functional units involved in a given operational function may or may not all report to the same management control center at the next echelon. If not, all the management control echelons involved in a given operational function will be accountable to some common higher echelon management control center.

Operational functions can be conceived as having a "tree" structure made up of management control centers branching downward from a single focus of control and terminating in functional units. Each functional unit may be part of several different structures, depending on the number of operational functions in which it participates. A *single* focus of control is often difficult to find and may therefore be thought to be non-existent. Further investigation will usually show, however, that the apex of an operational function coincides with a management control center in which resides the span of control necessary to make decisions affecting the *routine* activities of functional units acting in their assigned roles as part of an operational function. It is never higher than the highest management control echelon in which such decisions are *usually* made.

It is important to understand that *an operational function is a class of one or more classes of actions*. That is, it is a class whose elements are sub-classes. For example, order entry may be considered an operational function. Some of the classes of actions [5] which make it up are: preparation of memo orders, checking of credit and terms, pricing orders, cutting tapes for teletype transmittal, etc. The individual actions are, of course: prepare *a* memo order, check the credit of *this* customer, etc. The collection of individual actions concerned with the entry of any given single order is not an *operational function* [9], but rather an actual *operation* consisting of a sequence of related action steps. An operational function continues to exist even when actual operations are not taking place. Note that the levels [3] involved in order entry consist of such things as purchase orders in transit, memo orders awaiting credit check, etc.

10. An **action subsystem** is the group of **activity centers** [4] involved in an **operational function** [9]. (Obviously an activity center can be part of more than one action subsystem.)

11. A **decision subsystem** is the group of **decision centers** [6] and **management control centers** [8] involved in an **operational function** [9]. (A decision center can be part of more than one decision subsystem.)

12. An **information subsystem** is a special **functional unit or units** [7] involved in an **operational function** [9], and whose **levels** [3] and flows consist of **information** [2] generated and used in the **action and decision subsystems** [10, 11] of other **operational functions** [9]. (See Fig. 2-3, where the levels used by the information subsystem are labelled as "Data Sets," and where the information subsystem itself is shown as containing a decision center (or programs) and an activity center (or processing). Another method of internally structuring the information subsystem will be given in Definitions 14 and 16; it will be illustrated in Fig. 2-4.)

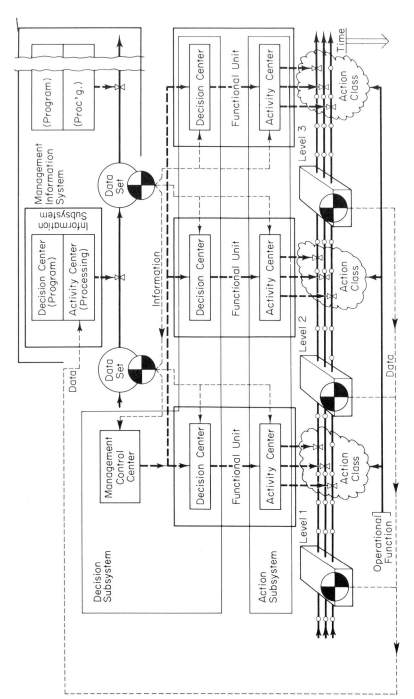

Figure 2–3. Schematic representation of Definition 13 (Management Information System).

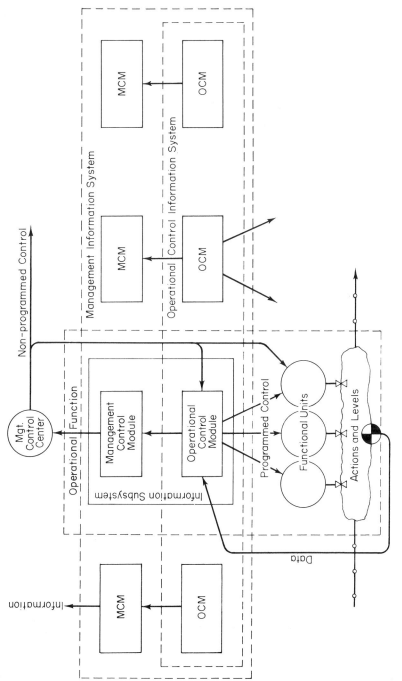

Figure 2–4. Schematic of the information system heirarchy.

35

An operational function can, therefore, also be defined in terms of these three kinds of subsystems. One of its subsystems, information, is itself "part" of an operational function whose other "parts" may be "parts" of other operational functions.

13. A **management information system** is an **operational function** [9] whose parts (corresponding to **functional units** [7]) are **information subsystems** [12] of other **operational functions** [9]. (Figure 2-3 is a graphic illustration of this which ties together the several notions defined above.)
14. An **operational control module (OCM)** is that part of an **information subsystem** [12] supporting the **functional units** [7] of an **operational function** [9]. (That is, supporting the action and decision subsystems of an operational function exclusive of management control centers.)
15. An **operational control information system (OCIS)** is all of the **OCM**'s [14] in a **management information system** [13].
16. A **management control module (MCM)** is that part of an **information subsystem** [12] supporting the **management control centers** [8] of an **operational function** [9]. (Therefore, a management information system is alternatively definable as an operational function whose parts are the MCM's and OCM's of other operational functions.)

Figure 2-4 is a schematic showing the relationships among the concepts defined in Definitions 13–16 in hierarchical form.

CONCLUSION

A Management Information System has been defined as consisting of parts of operational functions. This is entirely consistent with Forrester's view that the information system is a network reaching into all parts of the firm—that it is the connective tissue which links all other systems. In another dimension it is seen as having an inner core called an Operational Control Information System, whose parts are parts of the Information Subsystems of Operational Functions. This layered view is derived from Anthony's hierarchy of planning and control in the firm. There is man-machine interaction at both levels. In the operational control area it is programmed (prescribed) interaction, and its extent is ever diminishing as we develop feasible ways to replace machine-like human behavior with machines. In the management control area resides the substantial residue of essentially non-programmable decision making.

Modules, which have been equated with parts of Information Subsystems, are the basic entities in the systems classification, whose discussion will occupy the better part of the next two chapters. In a sense modules are the "species" in a systems taxonomy. The main burden of the claim that planning is a process whose elements can be formally defined and systematically related rests on the tenability of the concept of the module, and on the ability to properly define and identify modules within the business.

REFERENCES

1. Harold Sackman, *Computers, Systems Science, and Evolving Society* (New York: John Wiley & Sons, Inc., 1967), p. 42.

2. *Op. cit.,* p. 5.

3. *Op. cit.,* p. 42.

4. *Op. cit.,* p. 43.

5. A. R. Zipf, "The Computer's Role in the 'Dividends or Disaster' Equation," *Computers and Management—The Leatherbee Lectures* (Boston: Harvard University Graduate School of Business Administration, 1967), p. 61.

6. John Dearden and F. Warren McFarlan, *Management Information Systems* (Homewood, Ill.: Richard D. Irwin, Inc., 1966), p. 6.

7. Jay W. Forrester, *Industrial Dynamics,* pp. 54, 57, 59.

8. Charles A. Myers, ed., *The Impact of Computers on Management,* p. 13.

9. Dearden and McFarlan, p. 46.

10. Hershner Cross, "A General Management View of Computers," *Computers and Management,* p. 16.

11. Forrester, p. 53.

12. *Op. cit.,* p. 94.

13. *Ibid.*

14. *Op. cit.,* p. 93

15. *Op. cit.,* p. 68.

16. *Op. cit.,* p. 69.

17. *Ibid.*

18. *Op. cit.,* p. 95.

19. *Op. cit.,* p. 86.

20. *Op. cit.,* p. 71.

21. *Op. cit.,* p. 93.

22. *Op. cit.,* p. 96.

23. Herbert A. Simon, *The New Science of Management Decision* (New York: Harper and Row, Inc., 1960).

24. Forrester, *Industrial Dynamics.*

25. Sherman C. Blumenthal, "Problems of Management Display in Advanced Business Systems," *Proceedings of the 6th National Symposium on Information Display* (North Hollywood, Cal.: Western Periodicals, Inc., 1965).

26. Simon, *The New Science* . . . , pp. 5–6.

27. Forrester, p. 98.

28. *Op. cit.,* p. 99.

29. Simon, pp. 49–50.

30. Pearson Hunt, "Fallacy of the One Big Brain," *Harvard Business Review,* Vol. 44, No. 4 (August 1966), pp. 84–90.

31. Robert N. Anthony, *Planning and Control Systems.* . . .

32. Anthony, p. 77.

Traditional management theory placed primary importance on the hierarchical job/task pyramid with its emphasis on vertical relationships. The modern theory considers the total system as composed of numerous units and subsystems which interact . . . with each other. Not only hierarchical but horizontal and cross relationships are considered.

Richard A. Johnson, *et al.*[1]

THE SYSTEMS TAXONOMY
OF AN INDUSTRIAL CORPORATION

INTRODUCTORY DISCUSSION

A taxonomy is an orderly classification based on certain specified traits and relationships. In this book the "objects" we are interested in classifying are information systems and their components. The traits and relationships by which the classification is to be made cannot be chosen arbitrarily, but should serve the planning objectives outlined in Chapter I (page 13). Two of these objectives are of particular interest at this point. First is the desire to avoid separate, overlapping development, operation and maintenance of different systems, where there is no compelling technical or functional reason for difference. Second is the need to define the interfaces between systems components in a fairly standard way so that they may be properly integrated to operate across whatever boundaries may be established for the independent development of the components.

The biological taxonomies have produced a proliferation of ultimate entities (species) that number in the millions. In part this can be traced to the desire and ability of biologists to uncover fine morphological distinctions within existing subclassifications. Our purpose is not to multiply entities, however, but to avoid their multiplication. Taxonomies both differentiate and aggregate, depending on whether one proceeds downward or upward in the hierarchy. It is necessary that we keep carefully to the path between the extremes of too many small systems species or too few very large ones.

One source of the multiplication of systems stems from the inability, especially in diversified and decentralized organizations, to identify and measure commonalities* and differences between existing or potential systems. As long as there remains no basis or framework within which to classify systems, then systems requirements will continue to be stated only in terms of the observed needs of this or that user. These expressions of requirements tend to be unique in scope because of the lack of a common frame of reference from one group or division to another. It is well to remember, however, that a taxonomy is merely descriptive, while a plan is prescriptive, embodying a course of action. The systems taxonomy is not the planning target, therefore. That must be defined in terms of the users' needs. But the need, once having been expressed by the user, can then be segmented and classified by use of a comprehensive taxonomy.

MODULES, THE TAXONOMICAL ELEMENTS

MODULE SIZE

What of the size of the taxonomical elements? In any hierarchical scheme of classification, such as is proposed here, systems are defined in terms of the ultimate elements postulated. These elements emerge at the lowest level of the hierarchy as it branches downward. The generation of an impractically large number of these ultimate elements is to be avoided. Henceforth these lowest-level ultimate elements will be called "modules." Modules are larger than, say, a closed subroutine within a program, and smaller than a total logistics program system. Do the definitions in Chapter II help in the job of further illuminating the problem of size?

An Operational Control Module (see Definition 14 and Fig. 2-4) is the major part of the Information Subsystem part of an Operational Function. It serves, therefore, one or more Functional Units, each of which carries out a least one type of action in controlling the flow rates between levels. Let us proceed for a moment by example. Suppose we take orders shipped, but not yet billed, as a level. There are several actions in the preparation of an invoice. One is to look up special prices, discounts, delivery terms, etc. Reference has to be made to product catalogues and customer master file records. Now we might consider at this point that another level exists, consisting of those shipped orders about which pricing information has been determined. Next there would be another set of

---

*We use the term "commonalities" as the Pentagon does, to mean not only "similarities," but also "functional and structural identities" or "interchangeabilities."

actions, such as extending terms for each line item, totaling the invoice, applying freight charges, taxes, etc. Here we have a level that might be called invoices submitted, but not yet paid, i.e., a sales order accounts-receivable level. There is then usually a wait for payment, or for the account to become delinquent, before further actions are taken. However, payment may be received for a number of orders, there may be partial payments on several orders, etc. Credit status (and therefore matters of account delinquency) depends on the payment status with respect to an accumulation of orders, not on individual orders. So at some point we have moved from dealing with individual items to dealing with groups of invoices by account. Such activities may occur at many places in the company—within every billing operation. How shall the modules be set up to control these activities?

The smaller a module, the more likely it is to resemble other modules with similar functions. If a module's only function were something as trivial as, for example, "extend terms and total the invoice," the previous statement would obviously be true, since this identical action can be found in every billing operation in the corporation (indeed among all enterprises). On the other hand, a module this small is unlikely to be able to stand alone and perform useful work at an economic cost. It would be difficult to justify the development of an information subsystem merely to calculate an invoice total, when the costs of satisfying the elaborate formalities of input/output associated with computer processing are considered. A module, therefore, should encompass a sufficiently large number of actions to be economically viable on a stand-alone basis. If a module were not economically viable, it simply would not (or should not) be implemented except in conjunction with one or more other economically undersized modules to which it is closely related. This argues, of course, against the creation of artificial levels such as "invoices priced, but not extended." If anything, automation should serve to reduce the number of levels, not increase them.

Module size criteria are, therefore, empirical: create no new levels; encompass what is economically sound, but no more than that, if possible; start with the existing operational functions, and base the modules on these, rather than vice versa. Computers have an organizational impact, as we have seen, but this is never gratuitous. One should not start out by redesigning the organization merely because that would make its architecture more elegant, or our systems-design job easier.

COMMONALITY AND STABILITY

In order for modules supporting similar operational functions to exhibit maximum similarity, they must be relatively insulated from the differential influence of various existing and evolving organizational arrangements. The fact that a new division may be created, a division which organizationally subsumes business or product areas previously part of long-established divisions, should not have the effect of invalidating the modules supporting the functions carried on by those transferred areas. In addition modules should be unaffected by variations in information requirements having to do with the personal style or preferences of the individual line managers. These will certainly tend to change over periods of time, and they vary widely among the managers of similar operational functions at any given time.

Operational Control Modules should remain relatively stable in the face of organizational and management change, even though the Management Control Module, or Information Subsystem, of which they are a part must reflect these changes. Our assertion of this is circular, of course, since Operational Control has been defined in Chapter II as containing those elements in the information-decision-action network that are, by their very nature, relatively unaffected by organizational considerations.

MODULE BOUNDARIES

Conceivably one could set about constructing a matrix whose rows are operational functions, and whose columns are types of actions. Eventually, through trial and error, multiple intersections of actions and functions could be eliminated, so that the precise scope of each operational function would be defined in terms of actions unique to it. The following kind of decision would have to be made repeatedly during this process: Does a given action type "belong with" the others in the function, or not? Could it equally belong with others in more than one function, and, if so, in which should it be placed? (Is determining which warehouse should fill an order an activity of the order-processing function or the distribution function?) If an action type can be placed in either of two functions, the two functions have an interface.

In part, the question of placement of an action type in one or another operational function becomes a matter of determining marginal cost or benefit. Taking it away from one function may mean that the module involved is no longer economically viable on a stand-alone basis, while the module in which it would be placed is overly enriched. Such a procedure is purely hypothetical, of course. The cost-payoff information needed is not so readily available, but could in principle be developed. Rather, in practice, one proceeds to break a major systems development into phases, not all of which would be implemented at the same time, but which would eventually be integrated. The segmentation is usually done on the basis of experienced professional judgment, and only after the fact is cost-payoff data determined. And the fact very often is, in the case of large, integrated systems efforts, that the sum is economically greater than the parts; that a segment, or, in our terms, a module, is often justified not because it is in itself so economically attractive, but rather because it contributes to a whole which is.

The boundaries of a module are determined when the levels of the module are specified. These levels are data sets (see Fig. 2-3), and data sets are also the interfaces between modules. These interfaces are at the module boundaries, and will be discussed next.

MODULE INTERFACES AND DATA SETS

Inputs to modules, whether these are in the form of single transactions or batches, originate either outside of the Operations Control Information System of which the module is a part (e.g., an on-line keyboarding operation), or from other modules within the OCIS (e.g., a queue of transactions—in a direct-access storage medium, a card deck, on tape, etc.). Modules may have several inputs reflecting various combinations of the two kinds of sources. Similarly, outputs from modules, whether in the form of single transactions or batches, will be delivered either externally to the information system (e.g., a printed report or visual display) or internally to other modules (e.g., via multiple item tape or disc queues). As before, a module may have several outputs consisting of combinations of these two kinds.

Modules may be segmented by the implementing group into a number of programs or "tasks" in order to meet certain hardware, software, or programming personnel restrictions that may bear no relationship to the functional orientation of the module boundary as a whole. This interior module structuring is of no particular concern here, provided the functional performance specified for the module is not affected. The data sets that modules operate on must be specified in the functional requirements. Any transient data sets that may be created by virtue of internal module segmentation are really intra-module buffers and have no functional significance as far as the operational function is concerned. The specifiable data sets, however, do have applications significance. These data sets include:

1. Directories of information (e.g., name and address vs. company code).
2. Tables (e.g., machine loading standards, reorder formulae, etc.).
3. Working files (e.g., open sales orders, scheduled material requisitions, shop orders, etc.).
4. Master files (e.g., inventory records, vendor records, etc.).

Different modules at different times may require access to these files for purposes of updating, querying, report generation, cross-referencing, etc. Files that are thus used by more than one module are "interface" files, whose content and organization must be specified by the respective module design teams (jointly, if necessary). In general the form (serial, random, etc.), the locations (centralized, decentralized), the key attributes (record fields), and the linkages (vendor to product to purchase order, etc.) must be set forth, but details of implementation may be left open by the designers.

The interface between modules, and between modules and the real world of Functional Units, often consists of a data set called a *working file*. It persists as an entity only long enough to provide a buffer between two or more asynchronously operating modules or input/output activities. Working files include transaction files used for inter-module communication. A file of finished goods shipments produced as a by-product of an order-processing module may be considered an input transaction queue for an inventory-management module. If the latter module is not yet implemented, this file may be output in hard copy form for further processing. Thus, transaction files or working files may be important interfaces of a given module with other modules, with manual systems or with unimplemented modules.

Operational Control Module segments (e.g., "job steps," in IBM jargon) which are highly time-synchronized, such as in real-time situations, usually process a single transaction at a time through an entire "excursion." (An "excursion" is the whole chain of processing routines called upon to process the given transaction from its first appearance as input to some module segment, until that module segment can do nothing more on that particular transaction.) Generally the transaction is picked up from a queue (data set) of one or more waiting transactions on the basis of a priority scheme of some sort, and at the termination of the excursion is put into another queue (data set). These queues can be considered working files, as they are the boundaries of real-time modules which interface with other modules operating at different pulse rates. Single transactions undergoing an excursion in a real-time environment may or may not act as the interface between modules. Single transactions, however, often constitute the content of the man-machine interfaces driven by the modules of a real-time system. Thus a queue with one (or no) transaction could be a working file.

The second type of file consists of a data set called a *master file,* which persists as an entity throughout the life of a system. Rather than being a buffer of data generated, for example, by one module and picked up by another, it is a permanent store to which one or more modules have access from time to time for reference, updating or report generation purposes. Master files are specialized in content and organization to meet the needs of routine, day to day Operations Control Information Systems.

The updating of master files generally coincides with the basic "pulse rates" or cycles of the routine activity being supported by the information sub-systems in question. The sources of transactions against these files may be dispersed throughout the company. Transaction statistics and the volume of records in the file are generally known. The varieties of transaction types against the file are fixed. The master files contain only that information needed to support routine operation.

A third type of file may be called a *data base*. This file is more general-ized in structure than the master file, and its contents include informa-tion needed for response to a wide variety of non-routine, management control needs. There is some duplication of information between master and working files on the one hand and data bases on the other. Ultimately, various data bases may be organized into a common corporate data bank which can be the focus of a fully integrated management information system endowed with powerful inquiry-response capabilities. However, for a while yet, these data bases will probably be independent. They will be generally, but not always, query-oriented (direct-access) and updated periodically on a schedule independent of the operations control sub-system "pulse rate"; the update source for a data base will be processed and summarized from the data sets of the Operational Control Modules. Data bases will be centralized; the data-base statistics, as far as volumes of queries, numbers of records, "hit" distributions, kinds of inquiries, reports requested, etc., will be more difficult to anticipate than is the case with master files.

THE INFORMATION NETWORKS

Forrester has postulated information networks as one of the several kinds of network found in industrial organizations; other kinds are money, personnel, orders, materials and capital equipment networks.[2] The systems taxonomist, in laying the groundwork for the segmented development of properly integrated systems, must go beyond this monolithic conception. He must recognize that not all information processes are equally strongly tied together in the company. This is a basis for initial subdivision of the universe of information processing in the business into conceptually (and developmentally) manageable parts.

This problem is multidimensional. If one starts with Forrester's net-works, it can be shown that certain functions, such as procurement, inven-tory control, distribution, etc., occur in more than one network. Thus, one could adopt the view that, rather than follow the boundaries of the other networks, the subdivisions of the information network should be organized along the lines of similarity of activity, regardless of the functional loci of parts of the activities; just as, for example, a purchasing system covers the procurement of raw materials, supplies or equipment for capital projects, plant maintenance supplies, etc. Regardless of which of these two approaches one might take, there is yet another dimension, that of the similarity of activity, however classified, across sub-corporate boundaries. Thus, one might conceive of a common order-handling system for all divisions, or a single purchasing system for all divisions, etc. Before we can be specific about the identity of modules, we must find out what systems the modules belong to.

Sackman takes a somewhat pessimistic view of the general problem of systems classification:

> . . . it is extremely difficult, if not impossible, to give an operational definition of classification categories that can be subdivided into independent, mutually exclusive, and exhaustive subcategories. . . . the greatest obstacle in the path of successful classification is the refusal to face up to the complexity of the task. Armchair deduction is not enough. Exploratory empirical induction is one of the first steps, based on a continuing census of computer-based systems, periodically updated to keep up with significant changes. The individual systems constituting the bedrock population data base should be empirically described. Numerous systems traits should be operationally defined and systematically collected on an exploratory and provisional experimental basis for each computer census. Reliability and validity of trait items should be empirically tested and kept up-to-date. The more useful traits will persist, others will be dropped, and new ones incorporated into the trait inventory to be tested in turn for their effectiveness. This type of experimental experience will lead to alternative classification schemes. The more successful classifications will evolve and change with the changing population, and as such, could be designated as evolutionary classification.[3]

If this were the only valid approach within the corporate enterprise, regardless of its validity for the entire universe of computer applications, the systems planner would be little more than a custodian of after-the-fact information on already developed systems. At best he would probably be confined to the "data collection" and "integrate later" approaches described in the previous chapter. But this cautionary view is significant; it should remain foremost in our minds as we proceed.

Among other analysts there is little hesitation in identifying business information systems. Dearden and McFarlan have postulated two kinds of business systems: major (one that affects the entire organization), and minor (not of minor importance, but one that applies only to a limited part of the organization). The major systems are financial, personnel and logistics; the minor, marketing information, R & D, strategic planning and executive observation.[4] Here one might ask questions of the following kind: Is marketing information confined to such things as competitive intelligence, or does it also include short-term sales forecasts? If it comprehends the latter, then it, together with such other data as existing stock status and product commitments, is a vital input to the production-planning part of the logistics system. If "executive observation" is at all analogous to Anthony's "management control," then, as we have suggested in the definitions in Chapter II, the major systems (Operational Control Information Systems) are really part of these "minor" systems.

Forrester suggests that in many situations the development of an industrial-dynamics model can be done without considering the interrelationships of all of the networks in the enterprise. Perhaps the following observation is equally pertinent for the systems taxonomist:

> The flow of money represents an accounting for completed trans-actions. Money flow, however, is not ordinarily the principal determinant of sales and manufacturing decisions. Only in marginal organizations . . . would the conditions of the money network limit the freedom of decision making. . . . Also it is reasonable to start without the flows of personnel and capital equipment, since plausible and interesting situations exist in which labor and plant availability are not the factors primarily controlling industrial operations.[5]

This implies a strong connection between the orders network and the materials network, and a relatively more tenuous one between these two and the others. Let us for a moment assume that the relative degree of interdependence here extends to the interfaces in the information network, and therefore that a major separation can be made at this point. The information "subnetwork" supporting the orders and materials networks will be called the "*L*ogistics *O*perational *C*ontrol *I*nformation *S*ystem" (LOCIS). The LOCIS is concerned with the primary flow and transformation of materials and services occurring between the company's interfaces with its suppliers at one end of the network and its customers at the other. It assumes a fixed manufacturing capacity represented by levels of capital equipment (tools, machinery, plant, buildings, transport, etc.) and of manpower. However, the design of the LOCIS does not necessarily have to be changed even if this capacity is variable (which it normally is), provided that the system is designed to be flexible and expandable enough to meet growth in demand and capacity. We shall make this assumption and analyze its consequences further on.

In the category of non-logistics operational control are systems concerned with other kinds of physical operations, as well as non-physical ones. These involve the whole area of physical assets control: facilities and capital equipment acquisition, construction, maintenance and repair, and certain services. This suggests that it may be useful to postulate a

"Physical Assets Operational Control Information System" (PAOCIS), which, together with LOCIS, would constitute a major category of systems called, say, "Physical Operational Control Information Systems" (POCIS). This leaves the money and personnel networks to be classified within a category at the same level as POCIS, which will be called "Administrative Operational Control Information Systems" (AOCIS). The sub-categories within AOCIS are "Financial Operational Control Information Systems" (FOCIS), and "Manpower Operational Control Information Systems" (MOCIS), both at the same level as LOCIS and PAOCIS. All these systems have interfaces with each other both at the management control level and directly with each other, at the operational control level. This will be brought out more explicitly as we proceed.

We noted previously that certain functions within more than one of these systems, such as purchasing, represent a sort of "hyperplane" which cuts across the preceding categorization in yet another dimension. If there were to be purchasing "modules" in, for example, LOCIS and PAOCIS, might they not be similar in design, and therefore physically combined to operate as part of a common purchasing "module"? This apparent dilemma in the suggested categorization is easily resolved. These "modules" may indeed be combined, except that unique interfaces with other "modules" would have to be preserved in the resulting module. Our categorization is interface-oriented, and thus admits of physically common modules which have parts which are conceptually parts of different systems. This is no more paradoxical than the concept of the public information utility, where a common system may serve different customers having similar needs for information services.

Our taxonomy is multidimensional. Three of its dimensions have already been identified: the hierarchical classification of systems, common functions among systems in different hierarchical branches, and common "modules" across divisional boundaries. There are other dimensions as well, and these tend to emerge as we attempt to flesh out the structure in greater detail; for example, the geographical distribution of the firm's operations will play a role, as well as the kinds of "logistical" businesses the enterprise conducts. As a case in point Franksen and Romer have classified four kinds of production: (1) disjoint purchase, non-custom; (2) conjoint purchase, non-custom; (3) disjoint purchase, custom; and (4) conjoint purchase, custom.[6] Many diversified enterprises engage in all four classes of production. In Chapter IV these production classes are defined and their probable affect on the different kinds of "logistics data processing" are assessed. Let us first turn our attention again to the systems hierarchy—specifically the Logistics Operational Control Information System (LOCIS).

We have chosen to consider the orders and materials networks of

Forrester jointly, calling them the logistics network (not to be confused with LOCIS, which supports that network.) Table 3-1 is a list of some of

Table 3-1. LEVELS IN THE LOGISTICS NETWORK

Materials Inventories

    Reserved at vendors.

    Stockpiles at mines.

    Stockpiles at ports.

    In transit—pipelines, barges, trucks, ships, rail.

    At receiving and inspecting locations.

    At raw material stockkeeping locations—tank farms, rail sidings, plant storage, etc.

    In-process storage at plants.

    At finished product stockkeeping locations—plants and warehouses.

    At packaging and shipping locations.

Sales Orders

    Orders received, awaiting sales-office processing.

    Approved orders awaiting transmission to shipping point.

    Unshipped orders at shipping point.

    Back orders on made-to-order production.

    Shipped orders in transit, unbilled.

    Billed orders awaiting payment.

Production Orders

    Production orders awaiting scheduling.

    Scheduled orders awaiting material.

    Scheduled orders awaiting work orders.

    Work orders in process.

    Completed work orders awaiting inspection and inventorying.

    Completed orders awaiting movement to packaging and shipping.

Raw Materials Orders

    Production orders awaiting raw-materials scheduling.

    Raw-materials orders awaiting requisition action.

    Requisitions awaiting purchase action.

    Replenishment orders awaiting purchase action.

    Open purchase orders awaiting delivery.

    Delivered purchase orders awaiting payment.

the typical levels in the logistics network. There is an interesting parallel trichotomy in both the materials and orders levels. There are several levels of raw materials, in-process materials, and finished materials. Corresponding to these are three classes of levels in the orders part of the logistics network: levels of raw materials orders, production orders, and sales orders. Flows occur between all the levels in each of the three orders areas before they occur between the areas. That is, for example, sales orders are processed and goods shipped or back-ordered, and saleable inventory "taken down," all in a continuous series of closely synchronized actions. Subsequently, for finished-goods inventory replenishment, production orders are generated which may be aggregated for economic lot-size production runs scheduled for a later date. The level of finished-goods inventory acts as a buffer between the order-processing and shipping actions and the production actions. As Forrester notes:

> . . . some organizations have succeeded in speeding up the flow of sales information and production scheduling to the point where the random-noise variations in the market can now be directly imposed on the production process. This tends to ignore the proper use of inventories for absorbing such variations. Carried to an extreme, the result of more timely information can be harmful. The effect can be to cause the manager to put more and more stress on short range decisions.[7]

This points up an inherent danger in the "top-down" approach described in Chapter II. The manager may assume that the problems of production planning would disappear if full and instantaneous knowledge of sales orders were available. Some of the validity there may be in critiques of so-called "real-time-management-information-systems"[8] surely resides in their protests against unthinking attempts to couple too closely those things which should remain only loosely coupled.

The effect of creating three sub-classifications in LOCIS according to the trichotomy discussed above—which is what we propose to do—immediately determines what kinds of modules there must be in these areas, viz., raw-materials control, production control, and saleable-product control. In this scheme there would be three "loosely coupled" subsystems in LOCIS; *R*aw *M*aterials *O*perational *C*ontrol *I*nformation *S*ubsystem (RMOCIS), *PR*oduction *O*perational *C*ontrol *I*nformation *S*ubsystem (PROCIS), and *S*aleable *P*roduct *O*perational *C*ontrol *I*nformation *S*ubsystem (SPOCIS). The modules within each of these would be relatively more closely coupled. More loosely coupled still are the two major categories of systems in the Physical Operational Control Information Systems (POCIS) area, viz., LOCIS and Physical Assets Operational Control Information Systems (PAOCIS). If the degree of "looseness of connection" were to be equated to the level of the systems hierarchy where measurement is to be made, we might then conclude that the most remote connections are those between the POCIS and the Administrative Operational Control Information Systems (AOCIS), which includes Accounting Control in one of its subcategories. Yet there are very substantial outputs of data between the POCIS and the accounting systems. The point is, however, that routine accounting can be considered almost completely decoupled in a temporal sense from physical operations. Accounting periods are selected for legal or traditional reasons that have nothing to do with the procession of physical events in the company. Thus, our measure of connectivity is a matter of time-relatedness and synchronization of information feedback, and not primarily one of rigidly periodic and unidirectional information flows.

So far our discussion has been confined to operational control, with no mention as yet of management control. A great deal about management control has been implied, however, in the discussion thus far. It might therefore be well to recapitulate. Figure 3-1 summarizes the hierarchical categorization of operational control systems already discussed, recognizing that there is still some distance to go, vertically, horizontally, and in other dimensions as well. Certain subcategories, not heretofore mentioned, have been included in the figure. These are *F*acilities and *E*quipment *C*ontrol (FEOCIS) and *C*apital *P*rojects *C*ontrol (CPOCIS), both under physical assets control (PAOCIS); *T*reasury *O*perations (TROCIS), which, together with *A*ccounting *O*perations (AOCIS), is under financial operational control (FOCIS); and finally three subsystems under manpower (MOCIS): Payroll, Benefits, and Personnel Administration. The definition and the rationale underlying the postulation of these additional categories of systems will be taken up shortly.

All of these operational control systems are, according to the definitional exposition in the preceding chapter, at the core of management control. In the somewhat theoretical construction in the early part of this chapter, information from the master and working files of the operational systems is abstracted and lodged in a series of management control data bases. Whether this physically takes place or not is unimportant to the following argument, since the notion is perfectly valid conceptually. From the data bases, four kinds of management control information are generated or requested:

1. Monitoring reports (periodic)
2. Triggered reports (human decision required)
3. Demand reports (on-line inquiry-response, etc.)
4. Planning reports (special analyses)[9]

Any of these four kinds of management information may (and usually will) combine data abstracted from several operational control files. This is especially true for management information types 1 and 4. For example, measurements of profitability presented in periodic reports may be expressed in terms of "profit centers." These centers may be at the intersections of certain production and marketing units, and therefore may

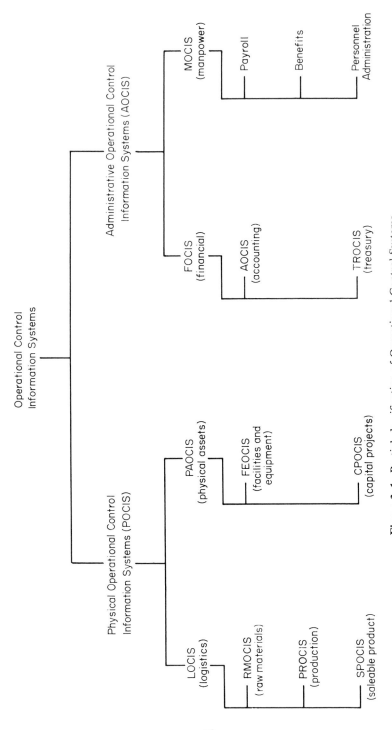

Figure 3-1. Partial classification of Operational Control Systems.

require the correlation of information derived from customer files, product files, and elsewhere. At higher levels of aggregation, profitability may be shown by product for all end uses, by customer or industry for all products, by division, etc. The tendency toward many-to-one correspondence between operational control information systems data sets and management information is similarly manifest when looked at from the viewpoint of certain kinds of middle-management responsibilities. Distribution and transportation management is concerned across the board with the movement of materials in all of the logistics and physical assets control areas, sometimes individually, but often on a joint basis, as when making freight-rate analyses among different modes of transportation. Production management is likewise broadly involved in many areas, from raw-materials scheduling to plant maintenance. Similar arguments can be put forth in the cases of purchasing, marketing, facilities, financial and personnel management control. Certain external information, not available in the operational control data sets, is also brought to bear in management control as well—for example, vendor advertisements in trade journals. It becomes clear that the moment we move upward from the level of operational control we enter a fuzzy area, one that defies the kind of logical approach discussed thus far. This does not mean that management control information systems development is not amenable to a systematic approach; it means merely that what has been described so far is not the whole answer but only part of the answer. Before pursuing this further, an open issue remains to be settled—that of identifying the operational control modules.

THE OPERATIONAL CONTROL MODULES—AN EVOLVING HYPOTHESIS

THE MEANING OF THE TAXONOMY

Earlier the notion of connectivity (or "closeness of coupling") among modules was represented as being of significance in how the branches in the taxonomy were selected; RMOCIS, PROCIS, TROCIS, etc. Actual systems which are developed may, for their own good reasons, include both closely and more remotely coupled modules. A user may have very valid economic reasons for wanting to develop a system which combines modules from several branches in a taxonomy, excluding others which, at first glance, would appear to be more "natural" candidates for inclusion than some of the modules selected to be implemented. For example, it is quite conceivable that a user would want to combine, say, order processing (from SPOCIS), accounts receivable (from AOCIS), and sales commissions (from Payroll). Therefore, *actual operational systems are collections of modules from among one or more branches of a taxonomy.*

Two or more actual systems may have some modules which have the same position in the taxonomical structure. That they have the same taxonomical name does not necessarily mean that they are similar or common modules. Their functional specifications within each of the different operational systems may be sufficiently unique to make joint development impractical. But they may not be unique, in which case the modules in question (not necessarily the entire operational systems) should be developed as common modules. (See Fig. 3-2.)

Module definition. Certain Operational Control Modules will be hypothesized at this point which, although consistent with the criteria set forth earlier, are arbitrary in the sense that other modules could have been selected to fit the same criteria. By identifying the modules as specified below and in the next chapter, we shall find that a rather acceptable looking architecture of systems results. Perhaps a simple and more elegant architecture could be built if we used a somewhat different set of module definitions. One cannot really judge this until such other possibilities are tried.

In using such unsystematic terms such as "simple" and "elegant," an appeal is made to the subjective aesthetic judgment of the systems architect. This is to some extent unavoidable. Systems designs, no matter how good, can always be improved, given the will and talent. In a sufficiently complex system it is practically impossible to achieve an ultimately simple design. However, systems which are relatively simple and elegant in design are usually found in practice to be operationally sounder and more economic than more complex systems which produce the same end product. There are principles in good systems design, and there are also good practices, the "arts" of the best practitioners in the trade, etc., but no comprehensive set of doctrines exists that, if followed religiously, will unerringly lead to a "best" systems design. In this situation an appeal to a sense of aesthetics is warranted, particularly at a stage in planning analogous to that of an architect's conception.

The motive for seeking a certain kind of economy in an architectural conception of an overall systems framework is not mere concern for superficial neatness. A fine teacher of philosophy, the logical empiricist Prof. Nelson Goodman, said: ". . . to economize and systematize are the same thing. Some economies are relatively unimportant and some apparent economies are spurious, but the inevitable result of regarding all economy as trivial would be a willingness to accept . . . [any elements] . . . that are clear enough to be admitted into the system at all." [10] A formal measurement of architectural simplicity in systems can probably be developed. It would involve not merely the number of modules, but also the number of interfaces or relationships among the modules, as well as the degree of consistency with which the criteria discussed earlier were

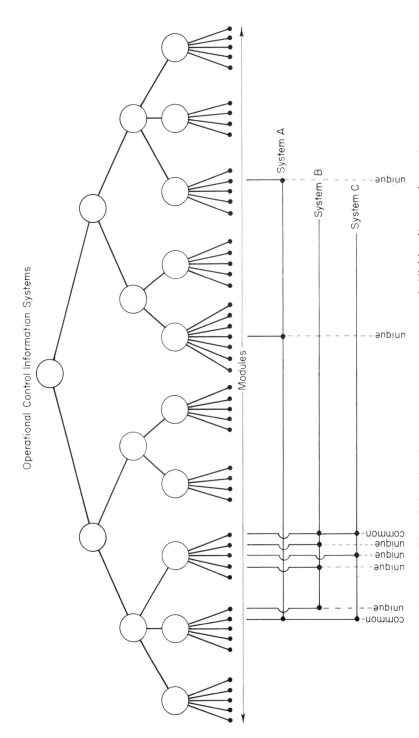

Figure 3–2. The relationship of a systems taxonomy to actual (divisional) operating system with common and unique modules.

used to choose the modules. The development of such a measurement is beyond the scope of this book. Even if one were available, it would be difficult indeed to establish a relationship between formal simplicity in the overall systems architecture and the overall lessening of the costs for all phases of all projects undertaken by the firm in fulfillment of the architectural conception. Thus, after exhausting the armamentarium of taxonomical rationale, our final criterion is unapologetically aesthetic.

Figure 3-3 depicts the hypothesized Operational Control Modules in each of the ten subsystem groupings (RMOCIS, PROCIS, etc.). Functionally similar modules, such as purchasing, are aligned horizontally in the figure. In Chapter IV these same modules will be depicted in a systems framework which illustrates the major interfaces and architectural relationships among them. These hypothesized modules may be considered to be the initial "pigeonholes" mentioned in Chapter II, page 19. As the review process shown in Fig. 2-1 takes place these "pigeonholes" may be expanded in number or scope, or otherwise revised, to conform more closely to reality as reflected in the actual systems proposals put forth by prospective users of systems.

MANAGEMENT CONTROL INFORMATION SYSTEMS

Operational control, and Operational Control Information Systems, consist of those routine activities and associated transaction-based data processing systems that would continue even if management went on an extended vacation (a purely hypothetical possibility, of course). We know what these activities are and can put our finger on them. We cannot so readily point to management control activities, nor prescribe what they are and when they should take place. This is in part because, as Anthony has pointed out, the really tough problems are not computer problems, but conceptual and even psychological problems: What is the proper measure of performance for a given area of responsibility, how often should the measurement be made, what information about the measurement is most decision-oriented, how is it best presented, etc.? [11]

Earlier in this chapter the role of a data base in management control was discussed. Anthony calls this a "data library." [12] The problem, as he puts it, is to:

> . . . develop a new concept that will guide us in answering [the] question [of level of detail in the data library] . . . . We want data at a much lower level of aggregation than we have ever stored before, but not so low that we exhaust feasible storage capacity, or so low that we use an undue amount of processing time in making summaries of it.[13]

Figure 3-3. Operational Control Modules (hypothetical) in an industrial company — OPERATIONAL CONTROL INFORMATION SYSTEMS

| | Physical Operations (POCIS) | | | | | Administrative Operations (AOCIS) | | | | |
| | Logistics (LOCIS) | | Saleable Product (SPOCIS) | Physical Assets (PAOCIS) | | Financial (FOCIS) | | Manpower (MOCIS) | | |
	Raw Material (RMOCIS)	Production (PROCIS)	Saleable Product (SPOCIS)	Property and Equip. (PEOCIS)	Capital Projects (CPOCIS)	Accounting (ACOCIS)	Treasury (TROCIS)	Payroll	Benefits	Personnel Admin.
Materials Scheduling	✓				✓					
Purchasing	✓			✓	✓	Accts./Pay	Cash Ctl.			
Receiving – Inspection – Storing	✓			✓	✓					
Inventory Control	✓	✓	✓	✓	✓	Inv Acctg.				
Distribution Control	✓	✓	✓	✓	✓	Dist and Frt. Accounting				
Sales Control			✓			Sales Accounting		Commissions		
Order Processing			✓							
Pricing and Billing			✓			Accts/Rec	Cash Ctl			
Scheduling		Production		Maint and Repair	Project					Crew Scheduling
Materials Requirements		✓								
Job and Process Control		Production		Maint and Repair	Project			Timekeeping		
Property and Equip. Control				✓	✓	P and E Acctg				
Schedule to Gross Pay						Labor Distribution		✓		Salary Schedules
Gross to Net Pay						Taxes	Paymaster	✓	Deductions	
Personnel Records Employee Plan Acctg.						✓			✓	
Stockholder Records						Dividend Accounting	Transfers		✓	✓
Investment, Pensions, Insur. Funds						✓	✓			
Tax Accounting						✓				

Figure 3–3. Operational Control Modules (hypothetical) in an industrial company.

This problem results from the desire to avoid the rigidly formatted and summarized information found in the traditional, periodically produced management report, and to substitute for it a more flexible and selective reporting capability, which can sort and summarize details in a variety of ways. This can now be done to a very limited degree: where the attributes by which we may wish to classify or aggregate information in a single file or set of linked files have been anticipated in advance, during the design of the file, its indices, and the file maintenance system. New reports can even be created on-line, in conversational mode, using a "light pen" and cathode-ray tube. More conventionally, new hard-copy reports can be generated by use of report-generator programs and report-specification languages.

Nevertheless we remain straitjacketed by the technology. It is very difficult to find a system which can produce management control reports that have not, at least in principle, been anticipated in the file design, even though the information they would contain is in the file. Of the four kinds of management control reports named on page 51, this deficiency in the technology only really affects the way the designer is constrained in his handling of monitoring and demand reports. Planning reports lie in the strategic area, and triggered reports are, almost by definition, rigidly defined in advance. Monitoring reports, presumably of the "actual vs. planned" variety, may lead the manager to want to probe more deeply into the details underlying a significant variance in an area under his control. This is ordinarily handled by routinely generating several levels of detail in the reports. Most of this detail will never be referred to, giving rise to bulky printouts and the repeated call for "management-by-exception" reporting systems. Rarely, however, is the manager able to define what constitutes an exception under all conceivable circumstances, with enough rigor to guarantee that he would never wish to examine what would then become non-exceptional (and non-reported) information. The potential exposure is too great for a manager to commit himself in this way with any finality.

A key objective of planning expressed in Chapter I is to insulate operational control systems from the need for repeated overhaul to make them adaptable to organizational change. Conceptually this has been done by postulating different files of data for operational control on the one hand and management control on the other. This makes practical sense too, in many cases, since a given management control report may be based on data culled from more than one operational control file. In fact most cost-accounting reports are based on data from many sources: labor distribution, material costs, plant overhead, etc. Very often the actual hard-copy form of these reports *is* the management control data base.

The management control data base includes not only cost-accounting data but also budgets, sales forecasts, sales analyses, customer credit histories, inventory levels, vendor performance reports, capital project PERT reports, transportation analysis reports, profit and loss statements, etc., etc. In the next chapter, we shall attempt to identify various segments of the management control data base and the operational control files to which they are related.

THE TAXONOMIES OF OTHER KINDS OF ENTERPRISE

The taxonomical approach to creating a framework for systems development can be applied elsewhere than in the multi-unit industrial corporation, organized into product-line divisions, to which many of the examples in this book apply. A prime characteristic required as well in the non-industrial as in the industrial case, if one hopes to apply these principles, is a certain parallelism of structure and function among several sub-corporate, "product-line" oriented, organizational units. Such parallelism is commonly found in a great many non-industrial corporations, which may or may not be organized into "divisions" as such. Examples of this "divisional" characteristic can be found among nation-wide retail store federations, state-wide banks organized by region, diversified service organizations, railroads with multiple operating divisions (often the residue of merger), newspaper chains, broadcasting networks with owned local affiliates, "conglomerates" representing combinations of several of these kinds of industries, etc.

In retailing, for example, there are two major organizational dimensions to the problem of developing a systems taxonomy in a multi-divisional enterprise: merchandising and operations. The merchandising organization usually consists of a number of "merchant groups": a merchandise manager together with a number of buyers, one for each department within his jurisdiction; plus such functions as advertising and promotion. On the operations side are the individual stores with their store managers and departmental sales forces, plus warehousing, superintendency, personnel, distribution, etc. The stores in a widely dispersed organization will tend to be grouped by region or metropolitan area. The data-processing function associated with these groupings will tend to be similar, that is decentralized, at least in part. An approach to an operational control taxonomy might begin with a breakdown into merchandising, operations, finance, and personnel functions. Inventory control and buying in the merchandising area might be further subdivided among staples, fashion goods, and "big ticket" merchandise classes. The analysis could then look for module similarity within and among the operational systems.

REFERENCES

1. Richard A. Johnson, Fremont E. Kast, James E. Rosenweig, *The Theory and Management of Systems,* 2nd ed. (New York: McGraw-Hill Book Co., 1967), p. 64.

2. Forrester, *Industrial Dynamics,* p. 68.

3. Harold Sackman, *Computers, Systems Science, and Evolving Society* (New York: John Wiley & Sons, Inc., 1967), pp. 85–6.

4. Dearden and McFarlan, *Management Information Systems,* pp. 7–9.

5. Forrester, pp. 138–9.

6. O. I. Franksen and M. D. Romer, "Industrial Production and Digital Computers," *Proceedings of the 20th National Conference of the ACM* (New York: Lewis Winner, 1965), pp. 455–468.

7. Forrester, p. 427.

8. For instance, see John Dearden, "Myth of Real-Time Management Information," *Harvard Business Review,* May–June 1966, pp. 123ff.

9. "New Management Reporting Systems," *EDP Analyzer,* Vol. 5, No. 1 (January, 1967).

10. Nelson Goldman, *The Structure of Appearance* (Cambridge, Mass.: Harvard University Press, 1951), pp. 59–60.

11. Robert N. Anthony, "Future Uses of Computers in Large and Complex Organizations," *Computers and Management—The Leatherbee Lectures 1967* (Boston: Harvard University Graduate School of Business Administration, 1967), p. 114.

12. *Op. cit.,* p. 117.

13. *Op. cit.,* p. 119.

By definition, when we use the words Integrated Management Information System, we refer to a very highly organized combination of personnel, equipment, and facilities performing data storage and retrieval, data processing, transmission and display, all in response to the needs of decision makers at all levels of the business.

Hershner Cross[1]

IV | A FRAMEWORK FOR SYSTEMS DEVELOPMENT

SCOPE AND PURPOSE

GENERAL

The definition of an integrated management information system offered above does not explicitly refer to the scope or functional comprehensiveness of the system. It does not say "all of the needs" or even "some of the needs," and might therefore refer to a system of somewhat more modest scope than that which is seemingly implied. Modest horizontally at any rate, for vertically it would, by definition, have to extend from the lowliest clerical "decision maker" to the Chairman of the Board. We have earlier suggested that perhaps most of the information flowing in an enterprise, such as informal interpersonal communications of various kinds, cannot be profitably computerized. Furthermore we have attempted to make a case for a step-by-step development of an integrated system for that substantial and vital residue of information handling that is subject to practical and profitable computerization, starting from the bottom up, i.e., in the operational control area.

If step-by-step development is not to result in "islands of mechanization," a framework is needed which would serve to weld systems applications into a smoothly functioning totality. Our premises for such a framework are these:

1. Management control must not impose additional data *collection* requirements on operational control systems.
2. Management control may impose additional requirements for data *classification* on operational control systems.
3. Functional integration exists first at the operational control level.
4. Operational control systems can be designed independently of, and can be made to accommodate themselves to, changing management control requirements occasioned by organizational rearrangements and evolution in managerial style.

A major planning problem is the achievement of interim, partial capability within an overall, long-range, integrated systems plan, while simultaneously serving the objective of permitting the integration of each new addition with those portions of the overall system already implemented. A complex, integrated system, implemented in phases over a substantial period of time, must be capable of accommodating itself to change. Changes can be expected to stem from three major sources:

1. Changes in details of the systems requirements and specifications that are an inevitable accompaniment to any development effort. No complex systems design can be expected to be completely airtight.
2. Changes in organization and company policies requiring reorganization in major aspects of the system which provide the basis for planning and control of lower-level activities. These changes may have their origins in considerations extrinsic to the information system (acquisitions, important new products, etc.); but they also may result to some extent from the actual use of portions of the system, and the experience from this being fed back into the planning process to alter the objectives of that process itself; and from changes in design made to reflect changes in system objectives.
3. Changes in technology. Over any extended period, say five years or more, systems technology can be expected to evolve through at least one major and several minor revolutions comparable to the past progressions termed "generations" of computer systems. Planning for and design of systems must not be so rigid as to forestall the possibility of taking reasonable and appropriate advantage of technological opportunities when there are definite benefits in doing so. Among other things this requires being able to foresee where the technological trends are leading, and leaving "adapter plates" in the design so that new developments may be accommodated without sacrifice of basic system integrity and previous investments.

These sources of change lead one to argue against adopting an inflexible framework. In developing big systems, timely redesign and revisions are both practical and necessary. Proposals for systems changes, arising at random times, should be clustered in one bundle to be produced and introduced all at one time. This periodic process results in a series of systems versions, succeeding in each other in time, and each refining and elaborating on the preceding version. This permits system change to occur in a planned and controllable fashion, and inhibits potential danger to systems integrity from a piecemeal approach. There must therefore be a limitation on the amount of detailed design constraints in the framework. These matters are considered further in Chap. IX, "The Management of Change."

As a practical matter the framework cannot initially embrace every area of potential or actual automatic information handling in the company, although this might be an ultimate goal. Nor can it merely confine itself to systems whose development is sponsored at the corporate level, since many, if not most, systems in a large corporation are, and will continue to be for some time, developed in response to individual needs of divisions or other subcorporate-level organizations. If such developments are ultimately to find wide applicability and also tie together, they will be able to do so only by adapting themselves to certain necessary constraints imposed by a framework. The desirability of such an approach is analogous to that taken in other areas, where corporate-wide policies have been promoted to achieve certain objectives that would otherwise be out of reach, were each business entity within the enterprise to retain complete autonomy. For example, there are undeniable benefits from having all divisions observe common practices with respect to performance reporting, personnel policies, organization, accounting, capital budgeting, etc. In addition to asking the divisions to observe certain ground rules in the planning of information systems (to their ultimate benefit, and the benefit of the corporation as a whole), certain systems are natural candidates for development by the corporation on behalf of all the divisions. A teletype message-switching system is one obvious example.

A divisional system developed within corporate framework constraints may be adapted for use by other divisions with assurance that it will interface with the rest of that division's systems, and also with corporate-wide systems. Because this approach will tend to optimize the use of scarce systems-development resources in the corporation, all divisions and corporate departments can look forward eventually to being on an equal footing in systems applications at a relatively high level of sophistication. Also the divisions themselves will be assured that their systems will properly interface with each other and with those of the corporate departments.

FRAMEWORK PROPERTIES

Our taxonomy served to identify the modules and classify them in terms of certain criteria. These criteria had to do with the "relatedness" of modules, exemplified in the taxonomy by the grouping of modules into "subsystems" such as RMOCIS. The framework specifies *how* the modules of such subsystem groupings are tied together, and how the subsystems are related to each other and to the rest of the corporate organization. Thus, the framework serves more precisely to define the boundaries and interfaces of the modules and subsystems. These boundaries include the working and master files that have functional significance, but exclude other data sets that have only intra-module significance. The latter are within the province of the system designer. Attempting to specify them at the framework level might lead to the undesirable rigidity cautioned against earlier.

Knowing, for example, that a certain master file is maintained by a particular module, but is accessed by another, indicates a certain natural priority in development. The second module would be plainly inoperable unless the former already existed. Development priorities, discussed further in the next chapter, also depend on local and global considerations related to the modules, subsystems, and even larger systems entities. A particular module may have a small payoff as an isolated development, but may be an essential part of some larger systems objective of great importance to the enterprise. Its implementation may, therefore, be among the first things to be undertaken, because of its technical precedence.

Framework modules are not systems specifications, even partially. They only specify the *scope* of systems. In a given enterprise there may be a requirement for several unique module versions, each having the same scope. The framework makes it possible to establish a series of studies, each confined to a module, to determine how many actual systems versions satisfying the module boundaries are actually required, with the assurance that the actual systems will interface properly with those developed in accordance with the scoping of adjacent modules.

FRAMEWORK DEVELOPMENT GUIDELINES

A framework encompassing every conceivable applications area in the enterprise is not needed before starting detailed development work in some areas. However, an initial version of an overall systems taxonomy should exist. As the process of systems review (see Fig. 2-1) takes place, the taxonomy will be refined, and this will eventually reflect itself in the framework as it, too, evolves. Given these considerations, certain guidelines to the development of a framework are in order:

1. The work should proceed in phases. Succeeding phases will add detail to and improve conceptually upon earlier phases, and will also incorporate new applications areas.
2. Each successive framework "model" (phase) should include the previous model as a subset, so that work already completed within a prior context does not have to be redone or undergo radical alteration.

3. Each phase should be directed as much as possible to the current systems-planning efforts. The framework effort should not necessarily influence development priorities, but should definitely be influenced by them.
4. Extensive analysis should not be considered a necessary precondition to the initial work of synthesizing a framework. Analysis should serve to refine rather than to substitute for sound conceptualization. This is quite different from saying that analysis should not precede the development of detailed functional specifications for implementation of various framework modules. It must, of course.

A FRAMEWORK PRESCRIPTION

RELATIONSHIP TO SYSTEM DESIGN

The relationship of the framework to system design can be best expressed in terms of the level of detail included within the framework. Given the detail already in a taxonomy, it is evident that the designers would be instructed to work on certain specific modules or groups of modules, rather than on, say, a "production and inventory control system." By showing certain relationships among the modules the framework further constrains the systems designer. There are, however, several levels of detail below the module level where the designer has considerable freedom. These levels might be considered as an extension of the tentative taxonomical hierarchy previously sketched (see Fig. 3-3).

J. A. Simpson suggests what these additional levels are.[2] His "SAPTAD" "levels" overlap our "modules" and "subsystems," although he uses other names. He identifies the following levels in a hierarchical systems taxonomy:

1. *S*ystems (e.g., logistics operational control)
2. *A*pplications (e.g., saleable product operational control)
3. *P*roject (e.g., order processing)
4. *T*ransaction (e.g., customer orders)
5. *A*ction (e.g., pricing)
6. *D*etail (e.g., special pricing terms or discount rules)

The examples are mine and reflect my interpretation of "SAPTAD." If they are appropriate, then the third or "project" level corresponds to the bottom or "module" level in the taxonomy of the previous chapter. Simpson calls the third through sixth levels "systems design" levels. The first two levels are "management" levels in the sense that, in specifying the entities at these levels, management has thereby somehow placed constraints on the nature and scope of projects the systems designers will work on. The framework goes beyond this to the project or module level, although this might be unnecessary in a non-divisionalized enterprise (however, see Chap. IX, section on "Standard Modules").

MODULES AND THE FRAMEWORK

The framework depicts the modules, their interfaces, master files, etc. This is not a high-level systems design for some particular spectrum of users in the company. Different functions may have widely varying relative importance to the various "businesses" in the corporation. For example, raw-materials inventory control is not as important to a business that extracts magnesium from sea water as it is to a steel-manufacturing business. A function represented by a particular module may be implemented in a very rudimentary way indeed for some particular business, or may not be implemented at all. In this event there has to be at the very least a "zero" version of this module for those businesses in which this function is non-existent. The purpose of this "zero" module version would be to preserve the relationship among all the adjacent modules in the system by serving as a bridge, and providing the necessary interfaces. Thus, the framework is truly a framework (if the tautology may be excused), and not a systems design.

Data sets that have the status of levels (see Chapter II) in the information network are explicit in the framework. These data sets include master files, working files, and all inputs and outputs at the level of operational control; i.e., management control reports, etc. are not included. These data sets form the operational control interfaces of the modules with each other and with the external world.

Since implemented modules can work together asynchronously, the framework should address itself to the individual module tempos. These may vary according to user needs and cost considerations, but in principle the framework should provide a clue to the range of appropriate tempos (real-time, daily, weekly, etc.). Often the specific tempo will be known with some precision. The modules of an integrated system, having potentially different tempos, provide a degree of flexibility in meeting user needs not always available in the monolithic systems concept. The user need not be limited in his choice of working method by the deficiencies of traditional batch processing, on the one hand; nor need he have to pay an unwanted premium for unnecessary on-line processing of inherently slow periodic functions, on the other.

A module may be implemented in a number of versions to satisfy justifiably unique requirements of different corporate subunits, such as divisions. A single version of an implemented module may exist in a number of "copies," each operating independently at different geographical locations, and perhaps all interfacing with other modules at the same or different locations, some of which may exist in a singular form, and others in multiple copies. Examples of multiple copy module versions might be local systems for process control or automatic warehouse applications. The effect of the geographic variable can be isolated from other considerations by first determining how many different module versions would be required in each instance, if all the facilities and resources of the company were concentrated at one physical location. Once that determination has been made, it then becomes possible to consider how many copies of each version would be optimum for a given geographical dispersion of the physical activities involved. Of course this latter consideration involves questions of the economies of multiple computer sites, communications load, and whether or not file centralization is required. Let us consider two possible situations in order to illustrate the point just made:

1. Process control computers would not in general be installed remotely from the plants they service, since communications costs would be excessive for handling the large volume of sensor data. Similar reasoning may prove to be significant in some cases where data-collection terminals or other multiple-terminal, high-volume data sources are used. This would be especially true when the details of most items of information are only needed at the local plant site, and the central or higher-level parts of the information system require merely summary data or knowledge of exceptions. Thus, the presence of small computers at some remote plant sites may be economically sound. (They should be able to get along without local analysts and programmers, by using their version of the standard applicable module, and perhaps they would be completely unattended.)
2. Order-entry and order-processing functions might share the facilities of a common nationwide order-processing network, using some type of teletype terminals or computer-data transmission facilities, or some combination of both, as well as mail and telephone where appropriate. A small number of order-processing module versions could run in one large central computer complex, each version processing orders for a certain type of "business" or certain divisions. Production and shipment information could flow from this center to other appropriate centers, which would handle the production and inventory activity for the actual plants and warehouses involved.

FRAMEWORK EXCLUSIONS

This matter will be more generally treated in a later section. Now it is only necessary to say that there are certain activities whose *internal* information needs are either so specialized, or so removed from the mainstream of information which deals with the operations of the business, that it does not appear desirable to consider them in detail when developing the framework. The attention given to such areas might consist of one or two interviews with their senior management to verify assumptions about their relevance to information-systems development and to determine the general nature of their information requirements.

Certain activities are considered possibilities for such minimal treatment during the framework development effort. It is recognized that such departments as Audit, Law, or Insurance, will exert an influence on the overall information requirements; however, their internal requirements for information may not be particularly relevant to the adequacy of the framework for the "mainstream" information systems development plan.

A FRAMEWORK EXAMPLE

QUALIFICATIONS

The first and simpler of the two framework illustrations in this section is that of a Manpower Operational Control Information System; the second is for logistics operational control. These framework examples are for a hypothetical industrial corporation and are not meant to accord with the

Table 4-1. MANAGEMENT CONTROL EXCLUSIONS FROM MOCIS AND LOCIS FRAMEWORK EXAMPLES

MOCIS
1. Recruiting and employment
2. Training and personnel development
3. Labor relations
4. Determination of compensation and benefits rules
5. Employee counseling and motivation

SPOCIS
1. Competitive analysis
2. Setting sales quotas
3. Cost-price-discount policy determinations
4. End-use analyses
5. Product profitability measurement
6. Long-term sales forecasts

PROCIS
1. Cost per run and economic lot-size analyses
2. Quality standards and control
3. Manufacturing methods and procedures
4. Production planning
5. Space and equipment layouts

RMOCIS
1. Vendor analyses
2. Quotations and terms
3. Make-or-buy analyses
4. Economic order quantity determinations
5. Physical distribution patterns
6. Materials planning and forecasting
7. Surplus disposal

actualities of any particular type of organization or firm. They are, therefore, no more than suggestive of how a typical framework might look.

These examples, applying as they do to a large and highly diversified company, must be generalized enough to fit all the variations to be found in such situations, as one proceeds from "business" to "business" or from division to division within a corporation. The most highly variable elements, particularly the management control aspects, are excluded from the framework except where it would be confusing or misleading to omit them. For example, a change in the benefits structure must update certain personnel records, and a path must be shown for this kind of management input. In general, however, the tapping of information for management control, from either a management control data base or, ultimately, the operational control files, is not included.

Table 4-1 lists some of the management control exclusions from the framework examples. This list is not exhaustive, but merely suggests the kinds of management control information feedback that occur in interaction with the operational control system, but which are virtually impossible to depict in the generalized fashion required of the framework.

The framework examples which follow identify and describe the elements in the respective systems and the way in which they might be arranged for development. This provides the basis for developing a set of functional specifications dealing with each systems element or grouping of elements. In accord with the conventions previously discussed these elements will be referred to as modules, and groups of closely interacting modules will be called subsystems.

MANPOWER—*MOCIS*

Each master file in the Manpower System is dedicated to one and only one subsystem, and is not accessed by other subsystems. However, a master file may be accessed by more than one module in a given subsystem. The information interfaces between subsystems consist solely of working or transient files—generated by one subsystem and used as input by another —and have no permanent existence in the system. Working files are merely temporary buffers holding data in readiness for processing by a subsystem. Master files, although updated from time to time, have an uninterrupted existence in the system and do not evaporate after being accessed and processed.

Figure 4-1 identifies the subsystems, their master files, and the subsystem interfaces (working files). The figure depicts five subsystems:

1. Data acquisition and control—versions of which may operate at each of the data-processing locations of the enterprise.

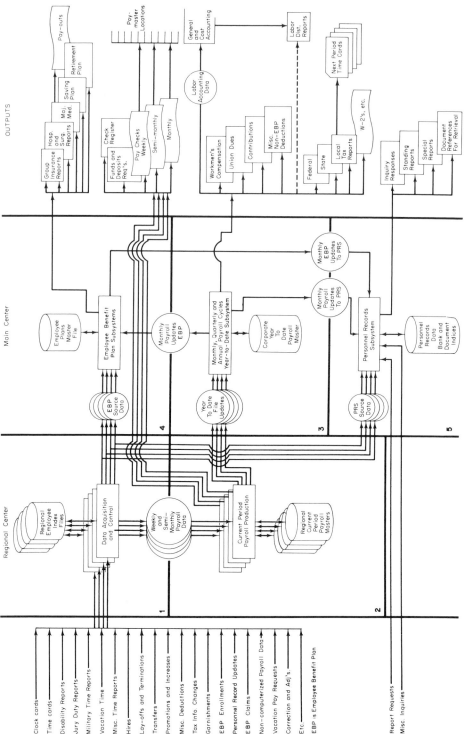

Figure 4-1. Manpower subsystems. Subsystems 3 and 4 may be consolidated.

70

2. Current period payroll production—also may run at each of the data-processing locations.
3. Monthly, quarterly and annual payroll (Year-to-Date)—run at one location for the entire organization.
4. Employee Benefit Plans (EBP)—also centralized.
5. Personnel records—also centralized.

After further analysis of file content and basic processing cycles, it may prove to be advantageous to consolidate subsystems 3 and 4 (Year-to-Date Payroll and EBP) and combine their separate files into one.

Several conclusions can be drawn from subdividing the manpower area into these four or five subsystems.

1. Input and check-preparation processing can be done as close to the source of data origination as possible. This has several distinct advantages as opposed to central processing:
   a. It accelerates the entry of data to the system, this reducing the interval between preparation of input, check production and check distribution.
   b. It minimizes the movement of a mass of paperwork from user to system and back. If data communications are used between field locations and the data-processing locations, this arrangement would also tend to keep communications costs to a minimum.
   c. It simplifies the problem of error handling by making it possible in many cases to refer unacceptable input back to the originators before further processing.
   d. It helps to distribute the manpower processing load more evenly throughout the complex of data-processing centers.
   e. It eliminates procedural complexities by requiring all manpower inputs of whatever variety which originate at a given location to be directed to one and only one data-processing center, namely the regional center serving that locality. (No inputs are sent to the main center.)
2. The overlap of duplicate information between the files is kept to a minimum within the constraint that the objectives in partitioning the manpower files as proposed are:
   a. To keep total file-handling time to a minimum by not passing monthly file data through weekly cycles, etc.
   b. To permit any output, report or information request to be handled by reference to one and only one master file.
   c. To allow the optimum organization of manpower-systems file data among a variety of storages (tapes, discs) appropriate to the processing requirements of each subsystem. For example, the requirements of payroll calculation and check preparation may indicate a file organized serially on employee number, while personnel records might require much more complex indexing and an entirely different ordering. A single file, whose structure would satisfy the requirements of both subsystems, would be optimum for neither.

3. Manpower subsystems need not all be implemented and cut over at the same time. If they were more closely interwoven, it would not be easy to undertake independent development of major pieces (e.g., Current Payroll) which could run independently of other pieces (e.g., Employee Benefit Plan and Personnel Records) scheduled to come later.

4. File data which ought to be consolidated and maintained centrally (for economy and because of the nature of the use of the information) are grouped into appropriate corporate-wide files.

Manpower Data Acquisition and Control. These subsystems operate at each of the data-processing centers. These "regional" subsystems accept any and all inputs generated in the regional area which update any of the master files in the Manpower System. A given input may contain data updating only one, two, or more master files. This subsystem can accept inputs arbitrarily in the form of punched cards, teletype, or from on-line terminals. In its initial version the system may accept only punched card or punched tape, or both, and process this input on a cycle basis. This cycle is presumed to take place at least daily in order that errors can be detected and recirculated as soon as possible, also possibly to meet the needs of one or another current payroll cycle occurring the next day, and finally to spread the "head-end" processing load evenly over the entire week. These subsystems will collect, verify, index, sort and disperse data to each of the other manpower subsystems. The outputs to the other subsystems are presumably written to magnetic tape, although eventually there is no reason that these outputs could not be stored on disc and subsequently forwarded directly over communications lines.

Current Payroll Production. Employees are paid through this subsystem. Each data-processing center handles the employees in its geographical area, although, because of the absence of timekeeping problems, it may prove convenient to handle all salaried (non-hourly) employees in only one center. The current payroll master file will contain *only* that information necessary to produce the next pay check for each employee. There will be no cumulative information at all except, for example, total FICA to date, in order to determine FICA residue, if any, to be deducted on the next cycle. The modules in this subsystem include:

1. Salary payroll calculation.
2. Hourly "schedule-to-gross-pay" calculation, including regular, overtime, piecework, incentive and mixed schedule time.
3. "Gross-to-net" and check production for all classes of employees.

Year-to-Date Payroll Subsystem. The basic cycle is presumed to take place monthly and run in conventional batch mode. If the basic cycle of the EBP subsystem is also monthly, there may be convincing reasons to combine the files of these two subsystems and make them into one subsystem. All monthly, quarterly, and annual reports are produced by these subsystems, as well as certain historical data destined for the Personnel Records Subsystem. If EBP is a separate subsystem, cumulative EBP information for the month is also produced as an output—perhaps on magnetic tape. The employee records in this file are quite variable in length, and should probably be organized in variable rather than fixed format, especially since they may be quite lengthy on the average.

Employee Benefit Plans (EBP). The primary reason this subsystem may not be combined with the monthly payroll is a difference in its basic cycle—for example, it may be semi-monthly rather than monthly. Also it is assumed that these files contain more than just year-to-date accumulations, and that certain data are carried over from year to year. If this is so, the file need not undergo annual purging, and might indeed require substantially different organization than the Year-to-Date Payroll master.

Personnel Records Subsystem. This is the "management information" data-base part of the Manpower System (the other subsystems are basically oriented toward routine operations). This subsystem should be designed to meet a variety of manpower information needs, including:

> Exempt salary data
> General personnel department data
> Skills inventory
> Mailing and telephone lists
> Medical and safety
> Security data
> Salary and benefits history
> Vacation records, etc.

Much of this data is related only by virtue of its applying to the same individual, but there are other common characteristics from a systems viewpoint:

1. The data is out of the main operational control data-processing stream.
2. Not all the needs for this data can be met by regular, periodic reports.
3. Much of the information is wanted in summary form, rather than as individual line items on a report; conversely, much of it is also wanted as an individual item of data on a single employee.
4. Output requirements are expected to be often on an "on demand" basis.
5. Records are extremely voluminous, which may require other than magnetic storage—e.g., microfilm document storage and retrieval.

6. Not all of the data is of equal interest or is accessed with equal frequency. Much of the data becomes archival with the passage of time.

A small part of this subsystem may be implemented at an early stage to satisfy known requirements, but much of it can be deferred until the other manpower subsystems have become operational. In its earliest phase, the personnel record might be maintained on removable disc packs which are periodically processed through report generators. This initial personnel record master file might include:

1. Employee number
2. Social Security number
3. Name
4. Home address
5. Next of kin and family data
6. Physical description; birth date
7. Position title and organization
8. Work location and supervisor
9. Telephone number
10. Salary history
11. Vacation and other time-off history

Later, the following information could be added to this basic file:

12. Medical and safety information
13. Security records
14. Skills and education
15. Company job history and performance evaluation
16. Previous business and military experience
17. Benefits history

The ultimate record may be so voluminous that only parts of it could be maintained in directly accessible form because of practical and economic considerations. If this be the case, the file could contain location references to microfilm documents which might be retrieved for the user. This referencing might be automatic or manual, depending on volume and on clerical economics. The Personnel Records Data Bank would be the only one in the Manpower System which would accept and respond to inquiries or requests for special reports. It might do this initially on a daily cycle, and later on-line. Updating of this file, however, would not be on-line, but would be handled through the regular updating mechanisms depicted in Figure 4-1.

Logistics—*LOCIS*

There are three subsystems in LOCIS, viz., Raw Materials (RMOCIS), Production (PROCIS) and Saleable Product (SPOCIS). PROCIS is perhaps most difficult of all to generalize satisfactorily from a framework point of view. The organization of production activities varies extremely widely depending on the product type. The operational control interfaces among the PROCIS modules are accordingly difficult to generalize. This is not equally true when the interfaces between PROCIS as a subsystem and RMOCIS and SPOCIS are considered. Figure 4-2 indicates the nature of these subsystem interfaces. In this example, we shall consider the interior framework structuring of each of these subsystems in turn, and as we do so we shall address the problems of generalization.

PROCIS. In Chapter III (page 48) mention was made of four classes of production. They will now be defined, after Franksen and Romer.[3]

1. Disjoint purchase, non-custom: finished product is the result of a long series of different manufacturing operations carried out on a few basic raw materials. Mass production of a few uniform products involving continuous operation is implied. Examples would be electric power, margarine, cement, paper, rubber, gas, oil, beer, etc.
2. Conjoint purchase, non-custom: finished product is normally the result of composing large numbers of different elements into a whole. Mass batch production of a limited number of different products is involved. A great deal of preparatory working up of materials may take place outside of the manufacturer's own operations, e.g., at subcontractors. Examples would be watches, cameras, television sets, automobiles, etc.
3. Disjoint purchase, custom: simultaneous manufacture, singly or in small series, of a large number of very different and often extremely complicated products, on the same production apparatus. A large number of different, standardized stock items are repeatedly used. Examples would be power transformers, rotating machinery, automatic control systems and special purpose machines and tools.
4. Conjoint purchase, custom: job manufacturing on a fixed production apparatus of very large, complicated products, in the shape of tailor-made plants or apparatus. Great uncertainties are involved. Examples would be ships, bridges, buildings, etc.

Both custom and non-custom products can be made-to-order. Custom products, of course, always are, while non-custom may be either made-to-stock or made-to-order. Mass manufacturing of the type involved in production classes 1 and 2 may involve few or many orders. Original equipment manufacture of thousands of special brand television sets for retailing by a large department store chain may involve only a single purchase contract. Mass production thus does not necessarily involve massive paperwork in the Saleable Product subsystem. This framework example

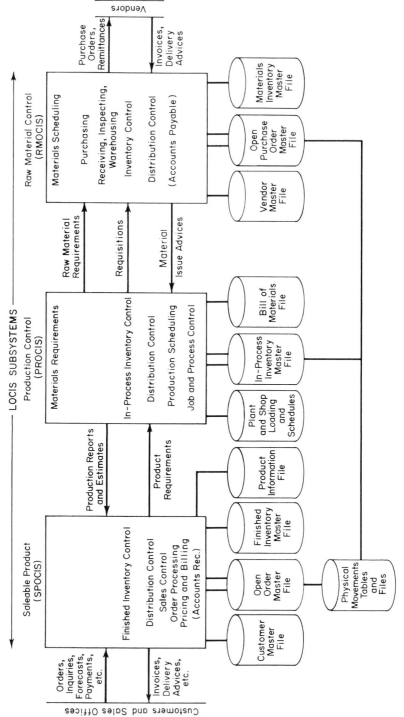

Figure 4–2. Logistics Operational Control Information System (LOCIS) (overall view).

will assume a mixture of mass production to-stock and to-order, and some custom production of the third class. The fourth class is not considered. This mixture implies a large volume of orders *in toto,* with little direct correspondence necessarily obtaining between order volume and production volume.

Product requirements in a manufacturing-to-stock situation are presumed to result from automatic reorders and back orders. These do not dribble into the system as they occur, but are batched for periodic scheduling according to the characteristics of the production apparatus. This apparatus is "tuned" on the basis of long term forecasts (usually 30 to 90 days or more) and cannot be profitably adjusted to abrupt changes in rates of demand. This "tuning" is the result of the production-planning cycle. Production scheduling, on the other hand, is concerned with producing a specified number of units of specified products in a specified period of time. Thus, while a production plan provides for the profitable scheduling of a certain range of demands, the schedules themselves prescribe precisely what is to be made and when. Thus, production control, as distinguished from production planning, is designed to serve certain limited operational control objectives, viz.:

1. To permit the least costly changes in schedules and operations to meet changes in forecasted, short-term requirements.
2. To make maximum use of given machine and labor capability.
3. To control the production apparatus in the sequencing, dispatching and routing of various jobs or operations.

These objectives can be achieved only within the constraints imposed on production control by the quality of the master planning, the methods of forecasting, rules for selection of economic lot-size, type of dispatching techniques used, and the possibly less than optimum physical heritage of the production apparatus. The most neatly arranged and automated production control system, with elaborate data-collection equipment on the production floor, can never overcome the handicaps of poor management planning and control, or poor decision rules built into the automated system.

Figure 4-3a is most closely representative of a "protocol" for a PROCIS framework that may show considerable modification and amplification in the details, if expanded to suit separately each of the first three production classes (disjoint purchase, non-custom; conjoint purchase, non-custom; disjoint purchase, custom). It is a starting point for each of the three, exhibiting their common structural outline. It includes the major *actions* (see Chap. II) found in all three, viz., receiving product requirements, exploding scheduled product requirements into scheduled raw-materials requirements, the updating of plant and shop schedules, produc-

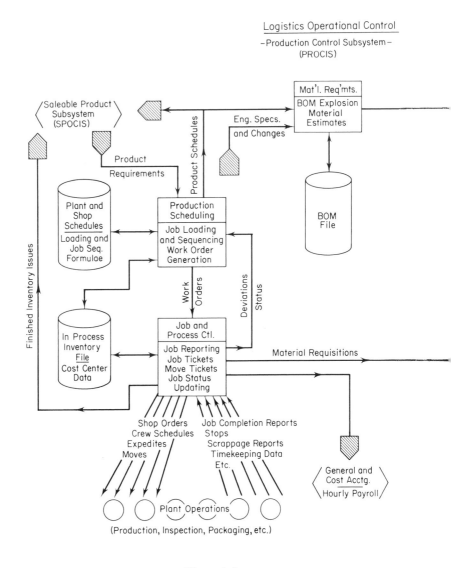

Figure 4–3a.

tion of work orders, requisitioning of materials, assignment of crews, reporting scrappage, updating in-process inventory, recording of job-step completions, and so on. The label "Plant Operations" is used in a very broad sense in the figure; it includes such "non-productive" operations as inspection, quality control, cleaning and packaging, etc.

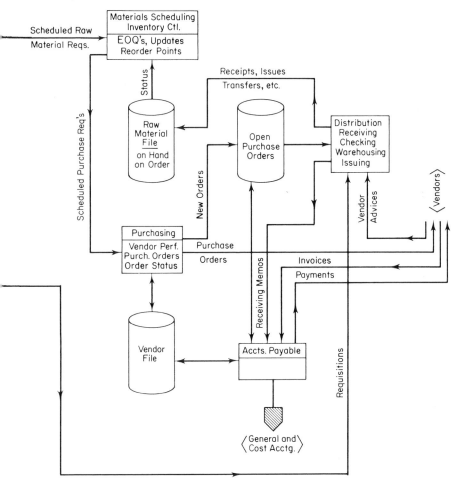

Figure 4–3b.

In detailing the PROCIS framework for a particular production class it is necessary to consider many more types of actions than are shown. For example, in production class 1, disjoint purchase, non-custom, we might include explicitly such things as mixing, weighing, grading, tapping, etc. Corresponding actions do not exist in class 2. Typical actions there might be unit assembly, sub-assembly, etc.—quite a difference, and one which serves to point up the futility of trying to develop a universally applicable approach to production control.

RMOCIS. Of the three subsystems in LOCIS, raw-materials control is most clearly applicable as a single system across product lines and production classes. The reason for this can be illustrated metaphorically by the converse to the pathetic fallacy, to wit: "The raw materials don't know what's going to happen to them in production and marketing." Exploded requirements are given, on-hand and on-order inventories are known, lead times can be ascertained by referencing the vendor files, economic-order quantity determination is based on decision rules built into the inventory control system, and so on. The same supplies ordered for two different divisions, destined to be made into entirely different products for entirely different end uses, would be subject to reasonably identical procurement procedures. The major source of difference might possibly be different distribution patterns, but these can certainly be handled by the same system with single versions of each module.

Some of the principal actions embodied in the RMOCIS framework (see Fig. 4-3b) are: receiving and processing scheduled raw-materials requirements, reserving raw materials, determining replenishment requirements, producing scheduled-purchase requirements, updating on-hand, on-order, reserved and available supplies, processing receipts, issues, transfers, etc., maintaining vendor files, selecting vendors, selecting transportation mode, producing purchase orders and transmitting to vendor, receiving vendor advices, checking receipts vs. purchase order copies, reporting receipts and issues, receiving materials, checking and warehousing, monitoring open purchase orders, receiving invoices and checking them for terms, and processing invoices for payment.

SPOCIS. This is perhaps the most challenging area in which to devise a framework, because the issues are not at all as clear-cut. That is, there is nothing that tells us very clearly that there are or are not such and such similarities and differences across product lines in various divisions that would tend to be reflected structurally in a common framework. Merely listing some of the principal types of actions in SPOCIS, as has been done in Table 4-2, is an indication of the functional complexity, and therefore the rich opportunity for diversity, in this area. For this among other reasons SPOCIS has been chosen for detailed case study in a later chapter (VII). A few things can be said, however, at this point. The type of framework shown in Figure 4-4 is applicable to those areas of business in which orders are entered at many remote locations, and where these orders compete for the products manufactured and inventoried at still other locations. This framework lends itself to a communications-oriented approach. It is too elaborate, and therefore unsuited, for businesses which

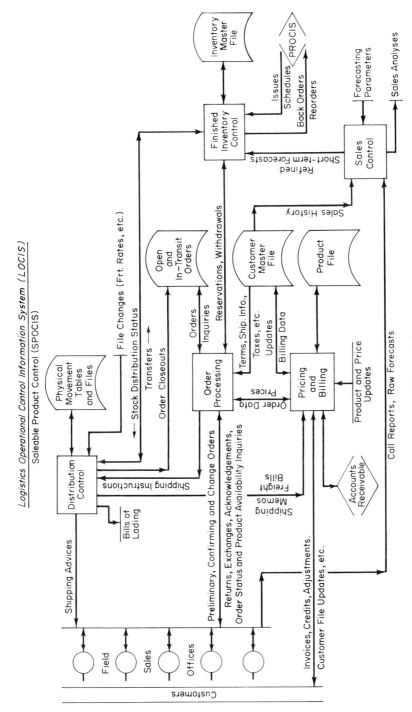

Logistics Operational Control Information System (LOCIS)
Saleable Product Control (SPOCIS)

Figure 4-4.

81

are conducted as collections of local production-sales-distribution complexes, or where warehouses are controlled by a single sales office. The illustration then is a framework for a single, company-wide, centralized SPOCIS, excluding certain business areas where a much simpler approach is called for. Regardless of these differences, the essential interfaces with the sales offices and with PROCIS would still apply.

Table 4-2. ILLUSTRATIVE ACTIONS IN SPOCIS

Order Entry
    1. Receive original and change orders
    2. Receive product information
    3. Relate customer need to product
    4. Receive customer data
    5. Receive customer inquiries
    6. Answer customer inquiries
    7. Transmit order status information to customers—price, delivery date, etc.
    8. Edit received information
    9. Establish priority
    10. Transmit order
    11. Reprocess order errors

Order Processing, and Pricing and Billing
    1. Calculate price
    2. Check credit
    3. Check for special charges
    4. Check discount and delivery terms
    5. Establish open order record
    6. Determine shipping location
    7. Reserve material for shipment
    8. Produce shipping orders and transmit to shipping points
    9. Select transportation mode and carrier
    10. Calculate freight charge
    11. Update product file
    12. Update inventory files
    13. Update customer file
    14. Update miscellaneous files—excess freight cost, etc.
    15. Produce and transmit shipping reports
    16. Receive and process production reports and schedules
    17. Update open order files
    18. Prepare and transmit customer acknowledgements
    19. Prepare and transmit invoices, dunning notices
    20. Update accounts-receivable file, process payments
    21. Generate data for distribution and production planning and scheduling
    22. Transmit order-disposition notice to sales office

Distribution (finished product)
    1. Determine optimum shipping location for positive lead time, etc.
    2. Replenish shipping-point inventories
    3. Determine routings for shipments—to customers
    4. Determine routings for interplant and warehouse shipments

5. Determine availability and schedule rolling stock
6. Receive updates for route/mode files
7. Edit and process route/mode updates
8. Receive, edit and process freight rate updates
9. Receive, edit and process updates for private-line transport
10. Determine distribution-cost standards
11. Prepare and transmit bill of lading
12. Receive and process freight bills
13. Process changes in estimated time of arrival—material in transit
14. Process transportation claims

Finished Inventory Control
1. Make forecasts by customer/product
2. Prepare refined forecasts by product (applying fixed decision rules)
3. Receive inventory status by location
4. Determine product requirements for forecast period for replenishment of inventory locations in accord with inventory policy
5. Generate product requirements

LOCIS and the framework objectives. There are certain modules in LOCIS which when implemented alone provide useful early capability. There are others that cannot operate by themselves. As a case in point, consider the SPOCIS subsystem. The Pricing and Billing module can operate without the others. The primary-file maintenance responsibility for the Customer and Product Information master files would be handled by this module. Confirmed customer orders, for which shipments have already been processed, would be periodically introduced for pricing, billing and general accounting purposes. As another example, the Order Processing module could not operate without Finished Inventory Control, but the reverse is not true. Inventory Reporting and Control is useful by itself, but Order Processing cannot be done without a regularly maintained inventory file against which reservations can be placed and shipments reported. If Order Processing is on-line, Inventory Control and Distribution Control must be too, although Sales Control and Pricing and Billing could operate in an off-line mode.

It is likely that many more versions of the Pricing and Billing and Sales Control modules will be needed to satisfy the diversity of requirements in a large corporation than would be the case with the Inventory Control or Order Processing modules. There might be only a single version of the Distribution Control module. If it can be demonstrated that there are in fact differing numbers of versions of each module, such a framework as this, even if not optimum in terms of module segmentation, is obviously to be preferred to any more monolithic approach, in which the number of versions of the whole subsystem would be equal to the number of versions of the most non-standard function in the system. The problem of module segmentation is illustrated in Table 4-2, where the division between Order

Processing module actions and Pricing and Billing module actions is difficult to establish for the general case.

REFERENCES

1. "A General Management View of Computers," in *Computers and Management—The Leatherbee Lectures 1967* (Boston: Harvard University Graduate School of Business Administration, 1967), p. 15.

2. "An Introduction to 'SAPTAD'," Bell Telephone Co. of Canada, presented at GUIDE 24, New York City, May 24, 1967.

3. O. I. Franksen and M. D. Romer, "Industrial Production and Digital Computers," *Proceedings of the 20th National ACM Conference,* 1965, pp. 455–468.

> *. . . each project parallels, in miniature, the ponderous steps of the master-plan-making procedure.*
>
> Robert H. Schaffer[1]

 V   **PLANS AND PROJECTS**

INTRODUCTION

A systems framework, no matter how refined and detailed, is not a systems plan. A *proposed plan* is a step-by-step prescription for achieving certain specified ends. It only becomes a *plan in actuality* when the performance of each of the steps has been approved, and resources allocated for their accomplishment. The steps become projects (which in turn have steps) only when carrying them out has become someone's specific work assignment. "Until then there are only good intentions."[2] The conversion of a proposed plan into a project (or series of projects) is the essence of executive decision making. The procedures by which this may be done in a rational way for business information systems are discussed in the next chapter. Planning itself fits into the thread of this entire book as the climax of an exposition that runs roughly as follows: concepts—framework—*planning*—organization for development. The anticlimax, to pursue the dramatic analogy, will consider the project study and proposal, the plan of *a* project, technical strategies, and the management of change.

A systems plan can be considered from two aspects: global and local. There is first the global "plan of projects," and second the local "project plans." The first, briefly, is a scheduled series of efforts leading to the realization of the totality of systems envisioned in the framework. It is evolutionary in character. In it are included the projects required to develop the systems delineated in the framework for those areas of the corporation already assessed. It is evolutionary because at any given time not all of the projects required to reach the ultimate goal for all areas will have been evaluated or known with certainty.

A key role played by this evolving plan will be described in Chapter VI (Procedure 3), which also has been mentioned in Chapter II (see Fig. 2-1), where this plan is one input to an "assessment process." In turn, the assessment process and its sequels, leading finally to management decision about a particular project proposal, are inputs to the evolving plan. A project plan, on the other hand, is another level of detail, developed when a project is approved, showing the scheduled series of events involved in the realization of a particular project in the overall plan of projects. In the next chapter, "Organizing for Systems Development," the creation and use of such a project plan by the project manager will be discussed, and the four "phases" in a project and their effect on project management, will be considered. A basis will be laid for this in the present chapter by describing the general form of a project plan.

The successive framework "models" mentioned in Chapter IV, each of which includes the previous model as a subset, have their counterpart in the plan of projects. This evolutionary continuum between the framework and the plan helps assure that work already completed in the context of a prior plan model does not need to undergo unnecessary alteration to accord with a new plan model. This concept does not mean that nothing, once done, is ever changed. It means rather that change is managed by deliberate planning, and is not permitted to occur willy-nilly as a reaction to narrowly and locally perceived needs and opportunities. The plan is both long *and* short range. It governs what is done near-term in ongoing projects, it includes a forecasted allocation of resources to future approved projects, and it targets a group of proposed projects for even more distant implementation. This latter, long-range aspect influences but cannot dictate the actual future course of systems development in the company. Future plan models will be directed toward emerging management objectives as they become known.

THE PLAN OF PROJECTS

THE FRAMEWORK AS FOUNDATION

The framework in its current version, evolving through the exercise of the assessment process already alluded to, is the foundation of the plan, and conceptually one of its more complicated elements. Its existence and influence on the plan serves to fulfill the planning objectives outlined in Chapter I more than any other item in the planning armamentarium, hence the copious discussion devoted to it earlier. The framework defines the application boundaries and their interfaces for all corporate units. Therefore the opportunity for assessing commonalities exists, and avoiding overlapping development becomes manifestly possible. It further provides the basis for determining the sequence of development by making clear the priorities from a technical point of view. It allows for the possibility of undertaking the development of large, integrated systems in manageable chunks, with the assurance that these chunks will properly interface with each other. At the same time it reduces the number of isolated "islands of mechanization" which might otherwise continue to be developed, operated, maintained and constantly changed or redone to meet new interface and reporting requirements. Lastly, because it distinguishes stable operational control elements from ever-changing management information aspects of systems, it serves to insulate and protect systems elements from the impact of changes in the pattern of management control and organization.

PROJECTS CONSIST OF MODULES

Projects to be undertaken in fulfillment of the plan have as their purpose the development of one or more of the modules in the framework, for one or more of the divisions or other subunits of the organization. These projects are separately proposed by the ultimate system users, are redefined after matching against the then-existing plan through a joint user–systems-staff assessment process, are then submitted for approval to management in the guise of user steering committees and a Systems Policy Committee,* and after approval are fed back into the plan to influence future proposals. Approved projects thus affect the plan as much as the plan affects proposed projects, and in the course of this updating and refining process the plan (and the framework) evolves.

Approved and ongoing projects, their schedules, the systems development resources allocated to them, and the forecasted availability of and requirements for these resources are part of the plan. Resource requirements are based in part on proposed projects, and in part on policy or other limitations placed on the acquisition of new resources. Costs and benefits by project, by groups of related projects, by taxonomical classification, by using organization, and for the enterprise as a whole, are included in the plan and kept up to date. Such information is useful in determining

---

* See Chapter VI for an extensive discussion of these committees and their functions.

priorities, in apportioning resources to realize the greatest returns, and to assure equitable distribution of resources among parties and applications contending for their use. For projects in being as well as those only on the framework "shopping list," it is vital to identify in the plan those which are interdivisional in scope, in order to advise the potential users to take this into account in their own planning, and to lay the basis for joint development taking all affected interests into consideration. It is clear that the plan must also stipulate as precisely as possible the effect of approved and anticipated projects on existing systems—Will they be replaced? Must they be modified? etc. Lastly, and very importantly, the plan must at all times provide a continuing basis for detailed hardware planning by setting forth the long-range technical implications of implementing the totality of projects in the evolving plan over the foreseeable future—perhaps five to seven years. This might encompass a gross plot of various loading parameters over time for different kinds of facilities—central processing units, peripherals, communications, mass storages, etc. —with an indication of upper and lower limits shown as an expanding horn enveloping the plot as it pushes out into a less and less clearly perceived future.

DEVELOPMENT PRIORITIES

Development priorities are determined by four particularly pertinent factors, among others. These are, not necessarily stated in order of their relative influence: technical precedence, payoff, available technology, and management objectives. Let there be no illusion that the first three of these, encapsulated in one naive formulation or another, absolve management from doing anything more than rubber-stamping the results. The reasons for significant management involvement are numerous and almost too obvious to dwell upon overmuch. For instance, the less experienced or less successful computer-using business may wish to confine itself for some time to the relatively unrisky applications, regardless of payoff, until a high degree of confidence in the systems organization is established. Or a firm may be faced with a necessity to devote most available resources to re-programming existing systems for a new line of computer equipment, simply because a presumably sound decision has been made to remove the older hardware by a certain date. Too, there may be imponderables in the situation not addressed by the tangible factors, such as competitors' activities *vis-à-vis* customer service type applications, and the like. The systems planning group cannot by itself determine development priorities, although its advice is indispensable to sound and informed management decision in this regard. It must recommend what these priorities ought to be, from its special technical and financial perspective. The Systems Policy Committee is the final arbiter *de jure* (allowing for appeals *in extremis* to higher authority by the potential systems users).

What is the nature of this special technical and financial perspective of the planning staff of the systems organization? It is, as has been indicated previously, a realization that systems should be developed from the bottom up; that is, starting with the module level. It is a corollary appreciation that there is no information generated internally (i.e., within the company) and required at the management control level that is not initially captured at the module level for use in operational control. Management information systems whose perspective is "top-down" are much in vogue, altogether too frequently because of the recklessly drawn analogy between management control in industry and military command and control. The rigid hierarchy of command in the military, and the need for instant, accurate, and coordinated response in singular tactical situations, almost unavoidably entail a monolithic, all at once approach to military command and control systems development. This is technologically very risky, financially very expensive, and the resulting problems of systems management are enormous. In industry the "tactical" situations are not unique, but tend rather to be repetitive; and with almost no exception tactical (more accurately, operational) errors are recoverable, or at least the survival of the firm does not depend on the rightness and consistency of a handful of urgent operational decisions, as national survival often does in this day and age. Therefore, the systems problems in industry can and should be approached in terms of breaking the data-processing universe down into small, manageable pieces, using available and proven technology, except only where there is a demonstrable correspondence to the command and control environment, and a proven case that the monolithic alternative is the best, all things considered.

Industry does and can continue to operate without "total-management-information-systems." To the extent that such systems would imply increasing centralization of control perhaps this happy state of affairs should continue. Our relatively free economy operates quite successfully without centralization of control. The analogy of the economy as a whole to the diversified corporation is more persuasive than the one of military command hierarchy to industrial management. Priorities for systems development in a company involve questions of return on investment, non-duplication of effort, technological precedence, risk, and so on; they do not rest on the alleged indispensability of a "total, integrated management information system" as the appropriate target of systems planning and development efforts. To postulate and then pursue such a target is not only to court technical disaster, but to lose sight of the basically economic objectives of systems planning in the company, outlined in Chapter I.

PUTTING ACTION INTO THE PLAN

Putting action into the plan is, of course, the cachet of many kinds of planning. Planning, if it involves merely the generation of lengthy, beautifully reasoned and thoroughly researched—but unread—reports, becomes an embarrassment to management. The characteristics of a systems plan that will tend to make it palatable, realizable and, therefore, effective in the field of action—in the *doing*—have been touched upon already, but let us recapitulate and amplify.*

1. The plan should embody moving forward on many fronts at the same time. This is the antithesis of the monolithic approach, with its attendant technical and financial exposure. Several projects, in the beginning reasonably small, involving many functions and organizational units throughout the company, should be going on simultaneously. This minimizes risk by distributing it. It also gets large parts of the entire organization immediately involved and concerned with the success of the plan.

2. The plan should allow for escalating slowly to larger and larger systems aggregations. Each of the early projects should be reasonably small, involving preferably no more than a couple of modules. As these small projects are concluded there will be motivational reinforcement through success, and a desire to proceed toward larger goals will become imbued in the participants.

3. In establishing priorities it is vitally necessary to begin with the urgent, but achievable. This may mean that those projects with the largest payoff are not necessarily first, if they tend also to be more complex, and to depend for their success on experience that can only have been obtained through a period of successful implementation of less ambitious projects.

4. The plan must provide for measuring achievement—Has what was promised been delivered? If not, why not, and what can be done to get back on course? This is too often an aspect of systems development more honored by lip service than by the serious respect and observance it deserves. Losing sight of the objectives by permitting chronic deterioration of performance in development and operation is the inevitable penalty of ignoring the doctrine of continuous evaluation. This doctrine is the essence of the scientific attitude so badly needed and so often sorely lacking in the systems profession. As Sackman aptly puts it: "System development may be conceived as an evolving set of hypotheses relating system design to system performance, subject to experimental verification throughout the life cycle of the object system." [3]

5. The role of the feasibility study or feasibility assessment (described in detail in Chapter VII) prior to establishing a project, is vital for defining precise goals. All established projects must have *precise* goals, with the necessary steps specified, including the spelling out of due dates, resources, responsibilities and measures of progress. Assumptions

---

* The following paragraphs find their inspiration in part from Schaffer's article. [1]

should be supported by data. The momentum of the systems organization and the planning staff, and the confidence of others in their work, is quickly lost when ever-changing goals seem continually to recede, because what was to be accomplished was never fully understood, could not therefore have been informatively and truly authorized by management, and cannot provide the basic element of management control.

6. Where goals must be changed, the plan must be updated and a new "model" created. Basic changes in goals, such as module redefinition, or changing the number of module varieties necessary to blanket the organization, should occur as a result of thorough study prior to project establishment. A series of such changes should be clustered in one bundle and incorporated into the plan all at one time, producing a new model of the plan, thus avoiding the slow attrition of the plan that would result from piecemeal change. The same thing can be said for individual systems development.

THE PROJECT PLAN

THE PHASES OF DEVELOPMENT

Four distinct project activities will be discussed preliminarily below, and in Chapter VI in terms of detailed procedure. These are Completion of Functional Requirements, Systems Specification, Programming and Testing, and Conversion and Cutover. Part of the justification for this division of a project as opposed to other possible ones resides in the fact that certain things are assumed to precede the establishment of a project, most particularly an assessment process and a feasibility study. The existence of a feasibility report makes it possible to talk in terms of a project as beginning with a phase called "*Completion* of Functional Requirements." This implies that the feasibility study, though it addresses itself to the functional requirements, as indeed it must, does so only to the extent necessary to satisfy the need for informed management decision making prior to project authorization—not to satisfy systems design requirements. The measurement of similarities and differences among functional requirements of separate corporate subunits occupies much of the typical feasibility study effort in a large and diversified company. This matter is so critical to the whole approach we have advocated for systems planning that much of Chapter VII will be devoted to it.

Other commentators on the systems-development process have also outlined the phases of a systems project. Laden and Gildersleeve have designated the first of these as a Survey, which is followed by Systems Investigation (data gathering), Systems Design, Programming, Filemaking, Clerical Procedures, Systems Testing, and Parallel Running.[4] The Survey and the Systems Investigation cover most of what we have considered to precede management authorization, viz., planning in general, the systems proposal and the feasibility study.[5] Systems Design in their terms includes preparation of functional requirements, and since the planning function as has been envisioned here was not considered as such, it also includes much of what we have relegated to the framework and planning function in general.[6] It also includes specification of the systems elements—programs, files, etc. Programming, Filemaking, Clerical Procedures, and Systems Testing are almost exactly parallel to what we have designated as Programming and Testing. Their Parallel Running phase is part of what we have called Conversion and Cutover. Thus, in the segregation of activities into defined phases for purposes of project management, we have not really proposed anything new.

Although Laden and Gildersleeve were talking primarily about batch-processing systems in their book, we find nothing very different when examining works on real-time systems. Head outlines the basic developmental steps found in real-time systems as Preliminary Technical Planning, Record Specification, Program Specification, Programming, System Testing, and Conversion and Operation.[7] Seemingly inevitable parallels to all these quite similar project structures can be found on further investigation.[8,9,10] This being so, perhaps we can safely proceed to discuss these phases as they are variously described in greater detail, confident that, though the names are different, the substance is essentially the same.

Chapter VII will deal with the structure of that part of the feasibility study which concerns itself with determining how many versions of a given module or set of modules are economically optimum for the multi-unit corporation. Let us assume that such a study has been completed, and that the results indicate that a single, common system is desirable in a certain applications-module area (such as Order Processing) to cover the needs of the entire organization, or major parts of it. There are certain things in the work of a project organization that should receive special emphasis in meeting this kind of a systems-development challenge, lest the potential overlap uncovered in the study not be achieved, or a system of such scope be compromised in implementation. It is not the intention of the following paragraphs to present a detailed checklist of the contents of each phase of a major project. This has been done for many different types of project more than adequately, and the reader is referred to several excellent sources.[11,12,13,14,15,16] Rather we shall confine our observations to the problems of some of the less well understood phases arising out of organizing projects for the special class of "common" systems mentioned above.

GENERAL OBSERVATIONS

One can conceive of a corporate-wide system (and even establish its economic worthiness) whose inter-organizational commonality resides in hardware and supervisory (i.e., non-application) software only. This alone would be worthwhile. In order to exploit the commonalities in applications software, efforts must be concerted in the following areas as well: (1) identifying the functions that are to be wholly common, those that are partially common (i.e., common for some of the included organizational units, but not all), and those that are unique; (2) defining these functions in terms of data-processing tasks that have non-overlapping scope across the spectrum of organizational units included; (3) specifying the common and unique master files; and (4) specifying the common and unique input/output message formats.

If all of the included businesses in the corporation are not to be converted at the same time (which is likely), then a schedule for the phased conversion of the system must be provided that can be used for scheduling hardware buildup, including peripherals. This is part of the Systems Specification, and ought to comprehend the following:

1. Central computer speed, storage, channel, core, tape unit, communications and peripheral interface requirements based on throughput and volume information derived from the Functional Requirements.

2. Provision for growth and margin for error in setting the above requirements.

3. Procedures for updating the system—adding businesses, adding file records, adding terminals, etc.

4. System segmentation (specification of "jobs" and "job-steps" in IBM jargon).

5. Specifying monitor functions (input/output handling, file access handling, error detection and recovery, clock-initiated tasks, operator communications, priority, record protection, performance measurement, switch-to-standby, etc.).

6. Support program specifications (utilities, test generators, single and multi-thread I/O simulators, debug aids, etc.).

7. Allocation of systems residence (core, extended core, drum, disc).

8. File structure (record formats, method of organization, channel-allocation scheme, indexing, coding, name-assignment procedure, access methods, etc.).

Because of its general perspective the above smacks of a communications-oriented emphasis, and indeed most systems of interest will include some on-line or on-line, real-time modules. These factors will be discussed more fully in Chapter VIII, "Technical Strategies."

We will address ourselves to some of the critical areas in three of the four project phases in the balance of this chapter, viz., Functional Requirements, Programming and Testing, and Conversion and Cutover.

FUNCTIONAL REQUIREMENTS*

Functional requirements need to be prepared in accordance with a standard that assures that changes can be incorporated as the project progresses, and that the form of the document assists in maintaining communications among all of the people involved on the project. The functional-requirements document and its amendments should always reflect the current statement of *what* is to be done by the system. Its format should be such as to be equally understandable to the functional experts in the user organizations, and to the technical experts on the systems-design team.

The functional requirements define the constraints placed on the system by its users. The data requirements, the data volumes, and the rate of processing are constraints imposed by the immediate users. The constraints of more remote users are imposed through the specification of interfaces with related systems. In general, therefore, the functional requirements are user-oriented. They define the job to be done and are not concerned with the method or methods of implementation; they define the problem without reference to the proposed solution. As such, the functional requirements are a basic reference for the system. Documentation of them is a necessary step in the development of the system, and updating of them is a prerequisite for the future evolution of the system. They are to be regarded as part of the permanent documentation of the system and not, as frequently happens, as a document to be replaced in due course by a set of non-functional specifications which reflects the hardware and software characteristics of the method of systems implementation. This being so, the functional requirements are and remain the appropriate documentation in the boundary zone between the user organizations and the project team. Agreement on a common language for the documentation is both desirable and logical. The conventions applicable to the functional requirements are neither numerous nor difficult. Adherence to them can be expected to contribute significantly to intercommunication between all parties.

Figure 5-1 portrays a "black box" concept of a system. The system involves input data, output data, data in master files, and rules for processing the data. The latter normally involve processing the input data against the file data (A) and producing some output data. Less frequently, no output data is produced by the (A) processing, or possibly the input data may be processed into output data (B) without reference to the file. Even less frequently, the file may be triggered to produce some output by something other than input data (C). The task of systems definition consists of defining the data, i.e., the elements outside the "black box," in

---

*I am indebted for the substance of the following paragraphs and the drawings to James Hammerton.

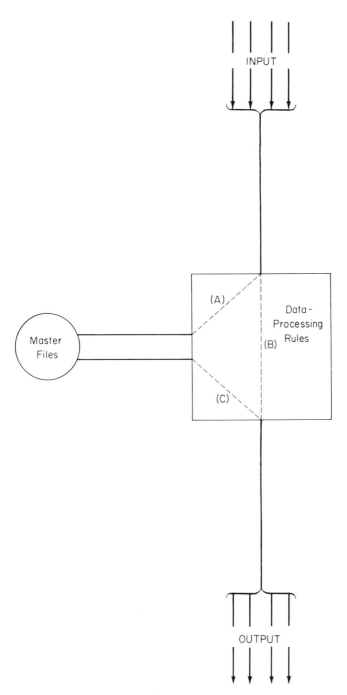

Figure 5–1.

terms of content, volume, and frequency of arrival or departure. The data processing is implicit in the input and output data definitions. However, since the interrelationships of the items of data are not normally obvious from an examination of the data definitions, the systems definition includes definitions of these interrelationships.

The *master files* contain data which are updated periodically and maintained perpetually, as distinct from working files, which are not updated and are normally used only once. The master files may be used by this system only, in which case definition of the file is required; or they may be used also by other previously designed systems, in which case the adequacy of the existing file definition needs evaluation.

The *inputs* and *outputs* are determined by the scope of the system defined in the feasibility study, which establishes the basic guidelines for systems definition. The scope of the system determines what part of the overall corporate framework is to be encompassed by the system (i.e., the modules included).

Input data definition includes specifying the source or sources of data, i.e., where they come from, what form they are in, and who is responsible for their production. If the system is being introduced to a formerly all-clerical system, the sources are printed forms of one variety or another. The relevant data on these forms are to be identified. The systems definition will not normally be concerned with how the data are transcribed into machine readable input, nor where the transcription takes place, although in some cases inclusion of this information may be a matter of convenience. Figure 5-2 shows inputs to the "black box" of Figure 5-1, some of which are machine readable. Normally, machine readable inputs are outputs from other mechanized systems.

The following guidelines are intended to assist in the determination of what to define and what to leave undefined, i.e., what to leave in the "black box":

1. If the control philosophy requires the transcription of a document into machine readable input at its place of origin, this is to be stated and the appropriate clerical procedure defined.
2. If the cost estimates of the feasibility study are based on a recommended method of transferring data between two locations, this method is to be specified.
3. Similarly, if the data are gathered from a number of source documents it may be necessary to produce a subsidiary source document as a key-punching instruction. In this case the production of the subsidiary source document from the primary source documents should be recognized and an appropriate clerical procedure specified.

In general, these guidelines are pragmatic, but they recognize the principle that the method of implementation is not part of system definition. How-

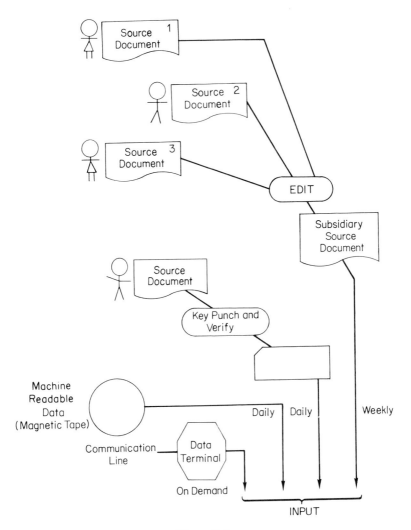

Figure 5–2.

ever, where there is only one meaningful method of implementing a certain input, no harm is done by mentioning this method.

Output-data definition includes definition of the destination of the data, i.e., where they go, in what form they are, and who is responsible for receiving them. Figure 5-3 illustrates some of the possibilities. As with the input data, there is a choice about what to define and what to leave in the "black box." Guidelines such as suggested above are applicable to the output data descriptions.

It will be understood from the above that the scope of a system determines the boundaries of the system, and that systems definition consists primarily of defining the boundaries. The "black box" is within the boundaries, and what goes on functionally inside the box is determined by the definition of the boundaries. Explicit definition of the contents of the "black box," therefore, should be left to the systems implementation documents, as it is not a part of the functional requirements.

TESTING

Testing (Programming and Testing phase) has been referred to as the *sine qua non* of scientific systems development. All is merely unverified hypothesis in the absence of properly planned and conducted tests. A systems design can in no wise be considered complete unless it includes detailed information on how the design is to be tested. Martin, in referring to real-time systems, has commented in this connection as follows:

> [Testing] cannot be separated in any of its phases from the design, implementation and maintenance of the system. This is probably the most important single principle for success in real-time testing. A design policy that aims only at the perfect running system and ignores its suitability for testing is unrealistic and will lead to chaos at installation time.[17]

Although designing the system so that it is testable is considerably easier in non-real-time systems, the point that Martin makes is no less valid for these cases, too. The kinds of tests, their sequence, and the nature of the test tools needed have been very thoroughly discussed by Martin,[18,19] Head,[20] and Sackman.[21] Sackman is particularly tough-minded on this point. He calls for treating operational specifications as working hypotheses continually subject to testing to determine that the system will "deliver the goods as promised."

CONVERSION

The conversion plan is no less important than the test plan: it belongs equally in the systems-specification phase of the project plan, and the plan-

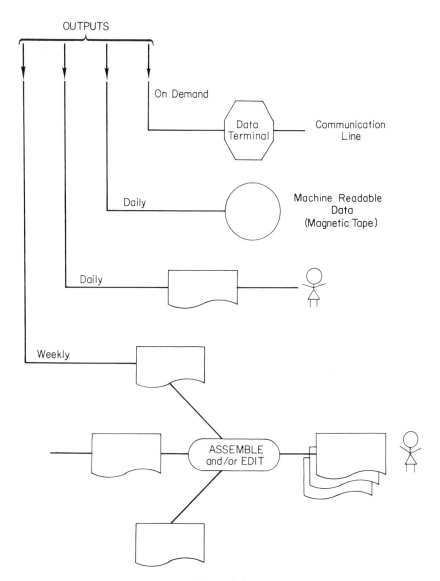

Figure 5–3.

ning for the two must be conjoint. One does not normally convert a major system all at once. What are some alternative methods of conversion by stages? Let us again use an order-processing–finished-inventory-control system as our example, and consider the alternatives.

1. Converting the entire system, but only applying it to one or more sales offices and warehouses at a time, not to the entire business at all locations. In this approach it is necessary to select carefully a mix of locations initially, that will give the most representative mix of business possible in order to fully exercise the system.
2. Converting a partial system—e.g., for all sales offices—at once, and subsequently adding other systems functions. Risk of failure early in the cutover period must be guarded against by providing capability for full fallback to the old system for all applicable locations, not for just a few. Plans must be carefully laid so that new functions of the system can be converted without risk to segments already operating.
3. Converting a partial system, applied to only one or more sales offices, etc., at a time, with subsequent augmentation. This is the safest approach, but it requires orderly preplanning if it is to avoid the potential problems mentioned in 1 and 2.

A potentially even more difficult problem is master file conversion. Many of the records to be included in the files of the new system are being maintained off-line in the old system under different formats. They do not "hold still" long enough to be taken out of the operational stream to be processed for conversion; and, once converted, two files, the old and the new, must be identically updated until the new system takes over. Moreover, not all of the records that will have identical formats in the new system have them in the old, particularly where the requirements of organizationally different corporate units are to be handled in common by the new system. Finally, if conversion is conducted in stages, and not all products or inventory locations are converted at once, there may be a problem at the field locations in having to handle transactions in two modes: entry to the new system for converted products, or entry to the old system for non-converted products, with all the attendant problems of later combining these two streams for billing, accounting and reporting purposes, not to speak of the procedural complexity involved in the first instance. These file conversion problems illustrate the decisions required of the project planners, the ultimate users, and the responsible managements, at the early stages of spelling out the requirements of a project.

REFERENCES

1. "Putting Action into Planning," *Harvard Business Review,* Nov.–Dec. 1967, pp. 158–166.

2. Richard C. Young, "Systems and Data Processing Departments Need Long-Range Planning," *Computers and Automation,* May 1967, pp. 30ff.

3. Harold Sackman, *Computers, Systems Science, and Evolving Society,* p. 206.

4. H. N. Laden and T. R. Gildersleeve, *Systems Design for Computer Applications* (New York: John Wiley and Sons, Inc., 1963), pp. 223–5.

5. *Op. cit.,* pp. 226–7.

6. *Op. cit.,* pp. 245–6.

7. Robert V. Head, *Real-Time Business Systems* (New York: Holt, Rinehart and Winston, Inc., 1965), pp. 76–7.

8. James Martin, *Programming Real-Time Computer Systems* (Englewood Cliffs, N.J.: Prentice-Hall, Inc., 1965), pp. 355, 367–9.

9. Sackman, pp. 172ff.

10. I. G. Wilson and M. E. Wilson, *Information, Computers, and Systems Design* (New York: John Wiley and Sons, Inc., 1965), pp. 138, 160ff.

11. Sackman, pp. 172–185.

12. Laden and Gildersleeve, pp. 223ff.

13. Head, *passim.*

14. Martin, *Programming,* pp. 287ff.

15. ———, *Design of Real-Time Computer Systems* (Englewood Cliffs, N.J.: Prentice-Hall, Inc., 1967), pp. 559ff.

16. Wilson and Wilson, *loc. cit.*

17. Martin, *Programming,* p. 253.

18. *Op. cit., passim.*

19. Martin, *Design, passim.*

20. *Real-Time Business Systems,* p. 292 and *passim.*

21. *Computers, Systems Science, and Evolving Society,* pp. 206–7, 289, 291, 332, 337–8.

If pressures rather than the executives are allowed to make the decision, the important tasks will predictably be sacrificed.

Peter F. Drucker[1]

VI   ORGANIZING FOR SYSTEMS DEVELOPMENT

INTRODUCTION

PURPOSE

This chapter deals with policies and procedures for governing the development of corporate information systems. Systems investigation, selection, priorities, budgeting, resource allocation, project monitoring and performance evaluation will be discussed. This discussion will formalize much of what has often been informal in the approach to systems development in the typical enterprise. Formalization is expected to have several beneficial effects.

> It will assist management in foreseeing the requirements for systems-development resources, and in deciding how those resources can be best allocated among competing demands.
>
> It will help assure the user organizations that systems developed on their behalf are consistent with their requirements, and that the development costs are properly estimated, budgeted, and controlled.
>
> It will help ensure proper coordination and control among the many phases and organizations involved in a systems-development effort.

Systems development encompasses all of the activities involved in a systems effort, beginning with a recognition of a systems need and ending with the satisfaction of that need. There are activities carried on directly and specifically in support of a given systems-development effort, and there are those indirect activities which are carried on in general to support all development activities collectively. ("Systems programming" is an example of the latter.) Systems projects as such are embedded within the entire scope of systems-development activities, and are only a part, although an important part, of the organizational matters with which we shall be concerned in this chapter.

PROBLEMS IN ORGANIZING FOR SYSTEMS DEVELOPMENT

If planning, development and implementation are to be corporate-wide, then the location of systems responsibility would seem to have to be at the corporate level. Information systems are potentially and actually so vital to the well-being of the divisions and other sub-corporate groups for which they are developed and operated, that an organization created to wield systems responsibility for the entire enterprise achieves a tremendous leverage over the line organization. The line organization might become justifiably tempted to frustrate and dilute this new power center unless a means is devised to equitably apportion and control systems responsibility. The line organization must somehow become a willing participant in systems efforts designed to serve the corporation's interests as well as its own—an objective that means compromise on all sides.

Control of systems development is obviously a sensitive matter. An even more critical concern of the various line organizations is the approval of projects to satisfy their needs. Here they must compete with each other for limited resources which reside largely outside their control. They are even required to express their needs (or to have them redefined) in terms of a planning framework not of their devising. Most galling of all, perhaps, is that where there is decentralized profit responsibility together with some measure of systems centralization, there will be considerable pulling and hauling over budget responsibility for systems development—but the line organization must ultimately pay, directly or indirectly, for systems development and operation. Direct allocation of systems costs is preferable to indirect allocation to corporate overhead for many reasons, not the least of which is that systems costs and systems benefits should go hand in hand. Where total corporate systems costs are absorbed in various budgets on a pro-rata basis, great injustices will occur. Perhaps the greatest cause of friction in a company is the allocation of costs of a centralized group to its customers. With the ebb and flow of business in each division, it is not too hard to demonstrate that hardware costs for the company as a whole are lower with centralized equipment. At the same time, however, in a situation where one or more divisions face sustained high loads, the costs allocated to these divisions may well be higher than if they had their own equipment.[2] Finally there is the question of who will manage the systems project: the line man with functional expertise, or the systems man with technical expertise? Unless and until questions like these can be effectively resolved, the prospects for corporate-wide planning, development and operation of systems, no matter how theoretically attractive, are doomed to slow, agonizing failure following an initial short, happy period of promise.

Throughout this book centralization of systems responsibility is unapologetically advocated. This entails organizational problems which must be faced, unless one is prepared to leave the arena when it comes down to the "crunch." To propose solutions is not to insist that they are necessarily right; but not to propose them surely labels one as a systems dilettante, not to be taken seriously when serious matters are at hand. We are encouraged in what otherwise might seem a rather moralistic advocacy of the centralization of the systems planning and development organization by a study cited previously, in which it was shown that 97 out of 108 manufacturing companies have created "top computer executive" positions, with key responsibilities not only for the EDP area, but also frequently for operations research, clerical systems, and *planning*.[3] The hallmark of organizational structures is constant change, so one cannot be right in an absolute sense in prescribing organizational solutions, but one may be right in those matters of principle which underlie proposed approaches. In that spirit is the balance of this chapter to be taken. A final few words from Whisler are appropriate here before proceeding:

> I expect that as business continues to follow the military in exploration of information technology, it will experience the same pains and difficulties in redefining organization and relocating authority and control that the military has had. A nice problem develops in trying to forecast shifts in the pattern of control in terms of any current organizational structure, when it becomes increasingly clear that the structure itself will be substantially changed as a consequence of technological development.[4]

THE APPROACH IN SUMMARY

Organizing for business systems development has received considerable attention in the literature. Perlman,[5] Canning,[6,7] Dearden and McFarlan,[8] Martin,[9] Middleton,[10] Head,[11] Johnson *et al.*,[12] and Laden and Gildersleeve[13] have provided insights based on their considerable experience. The specific approach outlined below and discussed in detail in the balance of the chapter is, however, my own. The general principles embodied in the approach are shared, I believe, with others.*

---

* Note, for example, citations 3 and 14 in this chapter, which refer to Booz,

The life cycle of a systems-development effort, as it would be conducted under the proposed policies and procedures to be discussed, would consist of the following five stages:

1. The user organization (division or department) is responsible for carrying out investigatory activities, with perhaps the help of internal or external consultants, leading to a determination of needs, and the preparation of systems-development proposals answering those needs. These proposals are approved preliminarily by a steering committee acting on behalf of the user organization management.

2. The systems proposals are jointly assessed by the staffs of the user and the central systems organizations in order to ascertain that all information necessary for the approval and establishment of a systems project has been provided. A report containing recommendations resulting from this assessment is placed before the user steering committee for final approval, and then before a corporate "Systems Policy Committee" acting on behalf of the corporate interest in allocating systems resources among competing user demands. Projects are approved (or not) at this point, and information in the report provides the basis for appropriate budget action.

3. The next stages of the systems-development project (that is, design, implementation, testing, and conversion) are carried out under the monitoring and control of a project organization, which is assigned manpower resources from the user and central systems organizations and other appropriate sources.

4. The data-processing or computer-operating organization undertakes activities, coordinated with the project schedule, to support the development effort in the areas of hardware procurement and installation, systems assurance, system-testing support, operations, and maintenance.

5. After the new system has "shaken down" operationally, its performance is evaluated by a "Systems Audit Team" in order to measure actual versus expected costs and benefits, and to determine the basis for improvements in this and future systems-development efforts.

Two key elements of this approach concern project authorization and project organization.

PROJECT AUTHORIZATION

A feasibility report is prepared during the pre-project investigatory and assessment activities. It is on the basis of findings reported in this document that specific projects are authorized and resources allocated to them. The purposes of this report are to: (1) identify the specific areas of the system being proposed that should initially be made into a project or projects; (2) develop complete data on the recommended project(s) for

---

Allen's study of 108 manufacturing companies, the "top computer executive," and the function of his organization.

informed management consideration; and (3) place the recommended project(s) in the context of other systems-development activities, including a determination of whether combining with other developments similar in scope is feasible, determining what "interfaces" must be provided with other systems, and ensuring the adaptability of the proposed system to business change and growth.

This information is presented to management together with a systems-planning staff analysis of the impact of this project on future resource requirements and other developmental activities. The objectives of this presentation are to: (1) assist management in weighing the relative payoff of proposed projects and other competing demands for resources; (2) help decide at what level support should be provided; (3) permit consideration of payoff relative to entire divisional and corporate posture in systems development; and (4) permit evaluation of technically feasible joint-development possibilities in the context of non-technical management objectives.*

Dearden and McFarlan have proposed that two techniques should be used in the feasibility study, viz., a form of present-value analysis, and a cash-flow format that does not require a distinction between investment and savings.[15] I agree with these proposals and have incorporated them in the "Procedures" that follow later in the chapter. The use of these two techniques minimizes the impact of progressively less certain estimates for future time periods by giving them less weight, and also indicates where different cash-flow patterns for different alternatives have close to the same value.

The key management activity at this point is the authorization of a systems-development project. The existence of a decision mechanism for this purpose, called the "Systems Policy Committee," is assumed. Its function, as conceived here, may previously have been performed by a variety of groups in the organization, which interacted as necessary to form a consensus in each case. The "Systems Policy Committee" is not intended to displace this desirable interaction and agreement, but to aid it with a formal and unifying organizational focus—one which can act on behalf of corporate and division management in making systems policy, and which is convened with some regularity for this purpose.

PROJECT ORGANIZATION

When we make reference to a systems-development project, we refer to some well-defined part of an overall schedule of activities authorized in

---

* Apropos here is the following observation quoted from the Booz, Allen study: ". . . when companies recognize the high cost of duplicate systems, they frequently acquire planning personnel to coordinate the efforts of systems analysts to ensure standardization of practices and procedures in data-processing systems. Professional systems analysts and planning personnel then recognize and move into the more sophisticated systems that need to be developed."[14]

furtherance of the corporate-wide systems plan. That we propose that a certain form of project organization (see below) undertake development work, as part of such a plan, should not be taken to suggest that this method is always the best method for systems development. It is not in fact desirable where the universe of development consists primarily of relatively small, isolated systems. In such a case, a functional approach may be preferred, with several resource departments each simultaneously involved with parts of several different small development projects. These resource departments might be, for example, management sciences (internal consulting), systems analysis, programming, and operations, each handing the small projects over to the next department after its own task is completed, much as in a job shop. For large, complex, less well-structured systems the functional approach simply will not do. There are no clean divisions between phases of a project, many phases go on simultaneously, development time is long, specifications are ever-changing, etc. Here it is essential that, for each project, there be a single focus of control over all phases of development.

When working with available technology, the differences between large and small projects are not so much the technical difficulties as the difficulty of the organizational and managerial problems encountered. The project- or program-management approach has arisen in answer to the demand for an improved organizational approach for large systems. Johnson *et al.* have defined this approach as involving ". . . the appointment of one man, the program manager, who has responsibility for the over-all planning, coordination, and ultimate outcome of the program." [16] Forrester might recommend a team instead of one man, because a one-man group is unstable in size,[17] but the essential point is that there should be ". . . only one Control Group for the whole system, and, indeed, one overall management." [18] Into this managerial nexus would be placed judgment, accountability and authority, simply because, as Hunt points out:

> . . . wherever judgment is, there accountability should also be found. By the same token, no one should be held accountable for a decision unless he is given the authority to commit the resources to carry it out.[19]

The project-management approach is not without its drawbacks. It is often in conflict with normal organizational structure, and thus the project manager, to operate effectively, must rely as much on his ability to influence other organization members as on the authority of his position.[20] The project manager cuts through traditional lines of authority by determining the when and what of project activities, while the functional (resource department) manager determines how and by whom support will be given.[21]

Middleton, in his study of 47 aerospace companies, reported on how well these organizations have met the objectives of achieving an assigned goal on schedule, within cost estimates, and complying to established standards, using the project-management approach. His findings are shown in Table 6-1 [22]:

Table 6-1. ADVANTAGES AND DISADVANTAGES OF A PROJECT-MANAGEMENT APPROACH

Major Advantages	% of Responses
Better control of development	92*
Better customer (user) relations	80*
Shorter development time	40
Lower development costs	30
Improved quality and reliability	26
Higher profit margins (cost improvement)	24

Major Disadvantages	% of Responses
More complex internal operations	51*
Inconsistency in application of policy	32
Lower utilization	13
Higher development costs	13
More difficult to manage	13
Lower profit margins	2

* Judging from the responses of the majority of organizations in the survey, we might expect that one could achieve better control of development, and better user relations at the expense of somewhat more complex internal operations.

These other significant points are made in Middleton's article[23]:

It is . . . essential the project manager have superior leadership ability. He must have administrative experience in [systems engineering]. And he must be skilled in planning, budgeting, scheduling and other control techniques . . . . A weak project manager cannot be made strong and effective by creating additional controls or a top-heavy project organization structure. . . . If the project manager is expected to exercise control over the functional departments, then he must report to the same or higher level as the department managers . . . . To be able to wield total control, a project organization must be responsible for:

1. [Definition of Functional Requirements] . . .
2. Task and Funds Control
3. Make-or-Buy Decisions . . . [e.g., Use of Outside Consultants]
4. Scheduling . . .
5. Project Status
6. Identification and Solution of Problems . . .
7. Project Change Control . . .
8. Associate or Subcontract Control . . .
9. [User] Relations . . .
10. [User] Potentials . . .

BUDGETING AND CONTROL

For authorized projects, the feasibility report contains information adequate for initial systems-development budgeting purposes. In order to define the budgetary responsibility adequately it is first necessary to discuss the budgeting philosophy of systems activities in general.

There are two major categories of systems activities in the company which require an allocation of resources: systems-development projects and systems support. Budgeting for systems development is primarily a user responsibility; systems support is the responsibility of the systems and data-processing organizations.

Specified quantities of systems-development resources are estimated in the pre-project stages for systems development, operation and maintenance. Outlays for the investigatory and analytic activities preceding implementation are relatively small compared with expenditures for development and operation of the systems themselves. Specific requirements for these pre-project studies are difficult to predict on a year to year basis, since their nature and extent is not always as clearly foreseen as are the requirements for previously approved projects. Thus, studies may be budgeted by the user organization on an experience or level-of-effort basis.

Systems-support activities include "systems programming," programming and operating systems research and non-project studies, systems and hardware planning, standards development, etc. These items are built-in, indirect cost elements of systems-development services provided directly to the user by the systems and data-processing organizations.

A systems proposal, particularly one covering a large number of functions, can be broken down into a number of phases, not all of which need be implemented at the same time. The separate phases, consisting perhaps of one or more modules, may be implemented as a series of projects, each with its own budget. Since few systems ought to be developed as small islands of mechanization, unrelated to other systems already in being or planned, small projects tend to be part of larger systems goals. If size were the only criterion by which a project became subject to the full scope of systems-management policies, then many elaborate systems could conceivably be built in small stages, outside the control of such policies.

Estimates of outlays required to commence or continue systems development and operation will often be known prior to a given budgetary period. As a minimum it should be known that a project of some generally established magnitude will be begun or continued in the forthcoming period. Budget provision for these efforts should be made by the user on the basis of the most up-to-date information available. Manpower forecasts can be based in part on these budgetary estimates.

The policy must also provide for a mechanism whereby "minor" changes in specifications, calling for additional work within an existing project, can be routinely handled without being subject to all the formalities associated with the establishment of a major project. Of course a series of such "minor" changes could change the character of the project radically, after it has been authorized and established. This potential abuse can be largely avoided by requiring every change which involves additional systems resources to be subject to some form of pro forma management review and approval. The cumulative impact of these changes can be measured by a central controlling authority. Budget provision for such changes are presumed to be built into the project budget as a contingency factor.

All projects are subject to overrun. This can be anticipated by the Systems Policy Committee, which may hold in reserve a certain percentage of total resources for just such contingencies. It may delegate to other groups, such as a Project Steering Committee, the discretionary right to negotiate for additional resources up to a stated percentage above the original authorization, provided the project contingency-factor control limit is not exceeded. If it should be exceeded, the matter would have to be brought before the Systems Policy Committee for consideration.

Continuing outlays for systems already operational will generally be known, so that budget provision can readily be made for them. Costs to be incurred within the data-processing organization for systems that are to become operational for the first time during the ensuing budget period must be estimated on the basis of documentary information developed during the project. This information should usually be available.

Minor development efforts unrelated to a specific ongoing project, such as the preparation of special one-time reports, may bypass the procedure, provided that they are reviewed periodically as a group by the Systems Policy Committee, or by a special steering body constituted for the purposes of reviewing these efforts collectively on behalf of the Policy Committee. Separate budget provision should be made for these needs, presumably unanticipated, under the category of "Non-Project Miscellaneous." Wherever possible these minor efforts should be undertaken within existing projects and should be treated as project changes. Where this is impossible or impractical, the effort should be made into a project, subject to this procedure, if the amount involved exceeds a fixed limit (say $10,000).

The proposed policy should incorporate provisions for appropriate control of all stages of systems development, from the recognition of the need for a system through its ultimate conversion and operation. This control is established by defining the scope of the separate development activities, their sequence, the organizations responsible, the formal documents, and management actions required at each stage. This is all summarized in Table 6-2. In this table, under "Stage IV," the four phases of systems projects, which were introduced in the last chapter, are placed in their proper sequence in the overall context of systems-development activities.

Table 6-2. SYSTEMS-DEVELOPMENT ACTIVITIES

Stage	Activity or Event	Summary
I Preliminary Analysis	1. Pre-Proposal	The translation of a recognized need or opportunity in the systems area into preliminary "working papers" as a basis for further study and definition.
	2. Proposal Preparation	The conversion of internal "working papers" of the user organizations into a document suitable for approval by the user Steering Committee and for communicating to the systems-development organization.
II Feasibility Assessment	1. User-Systems Staff Assessment	Determining the study needs, if any, to convert a proposal into a formal project-authorization document for final management action.
	2. Additional Study	Preparing recommendations and back-up information for management authorization of a project or projects (Feasibility Report).
III Management Consideration	1. Presentation	Providing the Systems Policy Committee with an informed understanding of the need for and consequences of authorizing a project(s) in the proposed systems area.
	2. Management Actions	Project approval (disapproval; referral for more information) and assignment of project responsibilities, resource levels, etc.
IV Systems Implementation and Control	General: Project Planning and Control (all phases)	Control of the project phases and accountability for project success; includes scheduling, budgeting, initiation of activities, technical review, and subproject control.
	Phase 1: Completion of Functional Requirements	Preparation of formal, user-oriented functional requirements in conformity with a "Guide to the Preparation of Functional Specifications," and their subsequent approval. (The "what")
	Phase 2: Preparation of Systems Specifications	Preparation of formal, technically oriented specifications for the implementation of the system (system design). (The "how")

	Phase 3: Programming and Testing	Implementation of the system design and pre-conversion testing.
	Phase 4: Conversion and Cutover	Phasing the tested system into full operation, including user-acceptance testing of the completed system.
V Data-Processing Organization Activities	1. Hardware Planning, Technical Assurance	Assuring that the data-processing organization will have sufficient facilities and will be able to assume responsibility for the operation of the system as it has been proposed and is being implemented.
	2. Hardware Procurement and Installation	The coordination of procurement and installation actions with project requirements and schedules.
	3. Systems Operation and Maintenance	Operation of the system, logging of performance measures, detection and correction of errors, and making minor improvements.
VI Performance Evaluation		The measurement of benefits attained versus benefits expected, and the recommendations for improvements in the system and in systems-development functions in general.

PROCEDURES FOR SYSTEMS DEVELOPMENT

The systems-development activities, summarized in Table 6-2, will now be outlined in detail. Each activity will be expressed in the form of a numbered "Procedure" with the following contents:

> Procedure name
>> Project stage, and
>> Activity identity
> Scope of the activity
> Objectives of the activity
> Related activities
> Responsible organizations and positions
> Documents used
> Documents produced
> Procedural steps

Each "Procedure" corresponds to an activity entry in the middle column of Table 6-2.*

PROCEDURE 1

STAGE I: Preliminary Analysis

Activity 1:   Pre-Proposal Activity

Scope: The translation of a recognized need or opportunity in the systems area into preliminary informal "working papers" as a basis for further study and definition.

Objectives: Ideas for systems work may originate anywhere in the corporation, most frequently in the potential using organization itself. Definition of needs and opportunities is not at this stage expected to have taken into account related efforts, feasibility, or availability of resources. It is necessary first to define the problem area and its magnitude in order that the user can place it in the context of his overall objectives in the systems area, and decide on the relative emphasis he wants to give the proposal. Specifically, the objectives of this activity are:

1. Definition of the problem area
2. Ranking of importance to user
3. Determination of the amount to be budgeted for a systems effort in this problem area for the coming planning period
4. Providing a basis for communicating about the problem with concerned management and staff people both in the user organization and outside it

Related Activities (See Fig. 6-1):
1. Succeeding: Procedure 2. Stage I, Activity 2—Preparing Proposal

Responsible Organizations and Positions:
1. User organization (division or corporate department)—originator
2. User's system group, if one exists, and/or the systems-organization consulting staff (e.g., the Management Sciences Department)
3. User management

---

* The section which follows is a detailed amplification of Table 6-2. The casual reader may wish only to scan it. The serious reader is advised to study it carefully.

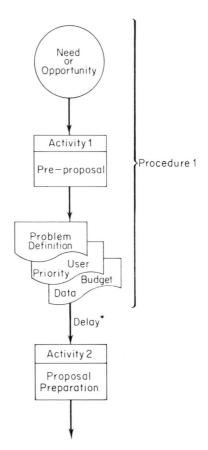

Figure 6–1. Procedure 1 and related activities. Delay* ensues between these two activities depending on the priority assigned by using organization. If given high priority, further action may take place without delay.

Documents Used: No formal documents

Documents Produced: No formal documents (internal memoranda only)

Procedural Steps:
1. At an early stage the person or group in the user organization responsible for overseeing and coordinating systems development performed for the organization, assumes responsibility for the pre-proposal activity, even though the ideas may have originated elsewhere.
2. The user's systems manager, governed by the policies established by his superiors for the conduct of his activities, prepares for his management the information necessary for them to make certain decisions. This information includes the description of a potential project, a general statement of its potential benefits and impact on the organization, its relationship to the user's ongoing developments or existing systems, its suggested priority, and the recommended amount of the systems budget that should be reserved for further work in the area over the ensuing budgetary period.
3. The management of the user organization must make a decision to authorize a proposal aimed toward establishing a project, based on the recommendations made to it by the systems manager. It must decide when and by whom this proposal effort is to be conducted.

PROCEDURE 2

STAGE I: Preliminary Analysis

Activity 2:   Proposal Preparation

Scope: The conversion of internal "working papers" of the user organization into a *systems proposal* as a basis for communicating with the systems organization.

Objectives: In government jargon this activity might be described as preparing a "request for quotation." The document will be referred to here as a "systems-development proposal"—that is, the user will propose that the systems organization undertake to develop the system described in the document. There is no intent to make this document conform to a standard set of ground rules with respect to form and content, but certain guidelines are suggested to facilitate subsequent study and negotiation. This is, therefore, *not* a formal procedure, since the systems organization ought always to be ready to discuss a user's requirements when the user feels the time is ripe for external consideration. There may be no clearcut division between Activities 1 and 2 in this stage.

Related Activities (See Fig. 6-2):
1. Preceding: Procedure 1. Stage I, Activity 1—Pre-Proposal
2. Succeeding: Procedure 3. Stage II, Activity 1—Joint User/Systems Organization Assessment

Responsible Organizations and Positions:
1. User systems staff
2. Management Sciences Dept. (optional)
3. User management

Documents Used: No formal documents (internal memoranda)

Documents Produced: The Systems Proposal. As a minimum this document should include the following:
1. A description of the system in terms of business functions included or significantly changed
2. A brief, preliminary description of the proposed systems concept— on-line, batch, type of communications, mode of input/output, etc.
3. A qualitative statement of the benefits expected, in order of importance (cost avoidance, improved service, improved timeliness, increased accuracy, etc.)
4. Relationships to any other of the user's systems in operation or under development, and to corporate systems (if known)
5. The amount currently budgeted for the proposed system
6. A statement of the importance of the need relative to other existing or forthcoming systems' development and to other management plans of the user

The proposal may also include other information that would ultimately have to be developed for final management approval. This information should be quantitative and specific, and should deal with cost/benefit, technical risk, resource requirements, work plan, etc. This so-called feasibility information is more fully discussed in Procedure 4.

Procedural Steps:
1. The user's management must decide:
   a. when it wants to present the systems proposal to the systems organization;
   b. what information about the system it wants to include; and
   c. whether "outside" help (e.g., Management Sciences Dept.) is to be called upon to render advice and assistance in preparing the proposal.
2. The user's system staff (plus Management Sciences personnel, optionally) prepares the proposal, with a set of recommendations as to priority, budget allocation, timing, etc. (See above: documents produced)
3. A presentation is made to the user's management, who decide to accept, reject, or defer. If revision is called for, Steps 2 and 3 are repeated.
4. When user's management accepts the proposal, a formal copy is forwarded to the systems organization with a request for further action (see Procedure 3).

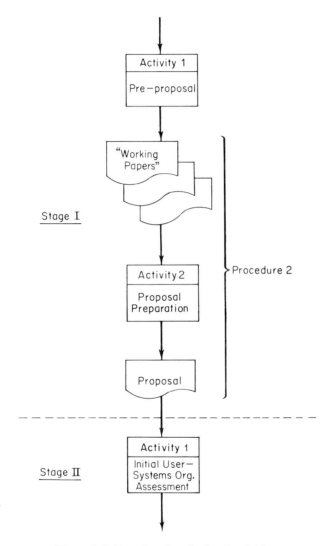

Figure 6–2. Procedure 2 and related activities.

PROCEDURE 3

STAGE II: Detailed Analysis (Feasibility Assessment)

Activity 1:   Initial User/Systems Organization Assessment

Scope: Determining the study needs, if any, to convert the proposal into a formal project-authorization document for final management action, and setting up a *study team* to conduct such study.

Objectives:
1. To determine whether proposal can and should be segmented into phases for sequential or parallel implementation.
2. To determine if phases of proposal are similar in scope to other planned or ongoing systems-development activities.
3. To define further detailed study requirements prior to recommending project authorization (including possibility of joint development of part or all of proposed system with that of other users).

If proposal is satisfactory as is, and contains adequate information in the form necessary for management authorization, the next activity in this stage may be bypassed. In this case the proposal *must* contain the information specified under "Documents Produced" in Procedure 4.

We do not necessarily presuppose the existence of a corporate-wide systems plan beyond that which already may exist as implied by the collection of systems in being, under development, and in earlier planning stages. As the corporate plan evolves it will become an important input to this assessment process, and, in turn, the output of this process will become an important input to the evolving plan. (See Fig. 2-1.)

Related Activities (See Fig. 6-3):
1. Preceding: Procedure 2. Stage I, Activity 2—Proposal Preparation
2. Succeeding: Procedure 4. Stage II, Activity 2—Additional Study

Responsible Organizations and Positions:
1. Central Systems-Planning Staff (systems organization)
2. User Systems Staff

Documents Used:
1. The Systems Proposal
2. The evolving "corporate systems plan," to the extent its existing scope encompasses the proposal area.

Documents Produced:
1. A memorandum specifying that the proposal is either presently adequate for management authorization purposes or needs further study.
2. In the former case, the joint preparation of a presentation to the user steering committee and the Systems Policy Committee for management authorization of a project.

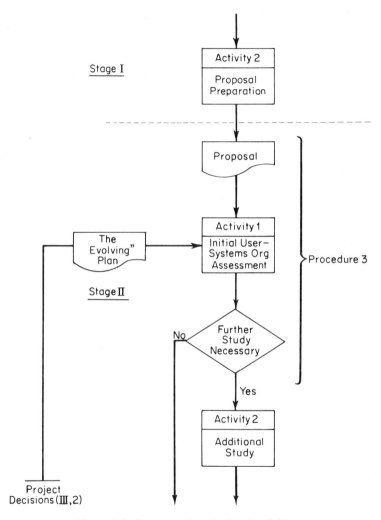

Figure 6–3. Procedure 3 and related activities.

Procedural Steps:

1. The systems organization assigns the proposal-assessment responsibility to its planning staff group, and informs the user organization.
2. The user- and systems-organization staff groups establish liaison for joint assessment of the proposal.
3. For systems proposals encompassing more than one functional area (for example, a large, integrated, logistics system covering, perhaps, inventory control, materials scheduling, purchasing, etc.) an attempt is made to segment the proposal into a number of modular phases which could be authorized separately, if desirable.
4. The sequence in which the phases should be undertaken and completed is determined based on "natural" precedence.
5. A determination is made of the possible similarity in scope of each of the phases to other proposed or ongoing efforts. This includes: (a) matching the proposals against an evolving and orderly systems classification; (b) segmenting proposals to fit the classification pigeonholes, or, if necessary, creating or redefining the pigeonholes to fit the proposals; and (c) evaluating against similarly pigeon-holed proposals for similarities and differences, and for properly defined interfaces.
6. The requirements for further study of those phases requiring early management authorization is determined, including the additional information to be developed.
7. Recommendations are developed for the size, composition and work plan of a *study team.*
8. With user- and systems-organization concurrence, a study-team manager and members are assigned to begin work.

PROCEDURE 4

STAGE II: Detailed Analysis (Feasibility Assessment)

Activity 2: Additional Study (Writing Feasibility Report)

Scope: Conducting a *feasibility study* and preparing a *feasibility report,* containing recommendations and back-up information for management authorization of a project or series of related projects.

Objectives:

1. To identify specific phases to be "projectized" initially.
2. To develop complete data on the project(s) for management approval.
3. To view proposed project(s) in the context of other systems-development activities, including: determining whether combining, in part or entirely, with other similar developments is feasible, deciding what interfaces must be provided with other systems, and ensuring adaptability of proposed system to business change and growth.

Related Activities (See Fig. 6-4):

1. Preceding: Procedure 3. Stage II, Activity 1—Initial User/Systems Organization Assessment

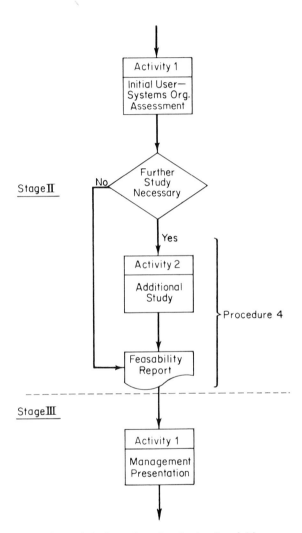

Figure 6–4. Procedure 4 and related activities.

2. Succeeding: Procedure 5. Stage III, Activity 1—Management Consideration Presentation

Responsible Organizations and Positions:
1. Study Team (created in Procedure 3)

Documents Used:
1. The systems proposal
2. Internal user "working papers"
3. The evolving "corporate systems plan," to the extent its existing scope encompasses the proposal area
4. Resource Utilization Forecast (see Procedure 6)

Documents Produced:
1. A *Feasibility Report* (data for management consideration and project guidance). The contents of this report include:
   a. description of the overall system in terms understandable to management.
   b. the specific scope of the phase(s) of the system for which approval is presently being requested.
   c. summary of findings, conclusions.
   d. specific recommendations.
   e. alternatives considered, approach selected for purposes of feasibility evaluation.
   f. effect of selected approach on operations, viz.,
      (1) people,
      (2) quality,
      (3) effectiveness,
      (4) costs and benefits (by project phases):
         —outlays by time period.
         —savings (personnel and other).
         —present value and discounted cash flow.
         —intangible, non-quantifiable benefits and probability of their realization.
   g. effect on existing and planned systems, and what is to be done with respect to those systems.
   h. probability of technical success.
   i. recommended plan of action:
      (1) phases to be approved and "projectized" now.
      (2) resources required, type and quantity to be assigned.
      (3) further study required prior to presentation of further phases for approval, and timing of the necessary preliminary studies.

Procedural Steps:
1. The study team develops its findings and reviews with the user, the manager of the systems organization and his staff, and other interested groups.
2. Revisions are suggested and made prior to presentation of the feasibility report to the Systems Policy Committee.
3. A Systems Policy Committee presentation is prepared by study team.

4. The systems-organization planning staff analyzes impact of study-team conclusions on future requirements and other developmental activities, and prepares a presentation of its findings for Systems Policy Committee.

Comment:

Before it is submitted to the Systems Policy Committee, the feasibility report of the Study Team is reviewed jointly by the user groups who are affected, or who were in some way responsible for the original proposal, and by the systems-organization planning staff. This review may modify the conclusions, or it may result in full concurrence with the report as it stands. If there should remain any important aspect of the report from which the users or the systems-organization staff dissent, this too would be reported to the Policy Committee along with the report itself.

PROCEDURE 5

STAGE III: Management Consideration (User Steering Committee and Systems Policy Committee)

Activity 1: Presentation

Scope: Providing the User Steering Committee and Systems Policy Committee with a *presentation* leading to informed understanding of the need for and consequences of authorizing the project(s) in the proposed systems area.

Objectives:
1. To assist in weighing the expected payoff of the proposed project and other projects competing for systems-implementation resources.
2. To help decide when and at what level of effort a project should be established in order to maximize the opportunity for significant progress without significantly impeding the progress of other important efforts.
3. To permit consideration of payoff opportunities in terms of contribution to the overall division and corporate posture in systems development, and not merely in terms of the merits of a project as an isolated system.
4. To present cost/payoff estimates and permit evaluation, in terms of management objectives, of joint development of proposed systems among more than one division, where there is no apparent technical or functional reason for different systems.
5. To permit consistency in the evaluation of this project against other proposed projects on the basis of uniformly complete and accurate information.

Related Activities (See Fig. 6-5):
1. Preceding: Procedure 4. Stage II, Activity 2—Detailed Study
2. Succeeding: Procedure 6. Stage III, Activity 2—Management Actions

Responsible Organizations and Positions:
1. Systems Policy Committee
2. User(s) steering committee(s)
3. Study team manager
4. System organization managers

Documents Used:
1. Feasibility Report (see Procedure 4 for description)
2. Resource Utilization Forecast (see Procedure 6)

Documents Produced: None

Procedural Steps:
1. Study Team presents its findings and makes its recommendations as to the establishment of a project and a proposed work plan showing scheduled resource requirements.
2. Systems-organization planning staff presents its analysis of the impact of proposed project on resources available and on other systems activities, and presents alternative courses of action.
3. Systems Policy Committee may request more information prior to making decision, or may take under advisement at this point pending decision.

PROCEDURE 6

STAGE III: Management Consideration

Activity 2:   Management Actions

Scope: Project approval and assignment of a *project team* with project responsibilities, resources levels, etc.; project disapproval or referral for more study.

Objectives:
1. To decide whether there is enough information about a proposed project and its effects to make an intelligent allocation of resources.
2. To allocate systems resources (principally systems and programming personnel) to this project, as compared to other proposed projects and other systems activities competing for them.
3. To select a start date for this project.
4. To assign management control responsibility for the project to a *project team,* in conjunction with the User Steering Committee.
5. To establish project steering responsibility and reporting frequency.
6. To determine benchmarks or checkpoints to be met prior to the approval of further phases of project.
7. To consider and make policy covering the general allocation of resources among projects, and between projects and non-project activi-

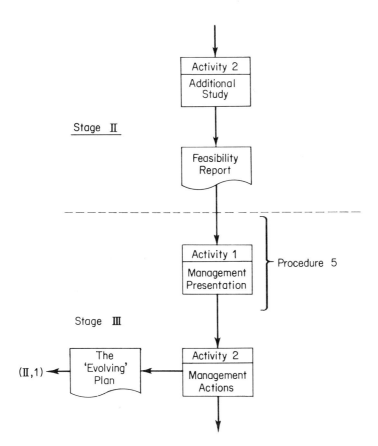

Figure 6–5. Procedure 5 and related activities.

ties, such as systems maintenance, "systems programming," systems studies, etc.

Recommendations as to priorities in terms of natural or technical precedence, and in terms of expected payoff, should be included in the proposals submitted. Payoff information may be based on no more than an educated guess, in which case management may decide that further analysis is required before a decision as to priority in the use of resources can be made, especially for major projects. It must also weigh the proposed user projects against other activities which may bypass some or most of this procedure in attempting to establish priorities, and, in turn, it must weigh all proposals before it against available or planned resources. The latter information would be available to the Policy Committee in the form of *Resource Utilization Forecasts,* projected a year or more into the future on an "evergreen" basis (see, in Chapter V, page 88, concerning the "expanding horn"). Existing projects may also find that previously assigned resources are inadequate, or that schedules must be altered. Requests for resource changes or major schedule changes may be submitted to the Committee. These requests must compete for resources against projects being newly considered.

Related Activities (See Fig. 6-6):
1. Preceding: Procedure 5. Stage III, Activity 1—Management Presentation
2. Succeeding: Procedure 7. Stage IV, General Activity—Project Control

Responsible Organizations and Positions:
1. Systems Policy Committee
2. User steering committee

Documents Used: Summary of management presentation material, based on Feasibility Report and Resource Utilization Forecast.

Documents Produced: Memorandum of decisions taken

Procedural Steps:

1. Assign a project team and project manager.
2. Select project steering committee (senior personnel independent of the project team).
3. Assign resources to implement project.
4. Concur if a major project change is necessary.
5. Establish project policies or relationships as appropriate.

Comments:

If further study prior to authorization is deemed necessary, the Policy Committee notifies the study team, defines requirements for ad-

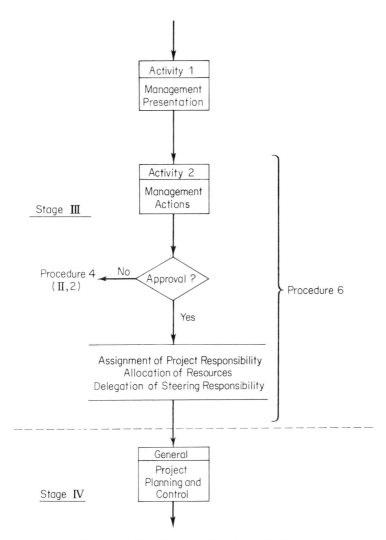

Figure 6–6. Procedure 6 and related activities.

ditional information, and sets a due date. Otherwise it establishes at this point a project and a project team, to start work as assigned priority dictates. The project team consists of permanent members (including a project manager) drawn from the user organization, systems-development resource departments, and other groups as needed, and "loaned" to serve on the team for the duration.

In some cases further study on existing projects may be deemed necessary before future phases are authorized. This would be true particularly if the scope of the original study did not carry through all phases to project completion, or if problems arose in the course of a project such that certain previously arrived-at conclusions were made invalid.

PROCEDURE 7

STAGE IV: Systems Implementation and Control

General Activity: Project Planning and Control (all phases)

Scope: Control of the project phases and accountability for project success. Includes scheduling, internal project budgeting, initiation of phases, technical review, and subproject control.

Objectives:
1. To provide technical and administrative continuity in the conduct of a project.
2. To provide a single focus for planning and control of the entire development effort.
3. To negotiate for and coordinate the efforts of personnel resources assigned to the project from several functional units, including the user organization, the Management Sciences Dept., the data-processing organization, and outside consultants.
4. To ensure proper coordination between the project team and other affected groups, including technical services, "systems programming," data-processing operations, the systems-organization planning staff, and the user's organization.
5. To periodically report progress to higher levels of management (steering committees and the Systems Policy Committee), and seek resolution of resource or schedule problems, if they occur, at the earliest possible stage.

Related Activities (See Fig. 6-7):
1. The Project Phases [see specifically Stage IV, Activities 1–4 (Procedures 8–11)]
2. Data-Processing Organization activities [see specifically Stage V, Activities 1–3 (Procedures 12–14)]
3. Stage VI, Performance Evaluation

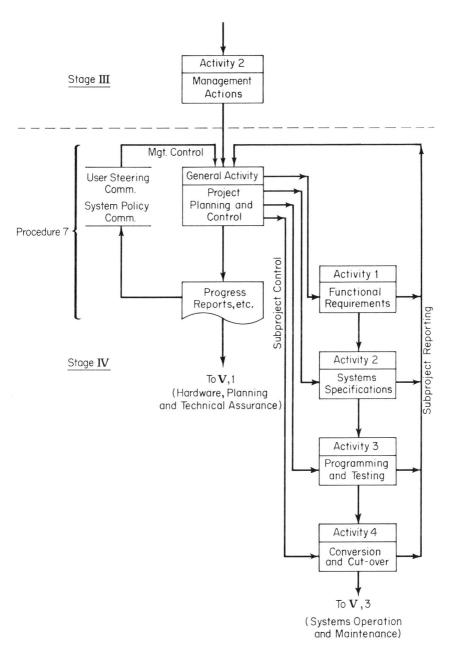

Figure 6–7. Procedure 7 and related activities.

Responsible Organizations and Positions:

1. Project manager (and his administrative staff, if any)
2. User steering committee
3. Systems Policy Committee
4. The data-processing organization
5. Managements of functional organizations supplying personnel resources or support to project team (including Management Sciences Dept. and the user organization)

Documents Used:

1. User "working papers"
2. User proposal
3. Feasibility Report (including "work plan")
4. Project authorization memoranda

Documents Produced:

1. Detailed schedule and budget by project phases
2. Manpower schedule
3. Monthly progress reports (actual vs. planned)

Procedural Steps:

The management of the Project Team is the keystone of the entire development process. In one direction it controls design and implementation, and in the other it is accountable upwards for the conduct and success of the project phases which have been authorized.

1. Each phase of the project is scheduled, budgeted, initiated, and administered by the project team internal management. The administration can be direct (where the working personnel from resource departments are assigned directly to the project team and report to one of its permanent members) or indirect (where the project team has given a "subcontract" for a well-defined piece of the project to another group in the corporation, or to an outside group). On critical but ill-defined pieces of work it is expected that the normal regime will be direct, otherwise indirect will be the usual case.
2. The phases generally applicable to a complete project leading from the approval of a project to the conversion of a major system would include functional requirements, systems design, programming and testing, and conversion. These phases are more fully discussed in Procedures 8–11.
3. The project team periodically reports to the project steering committee. It should routinely report the percentage completion of various activities, planned versus actual expenditure, present deviation, forecasted deviation at the future completion of each activity, and a summary covering all activities collectively. If existing or expected deviations require schedule or resource-allocation changes, these should also be presented fully to the steering committee at these reporting and review periods.
4. The steering committee in turn should decide whether it can take the

necessary action, or whether the matter must be referred to the Systems Policy Committee. If referred, the Systems Policy Committee may decide that further study is necessary before a final decision. Certain major project decisions will involve acquisition of facilities. Such requirements are communicated to the data-processing organization (see Stage V).

PROCEDURE 8

STAGE IV: Systems Implementation and Control

Activity 1:   Completion of Functional Requirements

Scope: Preparation of formal, user-oriented *functional requirements* and their subsequent approval.

Objectives:
1. To conduct this Activity in such a way that both functional and technical experts can commonly contribute and communicate about systems requirements, cost tradeoffs and performance criteria.
2. To communicate to the systems designers a complete and comprehensive specification of precisely *what* the system is to do from a functional point of view.
3. To communicate the same information to the user, so that he may give informed approval to these specifications prior to commencement of design and development.
4. To minimize the time and cost of the cascading effect of changes in functional specifications during later phases of development, by requiring formal "sign-off" of a specification document.
5. To provide to those who will manage specific subprojects a basis for detailed estimates of time and cost expenditures required to implement various parts of the system.

It is unusual to complete the functional requirements before some design activity is commenced, nor is it necessary, provided that the preparation of functional requirements has an adequate lead. It is extremely important, especially for large, complex efforts, to separate this type of user-oriented analysis on the one hand from technical systems analysis on the other, lest the two become so intermixed that the user fails to understand precisely what he may be getting for his money until after the system is in operation.

Related Activities (See Fig. 6-7):
1. Concurrent: Procedure 7. Stage IV, General Activity—Project Control
2. Preceding: Procedure 4. Stage II, Activity 2—Additional Study (Feasibility Report)

3. Succeeding: Procedure 9. Stage IV, Activity 2—Preparation of Systems Specifications

Responsible Organizations and Positions:

1. "Functional Requirements" subproject team
2. Project manager
3. Functional organizations responsible for or supplying manpower to project
4. Project steering committee

Documents Used:

1. Feasibility Report
2. Work plan (schedule and budget, as negotiated)

Documents Produced:

1. Subproject progress reports
2. Functional Requirements document
   a. narrative description of system functioning and characteristics
   b. data specifications (the identity and data contents of input transactions, output reports and items, and master files to be maintained)
   c. the processing of the data required
   d. time-related parameters and volumes
   e. interfaces with related systems
   f. control requirements
   g. conversion planning guidelines
3. Performance criteria (acceptance-test requirements)
4. Updating of the cost and savings estimates in the Feasibility Report
5. Systems training requirements

Procedural Steps:

1. The project manager negotiates with functional groups (such as the Management Sciences Dept.) for the conduct of a subproject for this phase; or, alternatively, negotiates for people to staff this phase to report directly to the project-management staff.
2. A subproject leader is chosen and assigned by the functional group responsible.
3. Manpower scheduled and committed to this phase is incorporated in the "Manpower Resources Utilization Report" provided by the functional groups to the Systems Policy Committee (or its staff).
4. The functional-requirements subproject leader prepares a detailed work plan under the guidance of and with final approval by the project manager.
5. The work of the subproject team proceeds, observing the ground rules for reporting and technical checkpointing established by the project manager.
6. The Functional Requirements document, or parts of it as completed, are received at appropriate times by the project steering committee, and formally approved by them.
7. Approved sections of the Functional Requirements document are reviewed with and turned over to the Systems Specifications team (see Procedure 9).

PROCEDURE 9

STAGE IV: Systems Implementation and Control

Activity 2:   Preparation of Systems Specifications

Scope: Preparation of formal, technically oriented specifications for the implementation of the system (*systems design* or *systems specifications*).

Objectives:
1. To specify precisely *how* the system is to fulfill the functional requirements and performance criteria.
2. To segment the implementation effort into manageable sub-tasks.
3. To define the subsystems and *how* they are to be integrated into the final systems configuration.
4. To specify the sequence in which the implementation tasks are to be performed, including scheduling and manpower requirements.
5. To determine and specify support tasks that must be performed.
6. To specify system testing, file creation and conversion steps.

Related Activities (See Fig. 6-7):
1. Concurrent: Procedure 7. Stage IV, General Activity—Project Planning and Control
2. Preceding: Procedure 8. Stage IV, Activity 1—Completion of Functional Requirements (Systems design and specification generally follows the completion of functional requirements, although some overlap would be normal and desirable.)
3. Succeeding: Procedure 10. Stage IV, Activity 3—Programming and Testing

Responsible Organizations and Positions:
1. "Systems Specifications" subproject team
2. Project manager
3. Functional organization responsible for or supplying manpower to subproject (e.g., the systems organization)
4. Data-processing organization

Documents Used:
1. Functional Requirements
2. Work plan (schedule and budget as negotiated)

Documents Produced:
1. Subproject progress reports
2. Systems specifications
    a. detailed systems configuration
    b. description of the application-program segments to be written
    c. description of the manual procedures to be written
    d. record and file designs (input, output, files, tables, etc.)

  e. description of the utilities and test tools to be developed or used (if not already available)

  f. hardware requirements (computers, peripherals, communications, terminals)

  g. data-management and operating-system requirements

  h. programming languages to be used

  i. test specifications and testing schedule

  j. conversion plan

  k. detailed manning requirements and schedule for programming, testing, conversion, and cutover

  l. detailed manning requirements for systems operation

3. Final updating of cost and savings estimates

4. Final updating of performance criteria

Procedural Steps:

1. The project manager negotiates with functional groups (primarily in the systems organization) for the conduct of a subproject for this phase —or he may, in unusual cases, arrange for the people who staff this phase to report directly to the project management staff.

2. A subproject leader is chosen and assigned by the functional group responsible.

3. The "Systems Specifications" subproject leader prepares a detailed work plan under the guidance and with final approval of the project manager and the subproject leader's manager.

4. Manpower scheduled and committed to this phase is incorporated in the Manpower Utilization Report provided periodically by the functional groups to the Systems Policy Committee (or its staff).

5. The work of the subproject team proceeds, observing the ground rules for technical checkpoints and reporting established by the project manager.

6. Approved sections of the specifications are reviewed with and turned over to the "Programming and Testing" team (see Stage IV, Activity 3).

7. Hardware, communications, and operating-system requirements are reviewed with the data-processing organization prior to hardware procurement.

PROCEDURE 10

STAGE IV: Systems Implementation and Control

Activity 3:   Programming and Testing

Scope: Implementation of the systems design, and pre-conversion testing.

Objectives:

1. To carry out programming and testing in conformity with the systems design and work plan (although some overlap in these two activities is normal, and although, in fact, there is feedback from programming and testing to systems design). Systems design (i.e., systems specifi-

cation, Procedure 9) continues as a function throughout programming and testing, but at an ever-diminishing level.
2. To assess whether the system will perform as specified and, if not, what modifications might be made in the functional or design specifications, at the least cost and delay, to make the system operate more effectively.
3. To develop formal and complete operating instructions and manual procedures for the system, and to assist in training personnel of the user and operating organizations.
4. To arrange with the data-processing organization for use of testing facilities and other systems support.

Related Activities (See Fig. 6-7):
1. Concurrent: Procedure 7. Stage IV, General Activity—Project Planning and Control
2. Preceding: Procedure 9. Stage IV, Activity 2—Systems Specifications (partially concurrent)
3. Succeeding: Procedure 11. Stage IV, Activity 4—Conversion and Cutover
4. Related: Procedure 13. Stage V, Activity 2—Hardware Procurement and Installation

Responsible Organizations and Positions:
1. "Programming and Testing" subproject team
2. Project manager
3. Data-processing organization
4. Computer-center operating department
5. User groups involved in systems operation at input and output ends
6. Project steering committee

Documents Used:
1. Systems Specifications
2. Work plan (schedule and budget, as negotiated)

Documents Produced:
1. Program documentation
2. Test-data specifications
3. Procedures and operating instructions
4. Training manuals
5. Data-collection forms
6. Test scripts & test results

Procedural Steps:
1. The project manager negotiates with the systems organization for the conduct of a subproject for this phase.
2. A subproject leader is chosen and assigned by the systems organization.
3. The programming and testing subproject leader prepares a detailed work plan under the guidance of and with final approval by the project manager and the subproject leader's manager.
4. Manpower scheduled and committed to this phase is incorporated in the Manpower Utilization Report provided periodically by the functional groups to the Systems Policy Committee (or its staff).

5. The work indicated under "documents produced" proceeds, observing the ground rules for technical checkpoints and reporting established by the project manager.

6. The subproject manager coordinates the use of testing facilities with the data-processing organization (Computer Center), in conformity with an agreed-upon level of use.

PROCEDURE 11

STAGE IV: Systems Implementation and Control

Activity 4:   Conversion and Cutover

Scope: Phasing the tested system into full operation, through a *conversion* process.

Objectives:
1. To permit the user organizations to formally accept the system prior to cutover.
2. To accomplish conversion with minimum disruption in operations.
3. To accomplish conversion at minimum risk to the user organization.
4. To accomplish conversion at minimum cost.
5. To phase the project team out of responsibility for the system, and to phase in the line data-processing and other operating organizations.

With many systems, especially large, complex ones, conversion and cutover may be accomplished in phases. The phases must be carefully planned and executed, with significant participation by the user organizations. Parallel operation may be called for during some of the conversion phases until a high level of confidence in the system is attained. The phases of conversion may include:

Build-up of and operation with the master files, a section at a time.

Conversion (one or more at a time) of the facilities, departments, shops, or offices involved.

Conversion of one subsystem module at a time (if it can usefully stand alone), in conjunction with the phasing-in of the files and user facilities. After all phases of conversion are complete the project as such is disestablished, and is replaced by routine systems maintenance, which is a responsibility of the data-processing organization. A residue of the project team may continue for some months after full operation commences, however, for correction of major operating problems pending complete shakedown and final evaluation of operating performance.

Related Activities (See Fig. 6-7):
1. Concurrent: Procedure 7. Stage IV, General Activity—Project Planning and Control
2. Preceding: Procedure 10. Stage IV, Activity 3—Programming and Testing

3. Succeeding: Procedure 14. Stage V, Activity 3—Operation and Maintenance
4. Related: Procedure 13. Stage V, Activity 2—Hardware Procurement and Installation

Responsible Organizations and Positions:
1. "Programming and Testing" subproject team
2. Project manager
3. Data-processing organization (Computer Center)
4. User groups involved in systems operations at input and output ends
5. Project steering committee

Documents Used:
1. Conversion plan (from systems specifications)
2. Procedures and operating instructions
3. Training manuals
4. Data-collection forms

Procedural Steps:
1. A conversion team is assembled from among the implementing and using organizations.
2. The project manager generally assumes direct responsibility for this phase initially, gradually turning over more and more responsibility to the computer center and user organization. At the conclusion of this phase the project team has only a residual responsibility, whenever major systems "bugs" are detected.
3. An acceptance test (or tests) is commenced, at the conclusion of which the user accepts the system.
4. Manpower scheduled and committed to this phase is incorporated into the Manpower Utilization Report.
5. After cutover is completed, the disestablishment of the project is negotiated with the user and data-processing organizations, who take over full operating responsibilities.

PROCEDURE 12

STAGE V: Data-Processing Organization (Computer Center) Activities (of the Project Team)

Activity 1: Hardware Planning and Technical Assurance

Scope: Assuring the Project Team that the data-processing organization will have the needed facilities and will be able to assume responsibility for the operation of the system which has been proposed and is being implemented.

Objectives:
1. To provide to the data-processing organization early information on project requirements, to satisfy the lead time necessary for hardware

planning and procurement. (Initially the data-processing organization should be made aware of proposals awaiting authorization, so that an even earlier assessment of long-range requirements may be made.)

2. To consult with the data-processing organization on hardware, software, testing, and operational specifications, as they are developed within the project, to assure that they are adequate and that they can be fulfilled.

Related Activities (See Fig. 6-7):

1. Concurrent: Procedure 7. Stage IV, General Activity—Project Planning and Control
2. Preceding: Procedures 8 & 9. Stage IV, Activities 1 & 2—Functional Requirements and Systems Specifications.
3. Succeeding: Procedure 13. Stage V, Activity 2—Hardware Procurement and Installation

Responsible Organizations and Positions:

1. Project manager
2. Data-processing organization (Computer Center)
3. Systems specification subproject team
4. User steering committee

Documents Used:

1. Functional Requirements (when available)
2. Systems Specifications (when available)

Documents Produced:

1. Memorandum of agreement

Procedural Steps:

1. Subsequent to examining the systems specifications, the data-processing organization must formally agree that it can fulfill the requirements imposed upon it by the specifications, or else it must suggest and negotiate revisions of the specifications which make them acceptable.
2. Unresolvable differences between the project team and the data-processing organization should be referred to the project steering committee and the systems-organization management for consideration and resolution.

PROCEDURE 13

STAGE V: Data-Processing Organization Activities

Activity 2:   Hardware Procurement and Installation

Scope: The coordination of procurement actions and installation measures with project requirements and schedules.

Objectives:

1. To provide facilities at the times and in the quantities necessary for program and system testing.

2. To provide facilities at the times and in the quantities necessary for conversion, cutover, and operation.

Related Activities:
1. Concurrent: Procedures 10 & 11. Stage IV, Activities 3 & 4—Programming and Testing, Conversion and Cutover
2. Preceding: Procedure 12. Stage V, Activity 1—Hardware Planning and Technical Assurance
3. Succeeding: Procedure 14. Stage V, Activity 3—Systems Operation and Maintenance

PROCEDURE 14

STAGE V: Data-Processing Organization Activities

Activity 3:   Systems Operation and Maintenance

Scope: The operation of the system, the logging of performance measures, the detection and correction of errors.

Objectives:
1. To provide the required operational services and facilities.
2. To perform routine maintenance in the system in the event of minor changes, operating problems, or system errors, and to provide gradual performance improvements.

Related Activities:
1. Preceding: Procedure 11. Stage IV, Activity 4—Conversion and Cutover
2. Concurrent: Procedure 15. Stage VI—Performance Evaluation

PROCEDURE 15

STAGE VI: Performance Evaluation

Scope: The measurement of benefits attained versus benefits expected, and recommendations for improvements in the system and the systems-development function in general.

Objectives:
1. To evaluate the system after operational shakedown, when relatively error-free performance has been obtained, by a disinterested party (i.e., someone other than the project team, operating organization or user)
2. To measure the tangible benefits actually obtained
3. To measure the actual development costs
4. To measure the actual operating costs
5. To compare these costs and benefits against those planned, and determine reasons for variance

6. To assess the intangible benefits obtained and compare them with those originally estimated
7. To recommend what should be done to bring system up to specification at minimum cost and elapsed time
8. To determine what phases of the general development procedure need strengthening
9. To determine the success of the systems concept employed, and to recommend whether or not it should be employed again for future systems
10. To recommend whether future phases of the system should be approved, and when they should be approved

Related Activities (See Fig. 6-8):
1. Concurrent: Procedure 14. Stage V, Activity 3—Systems Operation and Maintenance

Responsible Organizations:
1. "Systems Audit Group"
2. User operating groups affected
3. Computer-center operations
4. Project manager

Documents Used:
1. Feasibility Report
2. Functional Requirements
3. Systems Specifications
4. Operating reports

Documents Produced:
1. Evaluation report

Procedural Steps:
1. The *Systems Audit Group* will study the systems documentation and determine the measurements to be made.
2. The team will devise the procedures necessary to make the measurements.
3. The cooperation of the involved parties will be solicited in obtaining the required information.
4. The collected information will be analyzed; conclusions will be drawn and recommendations developed.
5. The conclusions and recommendations will be put into a report and presented to the project manager, user steering committee, data-processing organization management and the Systems Policy Committee.
6. At its discretion management will act upon the recommendations, and consider the possibility of continuing or reestablishing the project, if major revisions are called for which involve resources beyond that which normal systems maintenance can provide.

Comment:

The Systems Audit Group should consist of people not involved in the original study, implementation, operation or use, but it must have the full

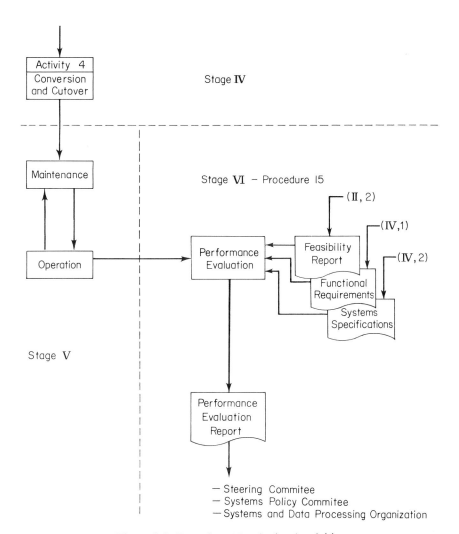

Figure 6–8. Procedure 15 and related activities.

cooperation of these parties. Therefore, it might be a separate group constituted for this purpose, an *ad hoc* group which would vary from case to case, part of an outside organization, or some combination of these groups.

The Systems Audit Group should be directly responsible to the Systems Policy Committee.

REFERENCES

1. *The Effective Executive* (New York: Harper and Row, Inc., 1966).

2. Justin A. Perlman, "Centralization versus Decentralization," *Datamation,* Sept. 1965, pp. 24–8.

3. Booz, Allen, and Hamilton, Inc., "The Computer Comes of Age."

4. Thomas L. Whisler, "The Impact of Information Technology on Organizational Control," p. 48.

5. Perlman, *op. cit., passim.*

6. "Planning for Data Processing," *EDP Analyzer,* Vol. 4, No. 6 (June 1966), *passim.*

7. "Building Corporate Data Systems," *EDP Analyzer,* Vol. 5, No. 4 (April 1967), *passim.*

8. John Dearden and F. Warren McFarlan, *Management Information Systems,* p. 48.

9. James Martin, *Programming Real-Time Computer Systems* (Englewood Cliffs, N.J.: Prentice-Hall, Inc., 1965), *passim.*

10. C. J. Middleton, "How to Set Up a Project Organization," *Harvard Business Review,* Vol. 45, No. 2 (April 1967), pp. 73ff.

11. Robert V. Head, *Real-Time Business Systems* (New York: Holt, Rinehart and Winston, Inc., Aug. 1965), pp. 99–100, and *passim.*

12. Richard A. Johnson, Fremont E. Kast and James E. Rosensweig, *The Theory and Management of Systems,* pp. 145–8.

13. H. N. Laden and T. R. Gildersleeve, *Systems Design for Computer Applications* (New York: John Wiley and Sons, Inc., 1963), pp. 223ff.

14. "The Computer Comes of Age."

15. *Management Information Systems,* pp. 25–6.

16. *The Theory and Management of Systems,* p. 145.

17. *Industrial Dynamics,* p. 364.

18. Martin, *Programming Real-Time Computer Systems,* p. 332.

19. Pearson Hunt, "Fallacy of the One Big Brain," *Harvard Business Review,* Vol. 44, No. 4 (Aug. 1966), pp. 84–90.

20. *The Theory and Management of Systems,* p. 145.

21. David I. Cleland, "Why Project Management?", *Business Horizons,* Winter 1964, p. 82.

22. Middleton, *op. cit.*

23. *Ibid.*

To get the facts first is impossible. There are no facts unless one has a criterion of relevance . . . everyone is far too prone to . . . look for the facts that fit the conclusion they have already reached . . . opinions come first . . . one does not argue them; one tests them.

Peter F. Drucker[1]

VII THE ECONOMICS OF A COMMON SYSTEM— A FEASIBILITY STUDY

INTRODUCTION

BACKGROUND

Chapter V related the systems plan (or "plan of projects") to the project plans, and emphasized the vital role of the feasibility study in spelling out the precise goals of a given systems project. Chapter VI gave further indication of how a specific project, in this sense, would be defined in a feasibility report prior to project authorization. *Completion* of functional-requirements specification is the first step shown *within* a given project (see Procedure 8 in Chapter VI), since the feasibility study (see Procedure 4 in Chapter VI) merely develops the functional requirements to the extent necessary to attain management approval leading to project authorization. The feasibility study is not intended to satisfy system-design requirements.

Another way of looking at this point was indicated in the "black box" concept of a system, in Chapter V. The details of what goes on inside the black box are a matter of systems implementation, and not a matter of functional specification (also called systems definition). The latter is concerned with defining the data outside the black box, and is expressed in users' terminology, or in language understandable to the users. Systems implementation descriptions should be of no concern to the users, as such, and need not be comprehensible to them. Thus the functional require-ments—which tell *what* is to be done by the system or subsystem, not *how* it is to be done—are to be roughed out in the feasibility study and ex-pressed in users' application terminology, not in systems language.

The output of the feasibility study, as described under Procedure 4 in Chapter VI, is the feasibility report. This report includes consideration of alternative approaches to laying out the system. One of these approaches is to be selected as the basis of the feasibility evaluation. The effect of the selected approach on the effectiveness of the system or subsystem, on its costs and benefits, and on the people involved in running and using it, is then to be covered in the feasibility report.

One of the problems facing a study team attempting to conduct such a feasibility study is to give adequate consideration to developing a general system or common system to take care of several distinct organizational entities (Divisions or Departments, perhaps) the work of which, although different in nature, somehow may present similarities. These organizational units would be candidates for using a common system if one could be developed under a reasonable project plan. This aspect of the feasibility study will be the subject of Chapter VII. Especially of interest to us will be how one might proceed in the absence of solid facts, since the feasibility study is often of necessity conducted at a very early stage of project defi-nition, with no firm quantitative picture of the various competing pos-sibilities at hand. The example to be presented in this chapter shows how, in the particular case of one divisionalized corporation, it was possible to develop a semi-quantitative method of evaluating such alternatives during the feasibility study. The simplification and linearization neces-sarily involved in this particular example indicate that the numeric results obtained should not be credited with great absolute significance. However, such an approach may sometimes serve the purpose of steering a feasibility study to a valid conclusion, on a rational rather than on a wholly intuitive basis.

STUDY OBJECTIVES

We shall now examine the case of the (fictional) XYZ Corporation. This case involves a system consisting of two modules in the Saleable Prod-uct Operational Control Information System (SPOCIS). The modules are Order Processing and Inventory Control (finished goods). These modules (for purposes of the study) are defined to include the following major functions: (1) order preparation, (2) check for credit as required,

(3) finished-goods inventory reporting, (4) checks for product availability, (5) shipping-point and means-of-delivery selection, (6) order entry, including transmission and editing, (7) order confirmation, (8) shipments reporting, and (9) maintenance of open-order files. Except for linkages the following functions are excluded: (1) inventory management, (2) production and distribution planning and control, (3) pricing and billing, (4) accounts receivable, and (5) sales and financial analysis.

The part of the overall feasibility study which concerns us here includes the following: (1) the requirements for the future order-processing systems of the various businesses in the corporation, (2) the similarities (commonalities) and differences among order-processing requirements, (3) the economics of the various alternative approaches to order processing, and (4) the kinds of technology available to implement the approaches.

The principal questions which the study attempts to answer are these: (1) How many different systems composed of versions of these two modules are required?, (2) What percentage of the sales and order volume can be covered by the systems version capable of handling the largest segment of the corporation?, and (3) If a common system is feasible, what are the alternative systems concepts to be considered, and which one should be selected?

APPROACH

A cursory examination of sales- and order-volume statistics showed that five of the divisions of the XYZ Corporation, selected because of their size and the similarity of their order-distribution patterns, accounted for the major part of both total sales dollars and order volume. These were the divisions that had a large number of sales offices around the country which "competed" with one another to place orders against a similarly large number of warehouses and plants. That is, the pattern of order placement by a single sales office on a number of different shipping locations tended to overlap the patterns of other sales offices in the same division. The remaining divisions, the majority, either consisted of a number of local, non-interacting, production-distribution complexes, or had a single production-distribution point, or dedicated warehouses located adjacent to each sales office.

Because of their similarity in both the geographical dispersion of their order-processing activities, and the need for a properly instructed central "umpire" to govern these activities according to rather complex sales-service and distribution-control rules, the five divisions were selected for study as potential candidates for a single, centralized order-processing–inventory-reporting system. The major opportunity for maximum payoff of such a single system lay with these five divisions.

The feasibility of a single system, as opposed to multiple systems for these five, derives primarily from the trade-offs between opposing cost influences. The first influence is quite obviously the economy of scale of one large system as contrasted with a group of several smaller ones. This kind of economy can be achieved by spreading the amortized development and operating costs of one system over a larger number of transactions. This is countered by increased development cost because of the complex design needed to handle the diverse requirements of all the different divisions involved; and, relatedly, the "pulsing" of this additional systems complexity by each transaction of the several varieties being processed. This additional complexity of program logic and communications, not needed by any single transaction variety or source, must be paid for by all. The challenge of our case study is to develop a measure of the economic trade-offs between increases and decreases in various cost elements as order-processing–inventory-reporting requirements and transaction volumes are aggregated into increasingly larger systems.

The diversity in order-processing characteristics of the five divisions collectively differs only in degree from that found within any one of them. Moreover, the similarities in these characteristics do not always follow organizational lines. For example, the requirements of the product lines within even one division are not identical in many respects, yet those product lines would presumably have to be handled within a single system, if one were to be planned for this division. For example, one product within one division is distributed from over 100 warehouses, other products from only a dozen regional locations. Similar comments can be made for other divisions. The several made-to-stock businesses in a given division have more in common (from an order-processing point of view) with the handling of such items in another division than they have with the made-to-order business in the given division itself. Clearly, if a single system covering all of one division can be developed, then in principle one can be developed for all five, if management so wishes.

For purposes of comparing five stand-alone systems with various combinations of the five into one or more aggregated systems, we use a cost-estimating procedure which assumes that each of the five would install a system similar in scope to the one in which they would jointly participate. That is, the operating characteristics and benefits (other than cost) will be the same for each business, whether it operates alone or in combination with others.

The *study plan* comprises four major tasks:

1. Defining a set of requirements satisfying the order-processing needs of the five divisions representing the major systems opportunity in the XYZ Corporation.
2. Postulating a typical (but hypothetical) division characterized by these requirements, and therefore representing a "model" or "reference" business as a basis for analysis.
3. Trying out various solutions on this "reference" business and evaluating them.
4. Selecting a solution based on this analysis, and measuring its effect when applied to the actual divisions, alone and in combination.

THE "REFERENCE" BUSINESSES

DESCRIPTION

In terms of order volume, the five divisions range from a low of 25–40,000 orders per year to a high of about 300,000 orders per year. The five have a combined total of over 600,000 orders per year. No single "reference" business could typify this range. Therefore, the following was done to overcome this:

1. Three "reference" businesses were postulated, each with a different level of activity. These were:

    a.   50,000 orders per year (200 orders per day)
    b. 150,000 orders per year (600 orders per day)
    c. 600,000 orders per year (2400 orders per day)

2. The ratios between orders and other types of transactions were made constant over this range, and conformed generally to the average of the ratios found in the five divisions. In the reference businesses the ratio of "other" transactions to customer orders are as follows:

    a. Change orders   0.10
    b. Line items   1.50
    c. Price quotations   0.10
    d. Inventory transfers   2.15
    e. Product inquiries   0.10
    f. Customer file updates   0.05
    g. "Made-to-order" orders   0.20
    h. Shipping orders   1.50
    i. All transactions   6.70

Volumes for the reference businesses were based upon statistics obtained from a survey of the five divisions. These volumes, keyed to number of annual customer orders, appear in Table 7-1.

The location of shipping points and sales offices and their volumes for the three reference businesses were postulated and plotted on maps. Table 7-2 is a summary of the number of such locations.

Table 7-1. STATISTICS FOR THE REFERENCE BUSINESSES*

Orders per day: (annual orders)	200 (50,000)	600 (150,000)	2400 (600,000)
Number of Customers	10	75	225
Number of Products	5	30	80
Number of SKUs†	20	90	250
Average Open Orders Per Year	3	10	39
Production Reports Per Year	42	132	528
Inventory Updates Per Year	114	321	1290
All Transactions Per Year	405	1155	4620

* Tabulated quantities are given in thousands.
† Stockkeeping units—an inventory location for a product.

The hypothesized mix of made-to-stock (80%) and made-to-order (20%) in the reference business also has an impact on order-processing characteristics. In the made-to-stock case the order can be placed directly on the shipping point, perhaps following an availability check. In the case of future delivery a reservation can be made against predicted stock balance at that time. Often the shipping point ships immediately on receipt of the order. However, in the made-to-order case, promised delivery date has to be obtained from the production-scheduling function.

Not all order-processing-related costs were included in the analysis. Where it was felt that differing systems approaches would not affect the cost of certain operations, these were excluded from consideration, since they would not significantly influence the net difference in estimated costs among the different approaches. Costs specifically included were: field office personnel (order entry points), communications and terminals, and central computer processing and systems maintenance. Costs specifically

Table 7-2. NUMBER OF LOCATIONS POSTULATED

	200/day	600/day	2400/day
Shipping Points	14	39	72
Sales Offices	4	23	46

excluded were those involving plant and warehouse personnel, inside sales effort, correspondence, etc. Development, training, conversion, etc., were treated as one-time costs, rather than amortized over the life of the system, and were not included as part of operating costs.

THE FOUR SYSTEMS CONCEPTS

Costs were analyzed for four systems approaches, called cases I through IV. These were:

I   Completely manual.

II   Manual order-entry processing, post-entry batch processing of confirmed orders for accounting and inventory-control purposes.

III   On-line transaction mode.

IV   On-line conversational mode.

In transaction mode the procedure contemplates an operator in the sales office who cuts a teletype tape from a manually edited memo order initially filled out by the sales correspondent. As the teletype station is periodically polled, the taped order would be transmitted as a whole to the computer, queued at that point if necessary, and processed in its turn. Transactions in error would be transmitted back to point of origin and reentered after correction. After successful order entry and processing against the customer, product and inventory files, a shipping order would be generated and transmitted over the teletype network to the selected shipping location.

In conversational mode the order entry clerk or sales correspondent is put directly on-line with, and under the immediate control of, the computer. The computer monitors and responds to each item of information in the order as it is entered, informing the clerk of errors or, for example, information as to product availability and delivery date, within 2–5 seconds of the completion of each of the 10 or 20 steps of the entry procedure. Effectively all of the processing of the order that needs to be accomplished at this point is completed by the time the entry clerk is finished entering the transaction. If the clerk or sales correspondent is on the telephone with the customer at this time, the entry of the order is completed on the computer terminal by the telephone call.

Costs were estimated for personnel, computer systems, and communications for the three reference businesses (200, 600 and 2400 orders per day). Personnel costs included those for clerical manning in the sales offices, which would vary depending on the systems concept. Personnel at the computer site (operators, maintenance programmers, etc.) were included in the category of central-site costs (i.e., computer systems). Personnel in the warehouse and plant locations were not included since their numbers would not be appreciably affected by the systems concept. Communications cost estimates were based on circuits designed to satisfy the geographical requirements of the reference businesses, the line speeds necessary for the different cases considered (e.g., low-speed for transaction and high-speed for conversational mode), numbers and types of terminals, remote interchange buffers, message switching, etc. Voice-communication costs were also considered.

Table 7-3 summarizes the three categories of operating costs based on order volume and systems concept. In Figure 7-1 the orders per year

Table 7-3. Reference Businesses Annual Operating Cost Summary*

Cost Element	50,000 Orders/Year				150,000 Orders/Year				600,000 Orders/Year			
	Case I	II	III	IV	Case I	II	III	IV	Case I	II	III	IV
Personnel												
Order processing	$120	120	53	24	$322	322	143	67	$1,478	1,478	576	264
Tape preparation (Case II)		19				36				96		
Manual inventory updating (I)	27				75				300			
Manual procedures staff (I)	12				16				24			
Sub-Total	159	139	53	24	413	358	143	67	1,802	1,574	576	264
Computer Systems												
Equipment		89	135	139		112	154	156		144	268	299
Other		26	58	65		31	72	91		43	96	132
Sub-Total		115	193	204		143	226	247		187	364	431
Communications												
Terminals	32	32	32	17	94	94	94	55	182	182	168	101
Lines & buffers	23	23	23	98	36	36	52	129	90	90	115	229
Message switching					30	30			72	72		
Voice	24	24	12	10	60	48	30	15	180	150	90	45
Supplemental					10	10	10	10	24	24	24	24
Sub-Total	79	79	67	125	230	218	186	209	548	518	397	399
ANNUAL TOTAL	$238	333	313	353	$643	719	555	523	$2,350	2,279	1,337	1,094
Cost Per 100 Orders (in dollars)			$626.00				$370.00				$222.80	

*Tabulated quantities are given in thousands of dollars.

151

are plotted against the annual costs for each of the four cases, and the points are connected with straight lines. This graph suggests that logarithmic curves might be fitted to the points to represent more realistically the intermediate values. However, the offset of such a curve from a straight line, once one is well away from the origin, would be slight and,

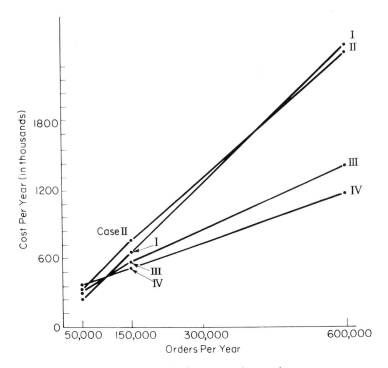

Figure 7-1. Reference business annual operating costs.

therefore, in this range we conclude that a simple linear interpolation to arrive at cost will provide sufficient precision for purposes of further analysis. In examining these curves it is clear, at least for the reference business, that cases III and IV provide significantly lower operating costs above 150,000 orders per year, and that the percentage difference between these two cases and cases I and II increases rapidly with the volume of orders. The manual system (case I) is least expensive at the low end of the range and most expensive at the high end. With conversational mode (case IV), the reverse is true.

THE "REAL" BUSINESSES

COST ESTIMATING FOR THE ACTUAL DIVISIONS

The cost per order processed has fixed and variable components. Modern order-processing systems, in common with most complex communications oriented computer applications, have a high fixed cost associated with their design, installation and operation. In the absence of countervailing factors, it is expected that there would be significant economic benefits from combining as many orders as possible into as few large systems as possible. In the case of each of the five divisions being considered there is wide diversity in requirements among the different product lines whose orders are to be processed by the proposed systems. Aggregation of the orders of these different product lines into combined systems will tend to increase costs because of the design complexity required to handle the diversity of requirements involved. Offsetting this are certain economies of scale that come into play, as the system costs fail to grow proportionately with increased volume. Manning inefficiencies are reduced, for example, as well as computer throughput costs per unit.

As a function of volume of orders, the three *computerized* systems concepts (cases II, III and IV) differ significantly in cost. In certain high-volume situations where the procedural complexity of order entry is severe, such as is represented by the case of Division A, a conversational-mode system may be feasible. Transaction mode is approximately midway in degree of innovation and implementation difficulty between cases II and IV. It is an appropriate systems concept for all five divisions. Since it was desired to evaluate the comparative economics of "go-it-alone" versus combined systems, an approach which is most generally understood and acceptable across the broad spectrum of the businesses was chosen. (To obtain simple comparisons, it is desirable to evaluate "go-it-alone" with system approach X versus "combined" with systems approach X. To compare go-it-alone with approach Y versus "combined" with approach X would have produced non-comparable results, making unnecessarily difficult the problem of evaluating the combination.)

The general form of the order-processing cost equation is: The total annual cost equals the sum of the products of each variable unit cost times the annual volume applicable to each, plus the sum of the fixed costs on an amortized basis.

There are variable and unit cost components for each *systems factor* (processing complexity, response-time requirements, etc.). The *elements of cost* are operating personnel, computer systems, communications, terminals, systems design and systems maintenance. The relationship between systems factors and the elements of cost can be shown by a simple matrix (Table 7-4).

In this matrix, cost component "$(2,3)$" represents the cost of communications due to the burden of meeting the systems response-time requirements. Each component in the matrix represents the costs due to the element of cost in its column for the system factor in its row.

For a system characterized by a certain processing complexity, a given spectrum of response-time requirements, a fixed topology or pattern of physical locations and their interactions, and a file size dictated by a given number of customers, products, etc., the following costs will tend to vary in complex ways as the volume of transactions increases:

Operating personnel
Computer systems costs (rentals, etc.)
Communications lines and equipment
Input terminals

The cost of systems design and development is treated as a fixed cost. Simplifying the analysis by treating personnel, computer, communications, and terminal costs solely as variable costs has two effects. First, it tends to make the results more conservative, since the economic benefits of combinations are less pronounced. Second, this equipment may not be one hundred per cent dedicated, and if not, the cost of adding new applications could be considered an incremental cost except in extreme circumstances (such as "conversational mode" order entry operating on dedicated real-time processors, operating outside an already existing teletype network).

The variable costs do not all vary in the same way as volume increases. Operating personnel costs will tend to vary with volume in one way, computer, communications, and terminal costs in other ways. With computer costs the economy of scale comes into play. For example, these costs may tend to vary according to the cube root of the volume squared.

For sufficiently large volumes (greater than, say, 50,000 orders per year) one might be able to make a simplifying assumption to the effect that the relationships between the variable-element costs (people, computer, etc.) are fixed. In other words, in sufficiently large systems, for every dollar spent on the computer, a fixed proportion of this is spent on people, etc., and to all intents and purposes these proportions remain relatively constant as the volume increases over a wide span. Actually, no reliable ῳy to develop a cost equation of the general form can be uncovered. ῒ relationships between each of the cost elements and volume are exceedʳ complex even in a given business, and to generalize for all businesses

Table 7-4. System Factors Cost Matrix

	1. People	2. Computer	3. Communications	4. Terminals	5. Design and Maintenance	
1. Processing Complexity	$(1,1)	$(1,2)	$(1,3)	$(1,4)	$(1,5)	$ Processing Complexity
2. Response-Time Requirement	$(2,1)	$(2,2)	$(2,3)	$(2,4)	$(2,5)	$ Response Time
3. Business Topology	$(3,1)	$(3,2)	$(3,3)	$(3,4)	$(3,5)	$ Business Topology
4. File Size	$(4,1)	$(4,2)	$(4,3)	$(4,4)	$(4,5)	$ File Size
$ Total Element Costs	$ People	$ Computer	$ Communications	$ Terminals	$ Design and Maintenance	$ Total Cost

is virtually impossible. That is why a base or reference business that typified a range of significant businesses was hypothesized, and estimated costs for it at three different volumes were developed. The results of this analysis, besides providing a fix on the unit element costs, established that the ratios between these costs did *not* remain fixed over the wide range of volumes of interest.

THE COST-DETERMINATION PROCEDURE

In summary, the procedure followed in obtaining cost per order for the separate divisions considered, and their combinations, was this:

1. A hypothetical typical division ("reference business") with all the characteristics of interest described—characteristics that exemplified those found in the actual divisions—was postulated. Volumes of various kinds of transactions (customer orders, line items, shipping orders, etc.) and file sizes (customers, products, etc.) were established. The numbers and locations of field sales offices, distribution points and plants were also defined. Manning requirements for order-processing personnel were developed, as well as computer, communications and terminal requirements.
2. These requirements were then subjected to a detailed cost-estimation analysis, and unit costs per order developed for people, computers, communications and terminals, assuming volumes of 50,000, 150,000, and 600,000 orders per year. For purposes of simplifying this presentation, design and installation costs of a transaction-mode system were based on an estimated figure of $1.3 million with a 5 year non-DCF straight-line write-off.* Maintenance costs included the necessary staff of systems and programming people assigned on a continuing basis over the life of the system.
3. Twenty "complexity factors" were defined as having an impact on one or more of the above cost elements. The *relative* cost impact of each factor versus each cost element was assigned, and a total factor unit cost and fixed design and maintenance cost computed.
4. For the factors which relate to volume (such as number of line items, inquiries, etc.) the ratio of these to orders was determined, and this ratio was compared to the same ratio in the reference business. From this comparison was developed a volume index for each factor to account for the effect of differing transaction mixes between the actual divisions and the reference businesses. In other words, two divisions with the same order volume, but widely differing average line items, will differ in their impact on costs. This index accounts for such effects.
5. A rating guide for each other non-volume complexity factor, on a scale of 0 to 10, was prepared. Each non-volume factor for each division was rated according to this rating guide.

---

* This simplification of course would not be acceptable in meeting the stipulations of the Feasibility Report contents described in Chap. VI (page 106). One such stipulation, for example, calls for use of discounted cash flow analysis (DCF).

6. A complexity rating index for each factor for each division was prepared. The rating of each factor for each division was then compared to the complexity rating for the reference business, and the ratio of the two provided a measure of how much more or less complex a given division was for a given factor than the reference business. This was necessary because the factor unit costs were developed for the reference business, and they would differ for any actual division according as it is more or less complex than the reference.

7. The variable factor base or reference unit costs were multiplied by the complexity rating index for that factor in each division and also by the volume index, to obtain an adjusted factor unit cost. These unit costs were summed to obtain total *variable* unit cost per order.

8. The fixed costs per factor were multiplied by another rating which reflected the maximum complexity which had to be designed into the system to handle the factor (rather than average complexity encountered for the variable unit cost computation). These fixed costs were summed to obtain total annual fixed cost, and then divided by the number of annual orders for fixed cost per order.

9. Costs were developed on this basis for each of the five divisions analyzed using reference unit costs at volumes above and below the actual volumes of the divisions. That is, if the actual division had a volume of 300,000 orders per year, reference unit costs were computed at 150,000 and 600,000 orders per year, and an interpolation made between the differing values derived from these two bases.

10. Costs were similarly developed for each reasonable combination of the five divisions, including very large aggregations (such as Division A plus Division B plus Division C) into a single system. Thus, the sum of the separate costs for each could be compared to the cost of a combined system handling all.

The economic effect of combination versus non-combination as alternatives for order-processing systems can now be approximated. For example, combining a "low complexity" business with a "high complexity" business increases the cost per order of the former and decreases the cost per order of the latter. The cost per order of the sum may be greater or less than the sum of the cost per order of each. This analysis can be extended to all of the five divisions and conclusions drawn as to the economic impact of combination into increasingly larger systems. These effects, if economically important enough, would indicate that the largest system that is technically feasible should be developed, and that the gains associated with it outweigh the obstacles to its development.

The following factors were identified as having an impact on order-processing costs. For weighting purposes, each could be isolated from the others and its impact evaluated independently for any business. These factors were classified under four major headings.

Processing complexity factors:
1. Pricing complexity
2. Types of orders (mail, telephone, etc.)

3. Priorities (including goods on allocation)
4. File maintenance and inquiry
5. Customer qualifications (including credit checking)
6. Variability of special instructions
7. Shipping-point selection
8. Matching customer need to product

Systems response factors (allowable time to complete):
9. Order acceptance
10. Shipping order
11. Shipping confirmation
12. Change order
13. Inputs to finished goods inventory (product changes)
14. Status inquiry
15. Order confirmation

Business topology factors
16. Order fulfillment pattern
17. Number of order entry points
18. Number of management control locations
19. Number of shipping points

20. File size factors
Number of customers
Number of products
Number of stockkeeping units
Average number of open orders
Number of route/mode combinations

EXAMPLE OF PROCEDURE

A complete example of the working of the procedure has been included for Division A, product line 1. The details and final results are shown in Tables 7-5a and 7-5b, in worksheet format. Table 7-5a contains the development of the estimated costs for the product line at 600 and 2,400 orders per day. Table 7-5b shows the interpolation to derive the

Table 7-5b. DIVISION A (PRODUCT LINE 1)—EXTRAPOLATED VALUES

Variable Cost/Order @ 150,000 Orders/Year = $ 4.5572
Variable Cost/Order @ 600,000 Orders/Year = 2.7224
Variable Cost/Order @ 120,600 Orders/Year = CPO (Cost per Order)

$$CPO = 2.7224 + \frac{600 - 120.6}{600 - 150} \times (4.5572 - 2.7224)$$

$$= 2.7224 + \frac{479.4}{450} \times (1.8348)$$

$$= 2.7224 + 1.9547$$

$$CPO = \$4.6771$$

Total Variable Cost/Year = 120,600 × 4.6771 = $564,060.

estimated costs at 120,600 orders per year. As shown in this example, the complexity of "shipping-point selection" (factor 7) is the same as in the reference business; at the same time the applicable transaction volumes are only 83% of those in the reference business for this factor. The costs per 100 orders ($13.77 at 600/day, and $4.15 at 2,400/day) are multiplied by the product of these two indices ($1.00 \times 0.83 = 0.83$) to produce the adjusted factor costs of $11.43 and $3.44 respectively.

RESULTS

TRANSACTION MODE

Table 7-6 summarizes the results of this analysis for seven combinations of the five divisions, singly and severally. Annual operating-cost savings of $0.53 million are estimated for a combined system consisting of Divisions A, B and C, as compared with three separate systems. In addition to these savings, of course, there are those stemming from the reduced fixed cost of developing one instead of three systems. Referring to the table, we note that the cost/order at the lower volumes lies close to the value for the reference business (with the exception of Division C). The combined systems costs lie significantly above the reference business costs at the larger volume. The increased complexity of the combined systems as compared to the reference system principally accounts for this.

Another perspective can be obtained by looking at the cost per order. Somewhat surprisingly, the lowest total cost per order does not occur at that combination which represents the greatest number of orders. The latter (case 7 in Table 7-6) is, in fact, only fourth lowest. Case 6, the lowest, does not include Divisions D and E. This does not necessarily mean that case 6 is the optimum. If Divisions D and E were separately implemented, the sum of the separate costs of these plus case 6 would exceed that of case 7, the combination of all of them.

CONVERSATIONAL MODE

The following discussion is based on the previous analysis. The estimated operating costs for transaction mode (case III) and conversational mode (case IV) for the reference business indicate the following:

1. At the Division A activity level (260,400 orders/year), the *reference business* costs are:

$750,000	for transaction mode
$660,000	for conversational mode

Table 7-5a. VARIABLE-COST ESTIMATION WORKSHEET (BASIS 100 ORDERS)

Business Entity: Division A-1 Complexity Rating Checked With: John Doe

Key Factor	Reference Business Estimated Factor Cost 600/Day	R.I.[1]	V.A.I.[2]	Adjusted Factor Cost[3]	Reference Business Estimated Factor Cost 2400/Day	R.I.[1]	V.A.I.[2]	Adjusted Factor Cost[3]
Processing Complexity:								
1. Pricing Complexity	$ 67.76	.88	.93	55.45	$ 36.22			29.64
2. Types of Orders	20.24	1.67	.91	30.76	12.91			19.62
3. Priorities (incl. Allocation)	21.18	4.00	.87	73.71	12.80			44.54
4. File Maintenance and Inquiry	5.87	1.11	1.31	8.54	2.41			3.50
5. Customer Qualifying	32.22	2.00	.91	58.64	12.89			23.46
6. Var. of Special Instr.	11.03	2.00	.91	20.07	6.59			11.99
7. Shipping-Point Selection	13.77	1.00	.83	11.43	4.15			3.44
8. Match Customer Need to Product	23.74	.71	.83	13.99	23.03			13.57
Systems Response:								
9. Order Acceptance	15.65	1.50	.82	19.25	7.34			9.03
10. Shipping Order	13.71	1.00	.83	11.38	4.41			3.66
11. Shipping Confirmation	11.60	3.50	.83	33.70	8.50			24.69
12. Change Orders	1.84	2.50	.10	.46	1.26			.32
13. Fin. Goods Inventory Inputs	1.47	1.67	1.47	3.61	.70			1.72
14. Status Inquiry	2.99	1.20	1.10	3.95	1.86			2.46
15. Order Confirmation	2.01	2.67	.91	4.88	1.95			4.74

(Right-hand R.C. R.I.[1] and V.A.I.[2] columns marked "Unchanged.")

Business Topology

		[1]	[2]			
16. Order Fulfillment Pat.	13.55	1.67	.83	18.78	12.71	17.62
17. Order Entry Points (#)	21.83	1.00	1.03	22.48	12.10	12.46
18. Control Points (#)	1.77	1.00	.25	.44	2.45	.61
19. Shipping Points (#)	32.71	1.00	.83	27.15	18.83	15.63
20. *File Size*	50.66	.69	1.06	37.05	40.39	29.54
Total Cost/100 Orders	$365.60	Cost/100		$ 455.72	$223.50	Cost/100 $ 272.24

Actual Customer Orders
(in hundreds)   1206

Total Cost/Year $549,600
                                    (Variable)

Cost/Order $ 4.56
                                    (Variable)

Actual Customer Orders
(in hundreds)   1206

Total Cost/Year $ 328,300
                                    (Variable)

Cost/Order $ 2.72
                                    (Variable)

[1] Relative Complexity Rating Index
[2] Volume Adjustment Index
[3] Reference Business Estimated Factor Cost ×
    Relative Complexity Rating Index ×
    Volume Adjustment Index = Adjusted
    Factor Cost

161

Table 7-6. ESTIMATED ORDER-PROCESSING OPERATING COST SUMMARY

(For Transaction Mode)

	Annual Order Volume	Total Variable Cost/Year	Variable Cost/Order
	(in year of study)		
1. Division A—Product Line 1	120,600	$ 564,060	$4.6771
2. Division A—Product Line 2	105,600	577,875	5.4723
3. Division A—all product lines	260,400	1,134,170	4.3555
4. Division B	162,000	705,040	4.3521
5. Division C	120,000	804,000	6.7007
6. Divisions A, B and C combined	542,400	2,111,670	3.8932
7. Divisions A, B, C, D and E combined	614,400	2,714,480	4.4181

ILLUSTRATION OF ANNUAL OPERATING SAVINGS THROUGH COMBINED SYSTEMS

(in millions of dollars)

Division A	$1.134
Division B	.705
Division C	.804
Total of separate costs	2.643
Cost of combined system	2.112
Annual Savings Potential	$ .531

2. At the Division B activity level (162,000 orders/year), the *reference business* costs are:

$575,000   for transaction mode
$537,000   for conversational mode

3. At the combined activity level (422,400 orders/year), the *reference business* costs are:

$1,029,000   for transaction mode
$870,000   for conversational mode

To develop a rough measure of the estimated costs for the *actual* rather than reference business, the following procedure was used.

1. From Table 7-6 the annual variable (operating) costs for transaction mode are:

Division A	$1,134,000
Division B	705,000
Total	$1,839,000

2. The cost ratios, at the indicated order volumes, of transaction to conversational mode for the *reference business* are:

at 260,400:   1.14
at 162,000:   1.07
at 422,400:   1.18

3. Applying these ratios to the transaction mode operating costs to derive an estimate of *conversational mode costs* for the *actual divisions* provides:

Division A	$995,000
Division B	660,000
Total	1,655,000

4. The cost of a joint Division A-B *transaction mode* system was derived as follows:

By extrapolation, Division A costs at 422,400 orders would be $1,663,000

In the same fashion Division B costs at 422,400 orders would be $1,398,000

If the systems were combined the estimated costs are assumed to be the average value of the above two figures, or $1,530,000.

5. Dividing the transaction/conversational mode cost ratio (at 422,000 orders) of 1.18 into this figure, the estimated cost of a *combined conversational mode system* is derived, and is about $1,300,000.

6. Comparing the figure from step 5 to the figure from step 3, the annual *operating savings* of a *combined* conversational mode system over two *separate* systems appears to be on the order of $355,000.

CONCLUSIONS

We may draw some conclusions, and add a few dicta.

1. A single, computerized order-processing system for these five divisions is feasible because all have similar requirements for a centralized

system in which information on inventory levels at various locations, shipments, customer data, etc., is rapidly accessible on a nationwide basis.

2. The cost per order, and therefore the overall cost, is decreased by combining businesses into a single system, even though the complexity of processing is increased. For example, the potential savings in annual operating costs for a combined system over five separate systems is in the range of $300,000 to $1.1 million.

3. The one-time development cost for a single system is no greater than the combined development costs of five separate systems, and may indeed be substantially less.

4. A single order-processing system embracing the five divisions would remove many administrative problems that arise when product-line responsibilities are shifted from one organization to another. No comparable shift in systems or procedures would have to be made. Organizational and accounting codes in the files could be changed rapidly.

5. Centralized, rapid-response, order-processing systems, capable of mate-

Table 7-7. COMPARATIVE BENEFITS OF CONVERSATIONAL-MODE VS. TRANSACTION-MODE ORDER PROCESSING (EXCLUDING OPERATING COSTS)

	Conversational Mode	*Transaction Mode*
1. Development cost	Greater than Transaction	
2. Operating cost		Greater than Conversational
3. Order-confirmation response	90–200 seconds	13–130 minutes
4. Order product-status inquiry responses	15–40 seconds	11–127 minutes
5. Controllability of distribution factors (shipping point/shipping date selection)	Flexible and direct	Indirect and difficult
6. Checking terms	Automatic	Manual
7. Order following and customer call-back	Minimal	Is substantially the same as a manual system
8. Vulnerability to obsolescence (likelihood of system requiring upgrading or redo within 5 years)	Low	High
9. Ability of system to handle response-time requirements of other businesses in the corporation	Complete	Partial
10. Effect of system overload	Slows down order entry	Shipping orders delayed
11. Temporary communications or computer outage	Everything stops (unless standby facilities available)	Order tapes can continue to be cut

rial reservation and shipping-point selection, cannot be successfully implemented unless and until complete and accurate computerized inventory records are being routinely maintained. These records must include finished inventory by location and in transit, on hand and scheduled, committed and available. The discipline of complete and timely production and inventory reporting must be developed for, and rigorously observed by, the field organization.

6. Most present computerized order-processing systems are subject to excessive delay between order receipt and delivery of the order to the shipping point (4–5 hours during peak periods). However, at the higher order volumes achieved through combination, it is possible to install high-speed communications coupled with an appropriate central system and field office procedure (i.e., conversational mode) to overcome such delays, with an attendant decrease in the systems operating cost. Moreover a rapid-response system offers opportunities to improve sales service and distribution control at the same time.

Table 7-7 summarizes the comparative benefits and drawbacks of transaction- and conversational-mode systems concepts, the only two economically plausible alternatives for a combined system.

REFERENCES

1. *The Effective Executive*, p. 144.

I am not aware of any other field of human effort where the result really depends on a sequence of a billion steps in any artifact, and where, furthermore, it has the characteristic that every step actually matters. . . . Yet precisely this is true for computing machines—this is their most specific and difficult characteristic.

John Von Neumann, "The General
and Logical Theory of Automata"

VIII TECHNICAL STRATEGIES

INTRODUCTION

In this passage Von Neumann was referring to massive computations, such as the inversion of high-order matrices, in which certain instructional loops are iterated thousands, even millions, of times. The observation, however, is no less valid in our present context, where the elements with which we are concerned are not so much the almost unendingly repetitive sequences of instructions (since successful execution of these is now a much less challenging problem to the systems analyst than when Von Neumann wrote), but the bewildering complexities of large, integrated, on-line, business information systems, involving human organizations, computers, communications, terminals, operating systems, data bases, etc. The purpose of this chapter is not to bemoan this complexity, but rather to comment on the broad technical implications of our preceding discussions, to identify and define some of the major technological elements with which we must contend, and to explore a possible synthesis of these elements that might satisfy the requirements previously set forth. Before proceeding, brief recapitulation of those requirements which we have imposed on a possible synthesis is in order.

From the framework standpoint, two kinds of "control" systems have been defined, *operational* and *management*. The first kind is concerned with that which is routine, stable, programmable, repetitive, and oriented to the discrete transaction. It is necessarily based on the detailed master file. Management control systems are non-routine, unpredictable, judgmental, intermittent in operation, but they are based on information periodically abstracted from the master files. They are, therefore, grounded on the existence of the operational control systems which maintain the master files.

Operational control systems are composed of modules with certain well-defined boundaries and characteristics. Modules receive data in the form of working files from other modules or from raw data sources generally remote from where processing is done. Output of processed data is often to locations remote from where processing is done, as well. Modules may have to communicate with many different remote sources and destinations. Some modules are required to operate time-synchronously with real-world events; others, asynchronously, in "batch" or off-line mode. This aspect will be of considerable concern to us in the ensuing discussion. Anthony remarks that "Data in an operational control system are in real time and relate to individual events, whereas data in a management control system are either prospective or retrospective and summarize many separate events." [1] While quite relevant to our discussion, this statement is not in itself an adequate formulation on which to base an important conceptual distinction in a technological synthesis. We shall see why shortly.

Operational control activities tend to be geographically dispersed, taking place at every location where the company maintains a facility, no matter how modest. This is much less true of management control, which tends to be centralized or regionalized at considerably fewer locations. Data processing (computer operations) may take place in part locally, regionally and centrally. Local processing, for example, may consist of input/output satellites and concentrators, perhaps coupled with job or process control at plant locations.

The development of modules and their later integration must take place in a certain sequence, determined in part by matters of technical precedence. For example, inventory reporting may have to be operational before order processing. Moreover, because of the technological and financial risks associated with the development of very large systems (which traditionally have encompassed, in our terms, several modules, and a *mixture* of operational and management control), we have advocated a step-by-step approach to development. This "bottom-up" process is also to be accompanied by capitalizing on opportunities for developing common systems, and by the integration of parts of such systems developed in adherence to precise scoping. Such scoping entails separation of management from operational-control requirements, so that the latter may exhibit a considerable degree of stability in structure and of precision in definition.

In consequence of all this a residual dilemma has been created: How can we satisfy management control requirements which have all the imprecision and instability ascribed to them? We can offer only partial answers. However, we have succeeded perhaps in confining the problem to a smaller portion of the system universe, whereas it formerly was more pervasive.

THE TECHNOLOGICAL ELEMENTS

ON-LINE AND REAL-TIME

In one of the early paragraphs of Chapter II Harold Sackman's definitions of "realtime" and "online" were quoted. The rather strange typography he uses is to distinguish modes of information processing as agent or subject, and "real time" events as environment or object.[2] In Sackman's terms both "realtime" and "nonrealtime" processing are "real time" events,[3] thus, he hopes, dispensing with the essentially verbal controversy over whether or not there is truly "non-real-time" data processing.* "Nonrealtime" processing prepares the system for action, while "realtime" processing conducts the action of the system to shape environmental events as they occur.[4] These events may occur over great ranges of time, from seconds to years.[5] While these terminological distinctions are semantically very useful to philosophical discourse, we are left with the problem of distinguishing at least two subspecies of "realtime" systems for purposes of technical discourse, viz., those in which the pulse rates are measurable in seconds or less, and those whose tempos are measurable in hours, days, weeks, etc. Henceforth we shall call the former "*on-line in real-time*" (or OLRT), and the latter non-OLRT (sometimes, but not always, "off-line") in recognition of the pragmatically inescapable fact that there are often overwhelming differences between the two from design and implementation standpoints.

There is a further reason for all this seemingly pointless definitional refinement. A large, functionally integrated, operational control system, or management information system encompassing an operational control system, is *ipso facto* an OLRT system embodying some non-OLRT elements. OLRT and non-OLRT modules can coexist only in computer–communications systems with OLRT capabilities. In this context non-OLRT processing is merely an operational mode of OLRT systems. The funda-

---

* Our use of "real-time" stands ambiguously for both Sackman's "realtime" and "real time."

mental orientation of the system's synthesis we seek from a hardware/ software point of view is, therefore, OLRT, with both operational and management control partaking in some measure of both OLRT and non-OLRT modes of processing. Multi-module systems benefit from being implemented on OLRT hardware and software by not being burdened with the necessity of accommodating their various tempos to the deficient and often plainly inadequate capabilities of purely off-line technology. Some of the inadequacies of off-line technology are manifest in a number of operational and management control situations; those situations in which OLRT must be considered have been summarized in an issue of the *EDP Analyzer*.[6]

1. Customer Order-Entry Systems where the product is perishable . . . or where competitive pressures are forcing faster customer service or better inventory control.
2. . . . to support irreversible transactions, where the decisions involve fairly complex analyses—granting of loans, credit sales, and such.
3. Control of highly interrelated operations, where if one operation falls behind schedule, many others are affected; an example is production control in the aerospace industry.
4. Collection of input data where there is a high likelihood of error in human operations.
5. Providing fast response from a data file . . . , e.g., military command and control, stock-exchange price quotations, police file of stolen cars, etc.
6. Where the service to a customer can be complex and must be performed in a short period, e.g., real-time savings banking.
7. As an aid to operating people performing their routine tasks, on a demand basis, e.g., text editing, file searching, etc.

Operational control by its very nature is "real time" (in Sackman's event-oriented sense), and was so even before the advent of computers. The introduction of computers into the stream of "real time" events has two noteworthy ramifications. The economics of computer operations require centralization of operational control, which previously was, and had to be, decentralized in order to be sufficiently responsive to the many local, ongoing, operational situations in the firm. Pre-computer coordination among these local situations was often slow and inexact, and thus the necessity for too much coordination was avoided where possible, even at the expense of maintaining large numbers of "levels" (see Chapter II) and "activities" to provide the buffers and control points necessary for sometimes ponderously slow synchronization to occur. (As an illustration, the Pillsbury Company shrank its grocery-products branch accounting offices from 33 down to one by 1960, with the introduction of computers.[7]) The second ramification is in the area of management control. Managers may not often require *up to the second* information, but they often want whatever information it is that they need *quickly*. Before files were computerized it was often possible to get information fast, at least on a localized basis, or even when it had to be assembled from several points through a series of phone calls. After (non-OLRT) computerization, managers at all levels, as a defensive measure, often demanded regular voluminous printouts to be able to satisfy their occasional needs for rapid access to data. "It is patently impossible to converse with [the files of a centralized] system without an on-line real-time capability. . . . the currency of the information dealt with is not nearly so important as the fast response." [8] So says R. E. Sprague, a prophet of OLRT long before many of the rest of us understood its significance in business. In fact there can be, and often is, "realtime" inquiry to files that are not even maintained in real-time. Finally, with the computer's algorithmic power available in real-time, the possibility of altering the *modus operandi* of business decision making in very fundamental ways becomes possible in principle. But there is still a long way to go before this becomes a reality. Among other things we must learn how to extend the "conversational principle" to unanticipated dialogues ranging over the contents of the entire corporate "data bank."

MAN-MACHINE INTERACTION

In the last chapter it was concluded that conversational-mode processing would play a significant role in logistics operational control systems. In the previous paragraph this approach has been generalized into something called the "conversational principle." Sackman defines this in the following way:

> Human performance in man-computer dialogue will vary with the similarity of the responding computer system to the real time exchange characteristic of human conversation in situations closely related to the operator task environment. As computer response time and message pattern deviate increasingly from realtime parallelism with the appropriate conversational and problem-solving norm, so will user performance deteriorate with regard to the achievements of system goals, leading to increasing compensatory, erroneous and maladaptive behavior toward the computer.[9]

Conversational interaction between man and machine is achieved by use of terminals. There are two distinct, although not necessarily separated, areas for the application of terminals: management control and operational control. As for the strategic planning area, Carroll, for one, points out that

> The requirements for access to global, current internal corporate status is clearly less important for the strategic planner, whose concern

is what might be beyond the corporate confines, than for the management controller, whose concern is what might be within.[10]

It is probable that terminals can be applied more readily in the routine administrative and operational areas, since the need and benefits may be more easily established in advance. Justification of terminals for management control tends to be more speculative. Managers may require less rapid response but higher-quality information display than the administrative and operational activities, whose requirements seem to be more predictable and more "realtime."

The current generation of managers generally finds it unreasonable (or unreasonably difficult) to communicate directly with the system, and will continue to require intermediaries for this purpose. As Hershner Cross observed,

> Today [1967] in our Company [General Electric] we have some 700 or 800 . . . visual displays, but relatively few of them are in the hands of General Managers. . . . they would rather leave the driving to somebody else; they would rather enjoy the fruits that the computer can turn out but not go through the pangs of understanding and working with it themselves.[11]

We conclude that in addition to an unquestionable requirement for terminals at the operational control level, there is a need for responsive data-base access by management, but not necessarily directly. This should change as available technology permits individual and group displays, interconnected to a "corporate data bank," to be used effectively and directly by those with only a rudimentary interest in or patience with the operational formalities previously connected with such use.

DATA BASE

Some technical aspects of the relation of the data-base concept to management control need to be discussed, particularly those where certain reasonable approaches are known to the author. In discussing them we are idealizing somewhat the notion that in management control the requirement for rapid access to information in unanticipated forms and levels of detail is paramount. If this were truly and unalterably so, it would surely face us with an insoluble conceptual and technical problem. What is required is not something ultimately elegant and efficient, and unobtainable, but rather something available at a tolerable cost. The concept of the management control data base as set forth in Chapter III entailed the periodic deposit in it of summaries of detailed information contained in the files of the operational control systems. The technical and conceptual requirements of this process will now be examined.*

The detailed records in the operational control systems are needed, but in a differently structured arrangement, to support the information requirements of management control. One essential of management control systems is the linking of information resident in a number of operational control master files. The latters' indexes are structured for efficient transaction by transaction processing through rigorously prescribed task excursions. If every possible cross-file linkage were to be provided in the management control data base, it might grow to astronomical proportions in order to contain the necessary indexes and directories. Barring this, an astronomical amount of computer time could be consumed in accomplishing the kinds of complex file searches necessary to assemble management control information from the detailed master files, if one were not able to provide the kind of complete index structures called for. A compromise is not presently to be found by trading off between complexity of indexing and length of file-search time, for such a compromise would be merely an aggregation of undesirables. The solution must lie elsewhere, namely in establishing cost versus value relationships for the data-base user.

The desire for information is essentially unlimited, but the necessity for paying cold cash for it will force a scale of relative values to be established. Since the costs of using the system must be compared to the values which the user receives, this comparison will be a vital part of the user's thinking during the systems-development process, as he attempts to distinguish his wants from his real needs. The cost–value relationship must be applied by the user to his analysis of requirements concerning the degree of detail, the age of data, the ease of retrieval, and the variety in formats maintained by his information system.

Having almost, but not quite, said that the solution to the data-base problem is to provide no flexibility, we will now recant, by enumerating certain techniques that will afford a measure of not to be spurned flexibility in data-base organization and use. And this has to do with what has come to be called "data management" systems and facilities.

DATA MANAGEMENT

An information system includes, first, the means for gathering, storing, updating, and retrieving data, and second, the means for converting such data into information for human use. In general, data-management systems are concerned with the first type of activity of an information

---

* The arguments in the next two paragraphs owe their substance to some notes kindly given to the author by Dr. Leon Davidson.

system, while specific user-oriented applications systems are concerned with the second type. Data management is a function of the systems software and is usually intended to be completely general in its applicability. What we basically require of data-management software is that it permit the modules (and their subdivisions) of an integrated, corporate-wide information system to be specified and developed independently of each other, and yet retain their capability of subsequently interfacing and interacting with each other within a network of computers and data files.

While information systems in one form or another have always existed in organized activities, the presence of modern computer systems has made possible the notion that systems can be developed which provide an all-inclusive network for collecting, storing, and processing data on a corporate-wide or division-wide basis. Such large-scale, integrated information systems might involve data storage on the order of 10^9 to 10^{10} characters. Organizing such masses of data and providing multiple user access on and off line, in a multi-programmed environment with many processors operating in parallel, has resulted in the development of elaborate operating systems to assist the user in coping with these requirements. As will be discussed in more detail later, a limitation of generalized operating systems is that they handle this data-management requirement in pieces—a computer at a time, a file at a time, an application at a time—not on a comprehensive, corporate-wide, dispersed, multi-computer basis. What is promised by the manufacturers (1), what is supported by them (2), and what is available from the software houses (3) goes something like this, to cite only the case of IBM systems:

1. Generalized Information System (GIS)
2. Operating System (OS), with very broad capabilities
3. Proprietary Data-Management Systems (DMS)

Sophisticated as the facilities these provide are, they all suffer to one degree or another from the limitations cited. They are designed specifically to meet the requirements of the bulk of the market—not for large corporations. Yet so long as even a large company confines its approach to developing islands of mechanization, these types of data-management systems will surely suffice. When a large enterprise has in the past ventured forth into large, integrated OLRT systems development, vast sums have been expended on the construction of special software, such as for the airlines (SABRE, PARS), the National Airspace System (for the FAA), etc. It is perhaps notable that all of these specially tailored operating systems involved networks of two or more computers. Generally our requirements, too, involve a network of computers.

The term "data management" as used here encompasses three types of related activities, viz., input/output control, systems control, and data-storage control. Conceptually the relation between these three activities and user programs in an information system can be depicted as in Figure 8-1. While this looks a good deal like a conventional operating-system

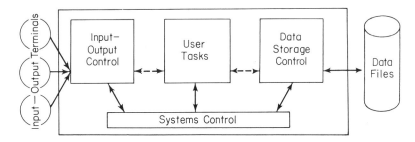

Figure 8–1. Relation between input/output control, systems control, data-storage control, and user programs.

schematic, we ask that our data-management concept apply to a network of processors as well as to single processors. That is, the kinds of systems implied by the framework assume a number of local input/output processors related (on-line and off-line) to a number of centralized file processors. Each input/output processor in general might handle several varieties of source data, intended for several different and perhaps only slightly related modules.

Input Control encompasses the functions of data collection, identification, verification, logging, editing, storing and forwarding. In this context storing and forwarding are not entirely analogous to that which takes place in a message-switching system, as will become clear momentarily. Input control consisting of these general functions is separable in place and often in time from all subsequent processing. The fact that the input process often takes place in the same location, and even in the same processor, as subsequent processing, does not preclude that it can be, and often is, accomplished remotely. This arrangement is common and easily realized in batch-processing situations; for instance, where transaction data is collected as it is generated, prepared for further processing, and forwarded periodically in a batch to a central computer location, either in the physical form of a deck of cards or a tape containing card images, or by communications lines.

This is equally realizable (and even more necessary) in OLRT processing situations, where each transaction must be time synchronized with further processing as it occurs—on demand. The transaction undergoes an excursion that may begin at a terminal, enter first one processor, then be forwarded on-line to another processor at the same or different location, etc., before the excursion is completed.*

With respect to input-control processing, the following characteristics certainly seem to be desirable:

1. Input control should always be accomplished on separate processors.
2. These processors may be arbitrarily collocated with other processors in the same computer, or may be separately located in dedicated computers, and in either case may be remote from or adjacent to the computers containing processors dedicated to subsequent processing.
3. Input control should be a function of the operating system (i.e., user-programmed tasks would *not* be involved in the input-control process). A separate input- (output-) control systems group would implement operating-system specifications to handle all input-control tasks on the basis of requirements in the system specification.
4. Applications programs should be effectively isolated from input control so that data is always accessed by them in a standard fashion (e.g., "If there are any input data of a certain type to be processed, get the next datum of that type from the standard location").

    [*N.B.:* Data coming from a teleprinter message-switching system would be treated by input control as if the source were an on-line terminal. The input processor(s) would be treated by the message-switching system as teleprinter (TTY) station(s).]

The implications of these desiderata, if realized, are these:

It is likely that every major facility or group of geographically proximate facilities of a corporation would eventually require local information-handling capability, some sooner than others. This local capability could include on- and off-line input/output terminal control, and perhaps some processing of strictly localized functions. It is desirable to capture data in error-free, machine readable form as close in time and place to its point of origin as possible. The original entry points in a given large metropolitan area might generate a large variety of transactions. A local computer with sufficient stored logic could handle such variety and hold the input processor for that metropolitan area. The benefits would include closely controlling the actual physical process of data entry as it occurs, automatically injecting repetitive information into the input data stream without the need

---

* The term "processor" as used here does not denote a computer main frame or central processing unit (CPU) in the conventional sense. *A processor is defined as an allocated part of a computer system dedicated to perform a certain job at a certain time.* If a main frame in the system is multi-programmable, a processor is that portion of a computer system devoted to one of the concurrent jobs being performed on it at a given time. If the main frame is not multi-programmable, the processor is a time partition of the main frame scheduled to perform a certain job. The term does not extend to time sharing in general, but rather to systems which are fairly rigidly scheduled.

for keystroking, eliminating the need for separate verification steps, eliminating duplicate transcriptions, drastically reducing the recirculation of errors in the system, reducing media costs (punched-card purchasing, handling, storage, transport, conversion, disposition, etc.), handling and forwarding real-time data and inquiries, and improving data-collection personnel environment (less noise, fatigue, etc.). Once a data-communications capability having substantial proportions exists, the economic justification for total on-line data input would be highly compelling. However, conventional data collection, followed by entry at input-processor locations, is by no means precluded in such a scheme of things, and would probably continue to be used widely in many situations.

Output Control encompasses the functions of receiving, storing, editing, formatting and presenting data in various forms for human consumption (or for automatic receptors as, for example, in process control). The same observations made with respect to input control concerning the separation of input from subsequent processing in time and place, etc., apply equally to output control. Therefore, with respect to output-control processing the proposed objectives are parallel to those for input control.

Data-Storage Control has a number of related objectives, some of which are handled in operating systems, some of which were encompassed within the original scope of IBM's Generalized Information System (GIS), and others of which were attacked in other systems, such as the CCC Corporation's MULTI-LIST, UNIVAC's IMRADS (*I*nformation *M*anagement, *R*etrieval *a*nd *D*isplay *S*ystem), GE's IDS (*I*ntegrated *D*ata *S*ystem), etc. The scope of data-storage control includes the functions of file organization, file indexing, storage allocation, storage and retrieval of file data by record or by class, relating data items in different files, and multiple accessing and sharing of files. Traditional approaches to the design of file structures do not adequately fulfill all these functions, and therefore do not ideally meet the requirements imposed by a functionally integrated information system.

More specifically the objectives sought are that

1. Data storage control be the interface between files (data sets) and user programs. This interface should be standardized such that data sets are self-defining to the user programs. That is, user programs should be able to operate on file data or records without being explicitly aware of formatting, types of physical residence, location of physical residence, or location within physical residence.*

---

* The technique referred to as the "self-definition of data sets" requires that format declarations (a term selected to distinguish it from IBM's "data descriptions") which characterize records in a data set are stored with the data set itself. Such format declarations would consist of mapping of field names, "pictures" (in the COBOL sense) and locations within the record. When these formats are changed,

2. File-accessing restrictions be specifiable to the system, as well as volume of response output desired, with the systems indicating the volume of the unoutputted residue of potentially responding records.

3. Some types of records be content-addressable by matching against a key field, on the basis of equality, or "between limits," or "greater or less than," etc.†

4. File records in a given data set be capable, on the basis of usage statistics or other criteria, of being allocated automatically to locations in a multi-level store consisting of a hierarchy of media varying in speed, capacity and cost.‡

5. Files be arbitrarily definable, nameable and then referable to by name at use time. Such "implicit" files may be subsets of an existing data set, or they may cross over two or more previously defined data sets (as in GIS) and not have to be explicitly defined prior to use. (See Fig. 8-2 for an illustration of the "implicit" file concept.)

6. It be possible for a special control-systems group to add attribute fields

---

the format declarations would have to be altered—but no changes in the user programs would be necessary. (Obviously operating-system data-management parameters might be involved in these changes, too, especially if record sizes are altered, or keyword positions, etc.) Assuming that a user program requires a different format for a given record (or, more generally, for a "data string") in a "self-defined" data set, it would supply its own format conversion by filtering the given data string through the respective format declarations, producing a new data string in the desired format. It would do this interpretively—one record (data string) at a time. This concept of filtering is common to many engineering fields. In the process of filtering, data-base control would need access to a glossary of synonyms in the event that the user employed different names for the data set. A similar approach has been used in ABACUS,[12] developed by North American Aviation. Another filtering approach has been used in the Keydata Operating System (KOP-3).

† If these data were structured in a multi-level storage hierarchy, specific records or summarized aggregates could be accessed by reference to a tree-like index or list structure. This would require the user to be thoroughly familiar with the complexities of this structure. Alternatively the user might access each datum by a datum key, if it were known, provided that the data-management system maintained a correlation between such keys and physical locations. A third accessing alternative might be to search the data bank by content (i.e., using lists of records having given field values, or logical combinations of field values). Using conventional memories, this approach would be impractical because of the excessive amount of time that would be required. This approach may prove not only viable, but optimal, if and when associative memories and associative mass stores become available. Search by content would presumably be used sparingly because of hardware limitations. Perhaps a special channel-control program could be developed to perform this function off-line. It could also perform the "counting" function to limit the volume of response.

‡ The problem of allocating records to locations in a data base in a multi-level store has been solved a number of times. If this is done periodically instead of dynamically ("realtime"), the problem is in fact much simplified. It does require, however, that in data sets for which this periodic reallocation is desired, certain usage data be maintained in each record. Statistical algorithms for accomplishing one kind of reallocation based on prior usage have already been devised.[13,14,15,16] If the reallocation is done periodically, only the recording of usage need be a resident part of data-storage control. Actual reallocation can then be treated as a separate off-line step. The off-line process can also handle the problem of purging files of inactive records, which then might be allocated to archival microfilm storage or discarded.

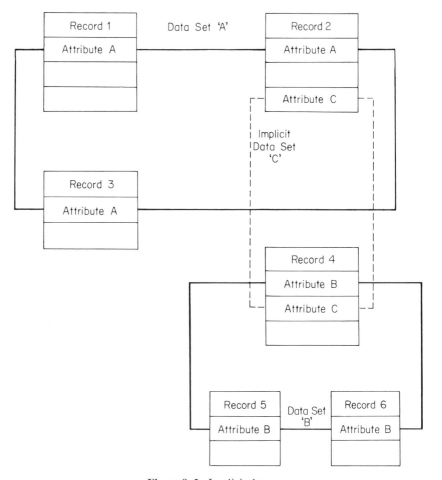

Figure 8–2. Implicit data sets.

to record formats, thus linking them to other records and classes of records by attributes at any level of indexing.

7. Data-storage control permit general file querying (possibly in semi-free format) without the mediation of a specially prepared user program. A query might refer to a previously catalogued data set, or to a newly specified "implicit" data set. Search logic could refer to record names or attributes, and be flexible in terms of kinds and numbers of logical operators permitted in a single data-set definition. Procedures on a defined data set might include operators such as "print," "display," "count," "sort," "total," "tally," "average," "list," "save," "delete," "store," etc. Newly defined data sets and procedures should be catalogable and sets and procedures recallable by name.

Systems Control is the traffic manager of the multi-processor network. Systems-control requirements are based on the following: input/output control is systematically separated, as we have proposed, from applications processing. Therefore, it may take place on physically distinct, and frequently remote, computers. Whether this is the case or not (the "not" pertaining where input/output is physically adjacent to applications processing, and may therefore be one of two or more concurrent activities on a single main frame or CPU) is often a matter of happenstance. Whether or not a computer site is at a plant or a warehouse does not usually affect the functions to be carried on. Thus, ideally at least, the applications programs implementing such functions ought to be isolated from considerations of the relative physical locations of the computing and the actual operations. The proposed data-management requirement permits the programmer to isolate himself from the details of accessing data from external sources or data stores, by allowing him to treat such data as if it were available in addressable memory. This means that systems control must, as one of its functions, act in effect as a data-paging supervisor, providing (in time-sharing parlance) a virtual memory system.

Another requirement for systems control is related to the partitioning of an application and its files for running on more than one processor, either concurrently, serially, or both; either in the same or separate locations, or both. Such partitioning may be a matter of convenience, efficiency or necessity. For example, an OLRT order-processing module may be providing product commitment information to an OLRT inventory-reporting module, while receiving product availability information from it. The two modules may be running in parallel on separate main frames. The information exchange between such modules, depending on its volume and urgency, might be variously accomplished as follows:

1. Direct, channel to channel, via cabling
2. Via shared main memory
3. Via shared auxiliary storage (drum or disc)
4. Via a dedicated communications link

5. Via a common-user message-switching system
6. Via off-line media: magnetic tape, punched cards, disc pack, etc. These may be physically transported or sent in off-line mode via communications and re-recorded at the receiving end.

Generally speaking, the performance capability of any one of the above methods is subsumed within the capabilities of any method higher in the list than it. It should be a matter of indifference how information is actually communicated between modules, provided that the linkage used meets speed and capacity requirements. It becomes an economic question at this point.

Systems control would reside in every main frame in the multi-processor interconnected network. Each computer (CPU) in such a network would communicate with every other computer via systems control. Also, since the tasks in a given module must be independent of whether input, output and file data are accessible in the same computer in which the module resides, or in a different computer, they communicate with input/output control and data-storage control via systems control. Of course, if input/output and files were on the same computer as the module itself, the formalities of systems control would be rudimentary; that is, it would recognize in such cases that it had no role to play and set bypass conditions within itself accordingly. Figure 8-3 clarifies these notions and depicts the relationships between the systems elements discussed.

In summary: (1) systems control should be resident in processor partitions within computers containing other processors requiring data communications (such other processors obviously contain input/output control also); (2) systems control between physically non-coresident processors should be a function of the operating system (i.e., module tasks should not be involved in this control process—a separate control-systems group should develop and implement operating-systems specifications to handle all data requirements); and (3) regardless of the actual method of data communications employed, module tasks should present and receive data to and from the system-control "interface" in a standard fashion.

One can reasonably expect that many of the features discussed above will be supported in operating systems developed for the use of large firms and other organizations requiring multiple computer facilities. They could also be of use within a single-computer installation with multiple processors (defined earlier).

The supervisory monitor of OLRT modules is the key ingredient of their operation. Data-management facilities are integral to it in part, and in part subordinate to it. That is, the monitor calls on all accessing, file and input/output facilities. It supervises the performance of all input/

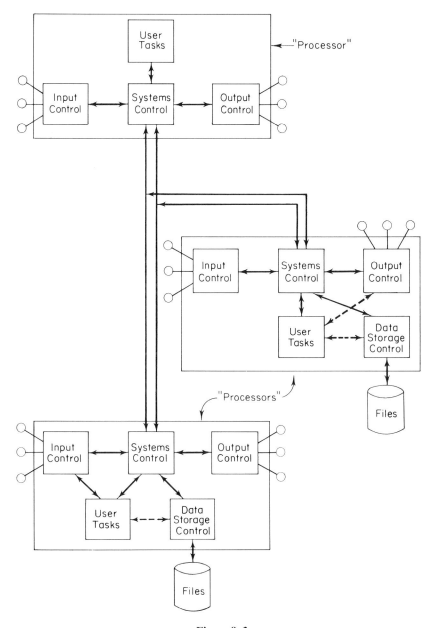

Figure 8–3.

output and file accessing in order that: (1) the system designer's choice of access methods be deferrable without delaying applications programming; (2) access methods be changeable later without affecting applications programs; (3) logic for error handling on access be a common function, and therefore handled by the monitor also; (4) records not be directly restored to the file by applications programs, because other tasks may be called by the monitor to do further processing on the same record; (5) the monitor be aware of restoration, to release the "protect" status of the record; (6) restart of a processing "event" after an error be possible, before the updated record has been stored; (7) it be easier to coordinate joint development of many programs using the same file records; (8) duplicate recording be possible, for backup purposes where necessary; and (9) the monitor can record channel- and device-usage statistics for the purposes of performance evaluation and improvement. Module tasks would therefore submit requests for data to the monitor.

The monitor is often called the "executive program" because it controls the sequence of tasks performed on various real-time transaction excursions, which are generally interlaced to allow interruptable processing when series of input/output and file accesses occur. In operating systems there is usually an interrupt handler and other task- and data-management features paralleling the functional characteristics set forth above. In such an environment the OLRT supervisory monitor and its subordinate applications tasks might run *as a job* under the operating system. In fact this is desirable for several reasons, not the least of which is the need for data-set compatability where the same data files are used in both the OLRT and non-OLRT jobs (the latter unquestionably running under the operating system)—off-line report generation from files updated in real-time, for example. However, if the system is occupied by OLRT jobs, continuously resident in the system over long periods, it is a drawback to efficient operation for them to have to be burdened with all the conventional functions of operating-system job management unneeded at such times. A cogent analysis of this matter suggested that a special OLRT supervisory monitor could be prepared for OLRT systems projects by "extracting from [the operating system] the necessary 'pseudo-hardware' to do this . . . [and at the same time] retain[ing] compatibility with the operating system services and facilities." [17]

Standard operating systems do not support OLRT systems resident in several machines, because they lack what we have described as "Systems Control." Generally speaking, these standard operating systems lack the ability to support very large numbers of terminals, OLRT oriented higher-level languages (e.g., JOVIAL), nonstandard configurations (multiple computers interconnected to multiple memories), and non-standard hardware (e.g., extended core memories). One is well advised, nevertheless, to accommodate his requirements to their existing scope, until such time as they are expanded in capability. This precludes the economic achievement (until a later time) of a *totally* integrated corporate-wide information system, but not the achievement of major parts of one.

HARDWARE, SOFTWARE AND COMMUNICATIONS CONFIGURATIONS

Hardware and communications for OLRT systems are available virtually off the shelf. This includes lines, line buffers, transmission-control units, central processors, and direct-access storage devices. The same state of affairs is true, as we have noted, in the case of software, with communications message-control facilities, reentrant code compiling languages, performance simulators, file protection, fallback and recovery, and dynamic core partitioning being available in standard operating systems. Perhaps the best way to illustrate the variety possible in integrated hardware, software and communications OLRT systems, if one is not limited to off-the-shelf items, is by reference to a few actual configurations that were designed to support large, integrated business systems.

The Programmed Airlines Reservations System (PARS) was designed to support in excess of 2000 airline agents and terminals, generating in the aggregate up to 55 inputs per second (about 10 inputs per reservation). The processing mode is mixed; that is, it is conversational mode for the airline's own agents, and is transaction mode (teleprinter) for outside lines. Most of the traffic during conversational-input entry is from the agent to the computer, but the computer does acknowledge each input segment within 2 to 5 seconds of entry.

1. The PARS Control Program:
   Message control
   Core and file allocation: 3 fixed block sizes for messages, records, working areas and program segments; up to five blocks for each allocation or entry.
   Queuing of work
   Priority of processing
   Scheduling of input/output
   Error checking
   Operator communications
   Fallback and restart
   System-performance statistics
2. The PARS off-line package (under an operating system):
   Symbolic library
   Object library
   Program-linking editor
   Program loader
   File recoup
   Utilities
   System measurement

3. PARS test tools:
   System test compiler (i.e., test-file generator)
   System debugging simulator (single thread)
   Remote-set simulator (magnetic tape–multiple thread)
   Real-time trace

4. Source language: Basic Assembly Language

5. Program size:
   Application programs: 170,000 instructions
   Control program: 30,000 instructions
   Test tools: 50,000 instructions
   Utilities: 20,000 instructions
   Support: 30,000 instructions

6. Continuous availability: 24 hours per day, 7 days per week

Figure 8-4 illustrates the terminals and communications supported by the system. The 1006 was the SABRE Terminal Interchange, to which 1 to 30 agent-set terminals could be interconnected. The 2948 Terminal Interchange supports 36 terminals. A maximum of 30 Terminal Interchanges connect to one high-speed circuit—a full duplex, voice-grade line. All circuits terminate in a 2703 Line Control Unit at the central complex site. Each Terminal Interchange (except the most remote) on each circuit has two receive channels (R) and one send channel (S) as shown in the figure. One R channel is to receive the cascading poll while the other can simultaneously receive data, following the polling regime outlined in the figure.

Because of the need for assured continuous operation, virtually all units were duplicated at the central site, with each unit involved in OLRT operation capable of being switched to either main frame. The arrangement is shown in Figure 8-5. The configuration includes two 360/65's, but smaller versions of PARS allow for 360/50's or 40's capable of handling lower message rates.

The Advanced Business System (ABS) was developed by a large manufacturer to handle its order processing, inventory control, accounts receivable, sales commissions and production-scheduling requirements as an integrated whole. It was designed to service 250 field locations with 1200 video terminals, generating a peak input rate of 2800 events per minute, with a response time of 3 to 5 seconds. In contrast to PARS, where the traffic is primarily from agent to computer, ABS is truly conversational; that is, sequences of data are displayed on the CRT terminal from which selections are made by the operator by hitting keys. Up to 20 such sequential selections may be required to complete a transaction. If codes (customer, product, etc.) are known, display calling can be bypassed in large part.

1. The ABS hardware:
   Terminals: 2260's (with 1053 slave)

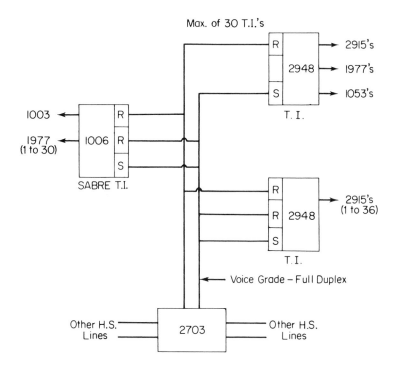

Figure 8–4. PARS—terminals and communication net.

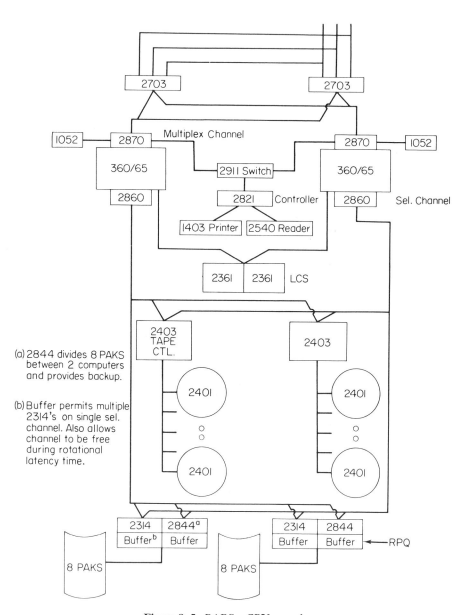

Figure 8–5. PARS—CPU complex.

Terminal interchange: 2848's
Remote multiplexer–concentrators: five 360/30's
Central CPU's: four 360/2065J's (1 megabyte plus Large
   Core Storage)
Discs: 2311, 2314
Drums: 2303
Data cell: 2321

The remote 360/30's act as "local" processor/concentrators for up to ten 2848 Terminal Interchanges. A wide-band, half-duplex channel handles the traffic between the "local" processors and the central site. This is shown on Figure 8-6. The central complex consists of *four* 360/65's, one of which is a standby for the other three. Central processors I and II (see Figure 8-7) are duplexed, sharing the processing load between themselves and processor III, which is exclusively devoted to data (file) management.

2. The ABS realtime software:
   OS/360
   BTAM (Basic Teleprocessing Access Method)
   Fixed partition sizes (8K, 16K)
   Special macro-language for application programs
   Basic assembly language for monitors and data-management programs

A special macro-language was developed for this project because the need for reentrant code eliminated COBOL, and PL/1 was not available at the time programming was to commence. The use of fixed partitions guaranteed that available dynamic space partitions were adequate for all tasks and working areas, minimizing roll-in/roll-out. The overall architecture of the ABS OLRT software operating under OS/360 is shown in Figure 8-8.

Allen-Babcock Computing Inc.'s time-sharing system merits attention because it illustrates one way to go about getting a workable data-management system. By installing an extra ROS (Read-Only Storage) as a control memory in the computer, wired to one's own specifications, one provides the special instructions (op. codes) needed to carry out certain data-management functions fast enough. Allen-Babcock had "list search" and "string evaluation" op. codes prepared by IBM in this way for their 360/50. Along with this, the use of large core storage (LCS) by Allen-Babcock permits the indexing of data management files in an LCS attachment.

A CONFIGURATIONAL SYNTHESIS

LOCAL INPUT/OUTPUT HANDLING

Figure 8-9 will be referred to extensively in the following discussion. It attempts to depict schematically how the various elements that have been previously described in this chapter might be embodied in an overall

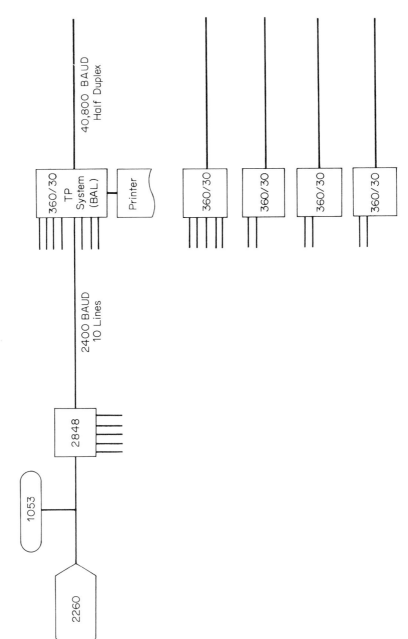

5 Lines to CPU Complex

40,800 BAUD
Half Duplex

360/30
TP
System
(BAL)

Printer

360/30

360/30

360/30

360/30

2400 BAUD
10 Lines

2848

1053

2260

Figure 8–6. ABS—remote terminals, communications, interchange-buffers, and line concentrators.

188

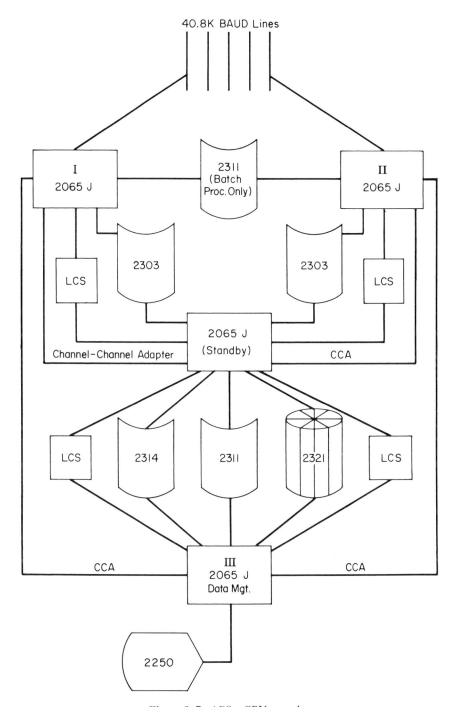

Figure 8–7. ABS—CPU complex.

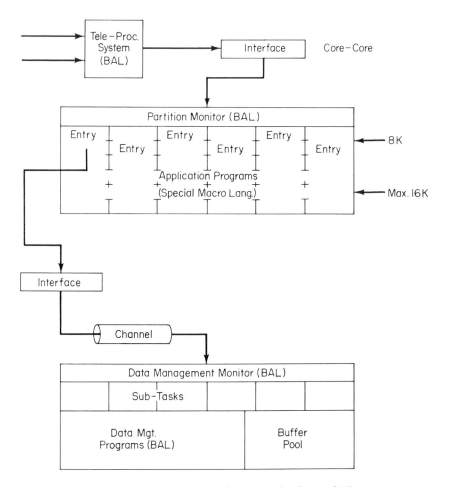

Figure 8–8. ABS—real time Operating System/360.

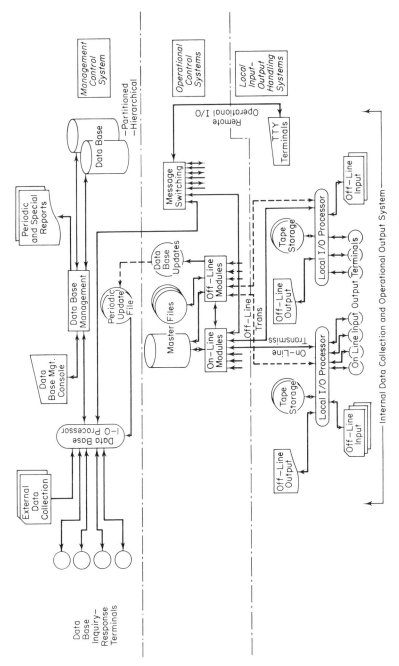

Figure 8–9. Configurational concept—integrated information system.

191

configurational concept. The processing elements in the configuration inter-communicate in two modes: on-line (shown by solid arrows), and off-line (dashed arrows). Both modes may use the same intercommunications facilities. The essential conceptual distinction between the two modes is that, in the case of on-line transmission, there is no appreciable delay between the input of a transaction by the local input/output processor and its subsequent transmission for further processing, while, in the case of off-line transmission, input data are accumulated on a storage medium such as tape and subsequently transmitted, either physically or by communications, in a batch. Data destined for off-line transmission and processing can be introduced into the local processor either by an on-line terminal or by punched cards. Data for on-line transmission and processing would always be input conversationally via terminals.

The so-called "local" I/O (input/output) processors shown in the figure are frequently remote from the centralized processors in which reside the applications modules, but there is no reason why some would not also be in the same physical location (and even collocated in the same main frame) as the applications modules, if these centralized locations were also near to operational activities generating substantial amounts of input. For locations which generate small volumes of data, or which are remote and isolated, the firm's teleprinter network, or even dial-up teleprinter service, provides alternative means of input. The figure shows the modules as stations on the teleprinter network. Actually, of course, there would be an interface between the message switcher and the module processor. In fact, this interface might connect through a local I/O processor rather than to the module processors directly. Output is also produced on the local I/O processors, both off-line and on-line. An example of the former might be payroll checks on a printer, and, of the latter, a shipping order on a warehouse terminal.

The local processors may, of course, reside in main frames containing processors concerned with other functions. These may include, for example, process-control modules. These main frames, like all those in the system concept being discussed, would include I/O, data-storage and systems-control functions.

OPERATIONAL CONTROL SYSTEMS

Operational control systems are sketchily represented in Figure 8-9. They consist of a large number of modules, both OLRT and non-OLRT, occupying in principle several main frames, and running concurrently in separate processors within each main frame and among the several main frames. Periodically (e.g., daily) data-base updates are extracted from the master files or from the working files of transactions in process. These are forwarded off-line, perhaps nightly, for updating of the management control data base. The computer main frames in which these modules reside also include I/O control, data-storage control, and systems control.

File inquiry that is part and parcel of operational control (a product availability inquiry, for example) is handled through terminals associated with the local input/output systems, even though management-level people may on occasion avail themselves of such inquiry facilities. The use of such a facility by a manager does not thereby make it a part of the Management Control system.

MANAGEMENT CONTROL SYSTEM

This segment of our configurational concept is the least well understood, in terms of implementing its more advanced and generalized manifestations in hardware and software. In its simpler, less flexible forms, however, it is a fairly rigidly structured information-retrieval system. The data base would in this case be partitioned into a number of separate but related structures containing various previously agreed-upon summary files and indexes. These structures may correspond to certain "natural" divisions of responsibility in the business, such as those between the marketing, production, distribution and financial functions.

Each of these structures in the data base might include, for example:

1. High-level summaries by
      department (product line)
      customer group (market)
      sales region
      time period (monthly, quarterly)

2. Intermediate summaries within the above by
      product
      customer/all locations
      sales office
      time period (weekly, monthly)

3. Low-level summaries within the above by
      product grade or size
      customer/location
      salesman or sales territory
      shipping point (daily, weekly)

These summary files might also contain frequently used analyses; trends by various parameters and combinations of parameters, actual versus plan; etc. Developing a method of setting up these data-base structures so that they do not continually fall apart because of the ever-recurring changes in the actual company and business structures—departmental reorganizations, market reassignments, product-line revisions, etc.—is the real challenge to be overcome in implementing this configurational synthesis.

REFERENCES

1. Robert N. Anthony, *Planning and Control Systems, A Framework for Analysis* (Boston: Division of Research, Harvard Business School, 1965), p. 78.

2. Harold Sackman, *Computers, Systems Science, and Evolving Society* (New York: John Wiley & Sons, Inc., 1967), pp. 226–7.

3. *Op. cit.*, p. 228.

4. *Ibid.*

5. *Op. cit.*, p. 234.

6. "Progress in Real-Time Systems," *EDP Analyzer,* Vol. 3, No. 9 (Sept. 1967).

7. Terence Hanold, "Management by Perception," *GE Information Systems Review,* No. 1 (1966).

8. Richard E. Sprague, "The Browsing Era," *Business Automation* (June 1967), pp. 53ff.

9. Sackman, p. 443.

10. Donald C. Carroll, "Implications of On-Line, Real-Time Systems," in *The Impact of Computers on Management,* p. 160. Note, however, his qualification immediately following: "This suggests little value in connecting the strategic planner to the corporate system . . . but several aspects argue to the contrary . . . [among these are] that *ad hoc* data can be combined with regularly available data for *ad hoc* decision-making." (p. 161.)

11. "A General Management View of Computers," in *Computers and Management—The Leatherbee Lectures* 1967 (Boston: Harvard University Graduate School of Business Administration, 1967), p. 18.

12. R. P. Larsen, "Data Filtering Applied to Information Storage and Retrieval Applications," *Comm. of the ACM,* Vol. 9, No. 11 (Nov. 1966).

13. S. C. Blumenthal, "A Dual Master File System . . . ," *Journal of the ACM,* Vol. 5, No. 4 (Oct. 1958).

14. R. L. Carmichael, *Dynamic Data Purging* (Canoga Park, Cal.: Data Systems Division, Litton Industries, Rep. #AT-TM2-64, May 13, 1964).

15. C. B. Poland, "Dynamic Flow of Programs and Data Through Hierarchical Storage," *Proceedings of the IFIPS Congress* 1965.

16. A. Opler, "Advanced Concepts of Utilization of Mass Storage," *Proc. IFIPS Cong.,* 1965.

17. Leon Davidson, "Operating Systems for OLRT," *Datamation,* Vol. 13, No. 10 (Oct. 1967), pp. 27ff.

Whenever possible, a system is conceived of in functional modules which interrelate to perform the overall task. Such a design makes both error correction and modification easier to carry out. A modification is introduced into the system as a new module wherever possible. The new module may be either an addition or a replacement for an already existing one whose action is to be changed.

Charles P. Lecht[1]

 THE MANAGEMENT OF CHANGE

THE DIMENSIONS OF CHANGE

In Chapter I (pages 11–13) we mentioned some of the kinds of change which affect the enterprise, and we said that these changes require continual innovation to ensure healthy growth and survival. We emphasize the impact of change for two reasons. First, the rate of change with which management must contend is accelerating. Each passing decade—or so it is said—witnesses more change than all the prior years combined. Second, since information systems reach into and pervade all the areas subject to this explosive rate of change—functional, organizational and technological —they too must change. The high cost of systems change should not be permitted to deprive the enterprise of information it needs to adapt to change.*

Large man-machine digital systems are traditionally costly and difficult to change, especially if the changes are radical. Often the "man" part is as difficult to change as the "machine" part. Many executives at or near the apex of the "man" parts are doomed to failure in a dynamic growth situation, because of inability to adapt. Similarly, systems are ultimately

---

* "The real cost of an information system is not that incurred to develop it, but that incurred by not having the information produced by it." (The original source of this caveat is unknown to the author.)

196

replaced in consequence of their internal inability to adapt readily to changing requirements. Cadell illustrates this type of maladaptation by citing the orders/capacity cycle in a growth business:[2] as orders come to exceed capacity to produce, the salesman-executives are superseded by the production executives, who achieve quick success. But after a relatively short period of ascendancy, as initial success results in capacity exceeding orders, the production executives are replaced again with the salesman-executives, and so on (unless they are those rare individuals with a genius for both kinds of management).

Many executives seek to buttress their stewardships against this built-in success–failure cycle by attempting to exercise an anticipatory rather than a reactive brand of management. But the delays in the information system, the lengthy decision–execution response times, and the tendency to under- or over-responsiveness often amplify or prolong the oscillatory nature of the problem. The parallel syndrome in the systems themselves is a tendency to continual incremental growth. System is piled on system, or a continuing series of minor enhancements is made to existing systems, in an attempt to generate relevant management information as a hopefully serendipitous by-product accompanying the production of increasingly vaster quantities of irrelevant, unused, or merely historic data. For systems, the success–failure cycle comes into play as a result of this very growth. Calvin M. Mooers holds that an information system will tend not to be used whenever it is more painful and troublesome to have the information it produces than not to have it. It is painful to receive more information than there is a desire for or an ability to cope with. The outward evidence is seen often in the large stacks of undigested material situated about managers' offices.

As the information pile-up occurs another system modification or addition is created to produce ostensibly only that which is wanted in the situation; but the preexisting *mélange* remains because of the unwillingness of anyone to take responsibility for retiring it. (Who might squawk?) This process is a form of change, true; but it is only marginally and fitfully adaptable change. Ultimately the patchwork collapses. Systems become moribund, and, like dead horses, no longer respond to the whip. The answer to this problem lies with the development of a new dynamics of adaptable systems growth, similar to the dynamics of organic growth— ever-changing but ever persisting.

SYSTEMS DYNAMICS

Corporate information systems or their major parts, in their separate en-tireties, are not things an organization acquires or discards lightly or frequently. Rather, after initial development, small parts of them are discarded and replaced at various times via a process known as systems maintenance and modification. Through this process it is conceivable that after a period of years hardly an original line of code may remain. Thus, systems must be looked upon as changing but somehow persisting entities with a continuing identity.

If systems, like individuals, experience such continuing growth and decay, in what does the persisting identity of such entities consist over a period of time, during which every component "cell" may be sloughed off and replaced? Perhaps this: Systems, like individuals, may be considered to have temporal as well as physico-spatial parts. To say, for example, that John Doakes at age 20 is the same individual as John Doakes at age 30 is, at the very least, ambiguous, if not plainly false. To be more precise we should rather state: "John Doakes at age 20" is a physico-temporal *part* of a persisting entity called "John Doakes," which also has another *part* called "John Doakes at age 30" (and many other parts as well). In fact, when we use names like "John Doakes" in ordinary discourse, we rely on context to reveal whether the use is a shorthand equivalent for a particular *part* of the referent, or is meant to designate the entire temporally persisting entity. This analysis of the meaning of continuing identity, while perhaps obvious, is revelatory and meaningful for our present purposes, because it offers us a vantage for reconsidering the dynamics of systems change, perhaps thereby illuminating better methods of coping more rationally with change.

Generally we cannot know in detail the conditions under which systems must operate several years hence, and therefore we cannot know the precise kinds of adaptions our systems must undergo to survive as viable entities. Yet in Chapter I (page 13) we have (audaciously?) set forth as one of our planning objectives the requirement of providing for adaptability of systems to business change and growth without periodic major overhaul (which would significantly include replacement *in toto*).

The systems planner–designer can take one of two basic approaches to this problem: he can attempt to manage the *problem,* or he can attempt to manage the phenomenon of systems change itself. In the first instance he is left with devising a means of coping with each requirement for change after it becomes manifest. If he follows the second course, he may be able to treat each requirement for change as an instance of a class of changes for which he has made provision in his systems plan. The latter approach is not only advocated, but its very possibility is embodied within the framework of modules we have attempted to develop earlier in this book. In this context modules represent classes of change.

Before proceeding to discuss this proposition further, let us review the sources of systems change. A major consideration in our approach to planning has been to provide for the achievement of an interim, partial capability while simultaneously serving a broader, corporate-wide systems objective. Related to this objective, and particularly relevant in implementing complex systems over long periods of time, is our emphasis on designing to accommodate changes. Recapitulating the discussion in Chapter IV (p. 62), these changes are of three types:

1. Changes in functional requirements and systems specifications. These changes are not only an inevitable accompaniment of any major development effort, since few systems designs are airtight initially, but also result from the fact that the corporate environment served by the system does not remain fixed after cutover.
2. Changes in organization and operating policy requiring reorientation in major design aspects of the system. These may even result to some extent from the actual use of portions of the systems which have been completed and cut over, the experience from which, when it is fed back into the planning process, alters the objectives of that process itself. Changes in systems requirements are then made, to reflect these changed objectives.
3. Changes in information-processing technology which, over any extended period (say five to ten years), can be expected to evidence at least one major and several minor advances equivalent to the past progression through "generations" of computer systems. This creates a problem of obsolescence—and an opportunity, in that one should not be so rigid in planning and design as to be unable to take reasonable advantage of technological advances when there are definite rewards for doing so.

All these types of change require the planner–designer of systems to leave "adapter plates" in his design so that modifications in requirements can be accommodated by a process of relatively painless replacement.

DESIGNING FOR CHANGE

PERSPECTIVE

The notion of a system as a persisting, adaptable entity comes from viewing the system as a collection of subsystems, which in turn are collections of changing modules. So long as the *relationships* among the component modules are unaffected by change—that is, so long as their boundaries remain constant—the integrity of a system, and, therefore, its continuing identity, is preserved. However, a change in these module boundaries is *ipso facto* a change in the system, and cannot be considered in the same class as a component change. A shifting of boundaries is a profound change because, once allowed in one module, it requires changes in the interfacing modules, and thus it tends quickly to spread its effects throughout all the other modules and files of the system. This ultimately leads to the discarding and replacement of the system, or major subsystem components, as a whole. Changes that, instead, are confined within the boundaries of a module may be accumulated and introduced all at one time, creating a new module "model." Different modules may be replaced by new models at different unrelated periods—some rarely, some frequently. The system as a whole persists throughout component-model changes. Designing for change requires selecting module boundaries in the first place which can withstand the impact of changes in business requirements, organizational structure, and technological advance.

CHANGES IN FUNCTIONAL REQUIREMENTS

Operational control modules will doubtless come to play a normative role in how the enterprise which follows our planning precepts adapts to change. Operational changes will come to be expressed in terms of the modules to which they apply. In other words, the classes of allowable adaptations will reflect existing module boundaries. Proposed changes which, because they might be improperly expressed, did not fall within one or another of these classes, would have to be redefined, so that each change as a whole, or in terms of its defined parts, would apply within specified modules.

The practical implications of this approach are not entirely clear since, within such a scheme, changes to related modules applied nonsimultaneously might involve the interface between them—for example, changing the length of a data field. Data filtering (see above, Chapter VIII), in this example, could handle many of the purely data-management aspects of this, but if the recipient module suddenly was presented with a twelve-byte field while it was still geared only to handle ten bytes, the resulting incompatibility could be disastrous. One possible answer might lie in the identification and separate treatment of changes affecting inter-module buffer files, so that the modules in question would be changed simultaneously.

CHANGES IN ORGANIZATION

These changes generally affect management control arrangements, but they do have an impact on the operational control levels as well. However, the latter would be confined to updating certain indicators or organizational codes in the master files. The codes might include, for example, designators for sales territory, product responsibility, etc. More importantly these changes would affect the data base and the hierarchies of data summarizations it contains.

In large corporations which have many organizational subdivisions, these types of changes can be expected with great frequency. In order to be able to handle them at a tolerable cost in time and money, at least three things are required, of which the first two have already been touched upon.

1. Physical and logical separation of management control and operational control processing and files. In this way, as we have seen, organizational change will have but minor effects on operational control modules.
2. A flexible data-base manipulation capability that will allow information formerly summarized in one segment to be shifted to another segment without elaborate reprogramming.
3. *Data standardization,* which is a needed practice not explicitly considered in our previous discussions. All organizational subdivisions in the firm must, in order to make corporate-wide systems a practical possibility, use the same data formats and codes in referring to customers, products, expense and income accounts, geographical locations or facilities, and so on.

TECHNOLOGICAL ADVANCES

There are two broad categories of change in this area (from our special perspective): changes which are module-confinable, and changes which are systems-wide. Very few technological advances will have implications which would be confined to the module level. There may of course be some dedicated or special-purpose gear serving single modules—for example, on-line data-gathering equipment on factory floors feeding only the Job Control module in PROCIS. However, since most of the technology that would be used is general purpose, changes in it, of which advantage is to be taken, will tend to have system-wide effects. The configurational conception outlined in Chapter VIII abjures almost entirely the use of dedicated hardware or software or communications.

Some of these technological changes will have little significance for the planner–designer in terms of preserving systems integrity. Preparing input on optically sensitive forms rather than card punching, or recording directly on microfilm instead of printing, might have important effects on cost/efficiency, but the necessary systems upgrading could be confined to the hardware in question and the data-management portion of the software, leaving the applications modules relatively undisturbed. This would be equally true for storage media—for example, the introduction of "photoscopic" memory to replace discs and drums. It would even be true for main frames, provided they were truly compatible with what is replaced (this certainly seems to be the trend, at least within any given manufacturer's product line).

The problem arises when radical technological change is considered and compatibility cannot be preserved. Such would be the case, for example, if practical and economically justifiable associative memories were to be introduced, to replace conventionally addressable memories. Associative memories simultaneously (i.e., in a single accessing cycle) search all locations for records having the same attributes. One could retrieve all orders for a given product received in a given time period, etc. In general, all items in storage having some specified Boolean combination of attributes could be simultaneously retrieved. The whole concept of individual master and working files might go out the window, with many of the old modules, to be replaced by a single corporate data bank with little of the complex indexing structures we know today. In the same category of profound technological advance would be laser communications, in which optical fibers might have the transmitting capacity of hundreds of thousands of voice channels. This might make feasible the complete centralization of all data handling and information, and not just some of the presently computerized aspects. Our prescription for the corporate information system might survive the impact of incremental change in technology; its tenability in the face of profound technological change, which could affect the very manner in which we conduct our affairs, is speculative.

STANDARD MODULES

The present high cost of systems change will increase the pressures for further standardization. Already this has led to standards in higher-level languages, data-interchange codes, compatible "families" of computers, etc. It may finally bring about industry-wide standards in word lengths, operating systems, and the like. This will have obvious beneficial effects in "liberating" the customer by providing him with competitive sources for hardware and software. Optimum advantage will accrue to the users, however, when and if they band together and adopt "processor" standards that would constrain applications software to operate within standard modules of core memory, peripherals, and external storage. Presupposing that all this comes to pass—and it is not unlikely that it could, given sufficient impetus from government and non-government users alike —it might then be possible to develop applications modules that are not only corporate-wide, but industry-wide as well.

An industry has grown up around the brokering of generalized business applications "packages," such as payrolls, savings accounting for banks, accounts payable and receivable, etc. Where these are applicable to a user's needs, he can often acquire a system for as little as 10% of the cost he might otherwise incur to develop it in-house. If standard operational control modules could be defined and agreed upon among a number of users, great savings could accrue through joint development efforts, *if* there were a prior basis established for this by the adoption of the kinds of standards discussed in the previous paragraph. Then the problem of adapting to technological advance would be considerably eased. Equally important, the shortage and high cost of analysis and programming skills would cease to be as great an inhibiting factor to more profitable and extensive business use of computer technology in the future.

CHANGE, THE COMPUTER, AND THE FUTURE OF THE BUSINESS ENTERPRISE

SPECULATION ON THE OFFICE OF THE FUTURE

Focusing on the typical business office, there appear to be only one primary and two subordinate reasons for people daily to congregate there for purposes of conducting corporate affairs. The primary reason is communication. In this category are included internal and external, verbal and written, man to man, man to machine, "one to many," "many to one," and "many to many" types of communication, taking place in formal and informal meetings, conferences, discussions and negotiations. The communication complex includes both the originators and receivers of communications, and those who are neither, but play an indispensable role as part of the communications channels, namely secretaries, file clerks, business-machine operators, telephone operators, and, on a different plane, computer programmers. As a subordinate reason, the office serves as a central store for information conveniently retrievable as needed. A not so obvious subordinate reason is to impose discipline by making people available to each other for purposes of communication at certain known and mutually agreed-upon times and places, and by allowing measurement of value given, and by providing a hopefully efficient and non-distracting working environment as a stimulus to productivity. As a byproduct of this daily foregathering of masses of people in central locations, those who support this sizeable primary group with services of various kinds add to the crowd: maintenance men, storekeepers, guards, waitresses, cleaners, etc.

It has occurred to some people in the computer business that it may become possible in principle to conduct most of these communications, and their attendant information-processing functions, more conveniently, economically and with greater efficiency without requiring these vast, struggling and expensive diurnal comings and goings. The day might come when, for example, an executive would be able to dictate a memorandum, including referenced material stored in the computer files, and incorporating graphics and tables which he will be able to arrange to his liking, with the sole aid of his "console." Given the desired distribution code for this memo, the system will then communicate it, depending on its urgency, to the consoles of the recipients, either when they are ready to study it, or by forcing in on their attention if immediate decision and action is required. If these consoles are not in the executives' own homes, they may be in a number of non-urban locations that might be called "management control centers," and which might also have facilities for group meetings augmented by group displays operated by a specialist. And if this ever comes to pass in business, would not much of the underlying concept be applicable as well to government, education, research, and elsewhere? The impact this could have on our urban way of life, and on our economy as a whole, is for the social scientist to contend with. One thought, however: the burgeoning problems of urban life may never be solved, but they may very well be supplanted by others of equal or greater proportions.

A number of observers foresee a "management information facility" centered on some form of group display which will become the focus of future management activity.[3,4,5] The view of these proponents is typified by Widener, who predicts that

> The formal desk will disappear as paper is replaced by display systems. Conference . . . tables will "get in the way" and will be traded in for comfortable, tilt-back swivel chairs that permit easier interaction between people and the displayed data. The atmosphere will be one of confident control, rather than the hectic, somewhat erratic pace we maintain today. . . . [The management information facility] will be on line to the computer through report interrogation consoles and large-screen, graphic displays. Management will be able to "hold conversations" with business systems, ask questions and get answers in seconds, probe problem areas in minutes, review actual trends and trend projections against plans.[6]

Rooms such as the one described, although not yet interconnected with computers, are becoming commonplace. Hanold, for example, reports: "Pillsbury has made a small beginning against the problem . . . by establishing an executive chart room which can have such electronic connections with the information system and such advanced display facilities as experience proves real use for." [7] The author has seen several such rooms. Particularly fine examples were set up by AT&T in Chicago and New York.

Sooner or later we will have the data-management and file-organization capability to create fully mechanized "chart rooms." How quickly they would actually be established remains a financial rather than a technical decision. In the meantime, business is occupied with creating the data base and extensive files necessary to manage its activities using computer systems in less spectacular fashion, and this, of course, is indispensable to further progress in the direction just described.

SPECULATION ON CORPORATE ORGANIZATION

If centralized information systems are constructed which, in principle, make information contained within them equally available to all who might need it, the continuation of the hierarchical power structure in business might be jeopardized. "To possess information is to possess power." [8] We do not yet have enough experience with these systems to make any firm generalizations about how they may ultimately change the organizational structures. One school of thought would have us believe that the inevitable result of pervasive employment of such systems will be a total recentralization rather than further sharing of power (see Chapter I, pages 5–7).

The market economy taken as a whole runs on a kind of self-correcting feedback principle, although it is anything but centralized when compared to even the most devoutly divisionalized (i.e., decentralized) corporation. Conversely, even the most decentralized organization is a long way from giving as much autonomy to its own various components as the market economy permits. The profit-center oriented corporation finds itself, in degree of authoritarianism, somewhere between the patterns exemplified by recent economic structures of the United States and those of the Soviet Union. Very few individuals in a large decentralized corporation really have profit responsibility and relative autonomy. Proportionately, a great many more profit centers with individual responsibility exist in the economy as a whole, which, despite its seemingly anarchic structure, has been held up to the world as a model of efficiency and productivity. To what extent might increasing computerization lead to more widespread autonomy within the enterprise, if this autonomy were to be manifested, as it is in the economy as a whole, by large numbers of profit centers?

Forrester suggests that in such an increasingly profit-center oriented organization,

> Some persons will offer personal services as advisors and consultants, others as contractors taking engineering and manufacturing commitments at a bid price, some as promoters and entrepreneurs to coordinate internal resources to meet the needs of the market, and still others in the role of informed investors to allocate the financial resources of the organization where the promise is greatest.[9]

Moreover, "Each man identified with a profit center would have a status similar to that of an owner–manager." [10] In making such an arrangement successful, policy making that permits a high degree of individual effectiveness becomes a most vital task for a small number of the most capable men in the corporation.[11,12] Such policy making

> . . . should allow freedom to innovate and should have the fewest restrictions compatible with the coordination needed to insure overall system strength, stability, and growth . . . [and] should be accessible, clear, and not retroactive. . . . Recent advances in the theory of dynamic systems and in system simulation using digital computers demonstrate that it will be possible to design internally consistent policy structures. . . .[13]

Not only would "Computers provide the incentive to explore the fundamental relationships between information and corporate success," [14] but also

> . . . they permit a rearrangement of the information system into a radical . . . shape with all files at the center . . . [providing] an information picture that is up to date and fully processed at all times . . . [and] directly accessible to persons who must now operate with too little information either to permit good management or to establish a feeling of security and confidence.[15]

Information monopolies would have to disappear, and along with them the control of individual behavior through the selective withholding and dissemination of information. The superior–subordinate organizational structure would be supplanted by a system of rewards based on carefully measured profit contributions, operating within a policy context that ensured consistency with corporate goals.

We have examined a point of view that implies that computers offer the opportunity to substantially enhance rather than further erode the importance of the individual in the enterprise. Whether or not this ultimately occurs, a period of increasing centralization will first have occurred, and has already started. As pointed out in Chapter I, the ultimate issue is very much in doubt, but it is well to keep in mind that computers and centralization do not necessarily go hand in hand.

SPECULATION ON SYSTEMS PLANNING AND CORPORATE SURVIVAL

McLaughlin contends that the firm is, in one sense at least, a mechanism for improving the efficiency of the productive process through organized innovation.[16] Since larger-scale operations tend to be more efficient, computer technology in a previously unconcentrated industry, like garment manufacturing, will lead to an increase in economies of scale and a resultant increase in industry concentration.[17] Thus, he argues,

. . . the forecast of business changes brought about by the mechanization of information processes will in general favor the large diversified conglomerate corporations, particularly those having large central information-machine operations.[18]

If in fact the "computer revolution" has, or comes to have, an impact corresponding in magnitude to that of the industrial revolution, then it may very well lead either to industry concentration where none now exists, or to the encouragement of more and bigger conglomerates, or both. Computer technology can have this impact because it is a general-purpose innovation, comparable in the ubiquity of its possible applications to the energy-converting machine. And its existence will make possible applications we cannot now foresee, just as television was not foreseen by the inventor of the cathode ray tube. Computer technology and its use has grown so fast because investment in this innovation has yielded efficiency improvements outstripping those realized from any other innovation in our time.[18]

Systems planning may evolve to the point where its practice permits the development of standard applications modules, to which smaller firms would be willing to adapt themselves, rather than the other way around. These firms might then be able to realize an increase in efficiency corresponding (to some extent, at least) to that in the giant corporations. More likely, however, this will not happen because of the lack of a centralized planning focus and authority in small firms. Increasing concentration may therefore be the result, and as this concentration leads continually to ever greater efficiencies through information-systems investment, the process will tend to accelerate, creating the kind of ultimate barriers to competition found in the automobile industry and elsewhere. The price of entrance will simply become too high, even for the most highly endowed entrepreneur.

If a future economy composed almost exclusively of giant competing conglomerates should come into being, information-systems planning might replace market planning or research and development as a major instrument of competitive weaponry.

REFERENCES

1. Charles P. Lecht, *The Management of Computer Programming Projects* (New York: The American Management Association, Inc., 1967).

2. Henry J. Cadell, "The Revolving Executive Chair," *Datamation* (Dec. 1966), pp. 45f.

3. W. Robert Widener, "New Concepts of Running a Business," *Business Automation* (April 1966).

4. Gilbert Burck, *The Computer Age* (New York: Harper Torchbooks, Harper and Row, Inc., copyright 1965 by Time, Inc.)

5. Richard E. Sprague, "The Browsing Era," *Business Automation* (June 1967), pp. 53ff.

6. Widener, *op. cit.*

7. Terrance Hanold, "Management by Perception," *General Electric Information Systems Review*, No. 1 (1966).

8. Jay W. Forrester, "A New Corporate Design," *Independent Management Review*, Vol. 7, No. 1 (Fall 1965), p. 11.

9. *Ibid.*, pp. 7–8.

10. *Ibid.*, p. 8.

11. *Ibid.*, p. 9.

12. *Industrial Dynamics*, p. 346.

13. "A New Corporate Design," p. 9.

14. *Ibid.*, p. 10.

15. *Ibid.*

16. John McLaughlin, *Information Technology and the Survival of the Firm* (Homewood, Ill.: Dow-Jones–Irwin, Inc., 1966), p. 107.

17. *Ibid.*, p. 179.

18. *Ibid.*, p. 196.

BIBLIOGRAPHY

BOOKS

Alderson, Wroe and Stanley J. Shapiro, *Marketing and the Computer*. Englewood Cliffs, N.J.: Prentice-Hall, Inc., 1963. The use of the computer at the strategic-planning level in marketing.

Anthony, Robert, *Planning and Control Systems, A Framework for Analysis*. Boston: Division of Research, Harvard Business School, 1965. A short, but cogent and well written treatment of the kinds of planning and control in the corporation, and of the levels of management exercising them. This is a seminal book for future studies.

Burck, Gilbert, *The Computer Age*. New York: Harper Torchbooks, Harper & Row, copyright 1965 by Time, Inc. A well researched and well written presentation for the manager–layman of a great many aspects of computer usage in business, with special emphasis on contemporary developments.

Computers and Management—The Leatherbee Lectures. Boston: Harvard University Graduate School of Business Administration, 1967. Papers and discussions by business leaders and professors.

Constantin, James A., *Principles of Logistics Management—A Functional Analysis of Physical Distribution Systems*. New York: Appleton-Century-Crofts, Division of Meredith Publishing Co., 1966.

Cyert, Richard M. and James G. March, *A Behavioral Theory of the Firm*. Englewood Cliffs, N.J.: Prentice-Hall, Inc., 1963.

209

Dearden, John and F. Warren McFarlan, *Management Information Systems.* Homewood, Ill.: Richard D. Irwin, Inc., 1966. A guide to current practice.

Drucker, Peter F., *The Effective Executive.* New York: Harper and Row, 1966.

Forrester, Jay W., *Industrial Dynamics.* Cambridge, Mass.: The M.I.T. Press, 1961. One of the most important and original books ever written on the science of management, this is indispensable to the serious architect of corporate information systems.

Head, Robert V., *Real-Time Business Systems.* New York: Holt, Rinehart and Winston, 1965. What they are, when they are called for, and how to do them, by one who has done some. Well written.

Johnson, Richard, Fremont E. Kast and James E. Rosensweig, *The Theory and Management of Systems.* New York: McGraw-Hill Book Co., 1967. The discussions of the organization and management of large systems efforts are of special interest.

Laden, H. N. and T. R. Gildersleeve, *Systems Design for Computer Applications.* New York: John Wiley and Sons. Inc.. 1963. One of the better books on the fundamentals of systems design. Its elements should be mastered by any one professing to be a business-systems analyst. Batch-processing oriented.

Lecht, Charles P., *The Management of Computer Programming Projects.* New York: The American Management Association, Inc., 1967. A detailed, step-by-step checklist, including worksheets, by one who has brought many projects to a successful conclusion without time and cost overruns. Strictly didactic in approach.

Martin, James, *Programming Real-Time Computer Systems.* Englewood Cliffs, N.J.: Prentice-Hall, Inc., 1965. A most thorough treatment of the subject.

————, *Design of Real-Time Computer Systems.* Englewood Cliffs, N.J.: Prentice-Hall, Inc., 1967. Immensely thorough. One of the best books ever written on systems design, real-time or otherwise. Must stand as a model for all writers on the subject. Can and should be used as a handbook and a reference as well.

Myers, Charles A., ed., *The Impact of Computers on Management.* Cambridge, Mass.: The M.I.T. Press, 1967. Papers and symposia with Forrester, Whisler, Leavitt, Carroll, Dearden, Beckett and others.

Sackman, Harold, *Computers, System Science and Evolving Society.* New York: John Wiley and Sons, Inc., 1967. A very ambitious and well written book that attempts to elevate real-time systems "science" to a central position in solving the problems of a complex and ever-changing industrial society. Useful especially for its insights and definitions.

Simon, Herbert A., *The New Science of Management Decision.* New York: Harper and Row, Inc., 1960. A seminal book for the management scientist.

Wilson, I. G. and M. E., *Information, Computers and Systems Design.* New York: John Wiley and Sons, Inc., 1965. Mostly about hardware concepts.

ARTICLES

Ansoff, H. Igor and Richard C. Brandenburg, "A Program of Research in Business Planning," *Management Science,* Vol. 13, No. 6 (Feb. 1967), B-219ff. Much of this is applicable to systems planning.

Blumenthal, Sherman C., "A Dual Master File System . . . ," *Journal of the ACM,* Oct. 1958. Earliest reported probabilistic algorithm for the movement of records among levels in a hierarchically organized store.

————, "Problems of Management Display in Advanced Business Systems," *Proceedings of the 6th National Symposium on Information Display.* N. Hollywood, Cal.: Western Periodicals, 1965. Unsolved problems of direct management–data-base interaction using a display subsystem interface. Possible approach suggested.

Booz, Allen, and Hamilton, Inc., "The Computer's Role in Manufacturing Industry," *Computers and Automation,* Dec. 1966, 14–19. Survey results.

————, "The Computer Comes of Age," *Harvard Business Review,* Jan.–Feb. 1968, 83ff. Survey results.

Brady, Rodney H., "Computers in Top-Level Decision Making," *Harvard Business Review,* July–Aug. 1967, 67–69. Survey results.

"Building Corporate Data Systems," *EDP Analyzer,* Vol. 5, No. 4. Vista, Cal.: Canning Publications, Inc., April 1967.

Carroll, Donald C. and Zenon S. Zannetos, "Toward the Realization of Intelligent Management Information Systems" in *Proceedings of the 3rd Congress on Information System Science and Technology,* Wash., D.C.: Thompson Book Co., copyright 1967, MITRE Corp., 151–167. A somewhat Utopian prescription of what is required.

Diebold Group, Inc., "Research Study Conclusions," *Computer Digest,* Aug. 1967, p. 8. Survey results covering 2600 executives in over 100 companies on management use of computers.

Forrester, Jay W., "A New Corporate Design," *Independent Management Review,* Vol. 7, No. 1 (Fall, 1965), pp. 5–17. A humanistic approach to business organization in the computer age.

Franksen, O. I. and M. D. Romer, "Industrial Production and Digital Computers," *Proceedings of the 20th National ACM Conference,* 1965, pp. 455–468.

Gray, Max and Herbert B. Lassiter, "Project Control for Data Processing," *Datamation,* Feb. 1968, 33–38.

Head, Robert V., "Management Information Systems: A Critical Appraisal," *Datamation,* May 1967, 22ff. Old salt in a new shaker. If you have not tasted it before, this is a good way to try it.

————, "Planning for Real-Time Business Systems," *Systems and Procedures Journal*, July–Aug. 1967. What the systems planner's (as distinct from the system designer's) responsibilities are.

Hunt, Pearson, "Fallacy of the One Big Brain," *Harvard Business Review*, Vol. 44, No. 4 (Aug. 1966), 84–90. Computers should not cause re-centralization. Convincingly argued.

Middleton, C. J., "How to Set Up a Project Organization," *Harvard Business Review*, Vol. 45, No. 2 (Apr. 1967), 73ff. Includes survey results. Not only how, but when.

Morenoff, Edward and John B. McLean, "An Approach to Standardizing Computer Systems," *Proceedings of the ACM National Meeting, 1967*, 527–34. Eliminating the reprogramming problem for everybody. But first the wolf and the lamb must compete on the lamb's terms.

"New Management Reporting Systems." *EDP Analyzer*, Vol. 5, No. 1. Vista, Cal.: Canning Publications, Inc., Jan. 1967.

Perlman, Justin A., "Centralization vs. Decentralization," *Datamation* (Sept. 1965), 24–8. Where the computer is leading us organizationally. Still another point of view.

"Planning for Data Processing," *EDP Analyzer*, Vol. 4, No. 6 (June 1966).

"Progress in Real-Time Systems," *EDP Analyzer*, Vol. 3, No. 9 (Sept. 1965).

Rowe, Alan J., "Information Technology in the 1970 Era." Unpublished manuscript, July 7, 1967, Department of Management, University of Southern California. Speculations by a professor of management.

Simpson, J. A., "An Introduction to 'SAPTAD'." Paper delivered at GUIDE 24, New York, May 24, 1967. Names the levels in a systems hierarchy as an aid to analysis and design of large information systems.

Sprague, Richard E., "The Browsing Era," *Business Automation*, June 1967, 53ff. An advocacy of management conversation with the computer.

"The Corporate Data File," *EDP Analyzer*, Vol. 4, No. 11 (Nov. 1966).

Widener, W. Robert, "New Concepts of Running a Business," *Business Automation*, April 1966. Describes the concept of an information-management facility ("chart room") with large-screen display.

Young, Richard C., "Systems and Data Processing Departments Need Long-Range Planning," *Computers and Automation*, May 1967, 30ff.

ADDENDUM TO BIBLIOGRAPHY

Blumenthal, Sherman C., "On-Line Processing," *Datamation*, Vol. 7, No. 6 (June 1961), 23–24.

This article was modestly overlooked by Sherm Blumenthal when he made up the Bibliography. It reports early on-line, real-time developments in the Air Traffic Control Computer project at General Precision Laboratories, where he was in charge of programming. Some of the concepts which appear throughout this book, such as the "excursion," are explained in this article.

I first met Sherm when he hired me as his assistant at GPL. As I now finish checking the manuscript of this book (which represents work on which we spent a recent year together), I feel that my inclusion of this article in the Bibliography closes a circle, not ending a relationship but providing a continuity and a thread of integration which in a way symbolizes the comprehensive and integrative approach which characterized the professional contributions of Sherman Blumenthal.

That this article and this book both represent a continuous position held by Sherm is indicated by the following extract from the review of the article printed in *Computing Reviews,* Vol. 2, No. 6 (Nov. 1961), Review No. 1161: ". . . [Blumenthal claims] that there have been many failures [in on-line systems] due to lack of a unifying theme without which the efforts of the programming team are uncoordinated." This book represents the culmination of his development of a unifying theme for applying computer systems to changing and growing roles in operating and managing the business enterprise.

Leon Davidson
September 26, 1968

INDEX